Jaguar Books on Latin America

William H. Beezley and
Colin MacLachlan
Editors

Addressing subjects as diverse as the region itself, the Jaguar Books on Latin America guide the reader through the myriad political systems, economies, and societies that comprise today's Latin America. Each volume in the series is edited by an eminent scholar in the field and gathers the most influential primary and secondary documents on a topic of central importance to the region's history and development. Together the Jaguar Books stand as a library of sources for teaching, as well as a useful reference for all those interested in Latin American culture, history, and current affairs.

Tropical
Rainforests

Tropical Rainforests

Latin American Nature and Society in Transition

Susan E. Place
Editor

Jaguar Books on Latin America
Number 2

A Scholarly Resources Inc. Imprint
Wilmington, Delaware

Scholarly Resources Inc.
104 Greenhill Avenue
Wilmington, DE 19805-1897

Library of Congress Cataloging-in-Publication Data

Tropical rainforests : Latin American nature and society in transition /
    edited by Susan E. Place.
        p.   cm. — (Jaguar books on Latin America ; 2)
    Includes bibliographical references.
    ISBN 0-8420-2423-9. — ISBN 0-8420-2427-1 (pbk.)
    1. Rain forests—Latin America. 2. Rain forests—Economic
aspects—Latin America. 3. Rain forest ecology—Latin America.
I. Place, Susan E., 1947–   . II. Series.
SD153.T76   1993
333.75'098'0913—dc20   93-4335
                                                          CIP

The paper used in this publication meets the minimum requirements of the
American National Standard for permanence of paper for printed library
materials, Z39.48, 1984.

Acknowledgments

In producing this volume I have been assisted by those whose aid and encouragement I would like to recognize. To begin with, a generous grant from the California State University, Chico, provided the time away from teaching that allowed me to complete this book. Also at CSU, Chico, Christine Crown and Chuck Nelson of the cartography lab in the Department of Geography worked cheerfully and expertly to create the maps from a disorganized mass of unrelated information.

I would like to thank Bill Beezley, who provided the original inspiration for this volume and kindly allowed me the opportunity to develop his idea in my own way. The generosity of the authors in allowing me to use their work in this anthology is also greatly appreciated.

Finally, I extend heartfelt gratitude to my husband, D. J. O'Donnell, for providing much useful feedback while this work was in progress.

Contents

Introduction

Several major events in 1992 focused attention on the environments of Latin America, revealing the dynamic relationship between nature and society and suggesting that we are in the process of rethinking our relationship with the natural world. The Columbian quincentennial, marking five hundred years of interaction between Europe and the Americas, stimulated a reevaluation of the consequences of introducing European technologies, economic systems, and social organizations into the Americas. The most recent phase in this relationship has taken place in this century, with the introduction into Latin America of an approach to economic development founded upon modernization. A strategy from Europe and North America, modernization is based on the adoption of Western technology and emphasizes high rates of economic growth that have caused many Latin American countries to incur large foreign debts. Part of this approach entails the expansion of the modern sector of the economy into "backward" rural areas that include the last remaining stands of tropical rainforest.

Another major event of 1992 was the United Nations Conference on Environment and Development (UNCED), or "Earth Summit," held in Rio de Janeiro. The contentious nature of this conference revealed both the political aspects of environmental policy and the importance of a healthy environment to economic development. Nature clearly plays an important but often unrecognized or seriously undervalued role in human economies. As a result of decades of environmental degradation, however, the necessity of maintaining environmental health is becoming increasingly obvious and has given rise to a new approach founded upon the maintenance of a healthy environment and respect for traditional cultures—sustainable development. How to accomplish sustainable development is an open question, especially since it challenges powerful economic and political interests that consider nature a free good that can (and even should) be used to increase economic output, whether it be by exploitation of tropical rainforests for quick profit, or conversion of the land to other forms of use, such as agriculture, ranching, or mining.

A society's perception of the tropical rainforest underlies and motivates its particular way of interacting with it. Part I introduces the reader to a variety of perceptions of the rainforest. The selections in Part II describe the impacts of the dominant modern approach to economic development on tropical rainforests and the people who live in them. The implications of these impacts and the arguments for saving tropical rainforests are discussed in Part III. Finally, selections in Part IV present alternatives for future development in tropical rainforest zones of Latin America, many of which raise the possibility of development as a process in which the natural environment and traditional cultures are preserved rather than destroyed in the name of "progress."

The American tropics (known to biologists as Neotropics) include a wide variety of forest ecosystems, from cloud forests on wet tropical mountain slopes to seasonally dry tropical deciduous forests and woodlands on the Pacific side of Mexico and Central America, and pine forests on the Caribbean side of Honduras and Nicaragua. Because there is more information published about it than about any other type of neotropical forest, most of the selections offered here focus on the tropical rainforest. A number of other forest ecosystems in Latin America, however, are equally (or more) endangered by the same forces that threaten the tropical rainforest. The natural distribution of rainforests in the Neotropics ranged from southern Mexico to southern Brazil (Map 1). The actual extent of rainforest today, though, is much smaller—and shrinking rapidly.

Humans have cleared vast areas of tropical forest in Latin America. Most of the forests of the seasonally dry zones of Central and South America have already disappeared, and tropical rainforests in the more accessible coastal areas have been decimated as well. Amazonia represents the last great contiguous expanse of tropical rainforest. Although perhaps only 15 to 20 percent has been removed so far, the rate of cutting has been accelerating so that now more than twenty thousand square kilometers are cleared each year. Projections based on current trends indicate that by the middle of the twenty-first century there will be no sustainable tropical rainforest left in Brazil. Only small, unsustainable remnants will stand. Because of the ecological characteristics of tropical rainforests, scientists now doubt that such patches of forest can survive in the long run, even if undisturbed by human activities.

Widespread tropical deforestation has a number of serious environmental, economic, and social implications. One of the most commonly discussed characteristics of the tropical rainforest is its high biodiversity. Occupying only about 6 percent of the earth's surface, these forests are believed to contain at least 50 percent of the world's known plant and animal species. Amazonia, the largest and richest of the tropical rainforests, contains at least 20 percent of the world's higher plant varieties and an equal proportion of the earth's bird species. Other areas in the Neotropics are also spectacularly rich in species, especially Central America, with the extra

Map 1. Natural Distribution of Tropical Rainforest in Latin America

diversity of habitat in its mountainous terrain and because of its land-bridge position between North and South America. Costa Rica, about the size of West Virginia, has more species of birds than all of North America.

Tropical rainforests are the most complex terrestrial ecosystems on earth. Structurally, they have many different life forms and are composed of several vertical layers of vegetation, each with associated faunas; this complexity allows a large number of different species to coexist in a given area. High biodiversity also implies that there is a large variety of genes and an abundance of different chemical compounds present in tropical rainforests. But a forest ecosystem is more than just an assemblage of species; it also represents the interactions between species, and the variety of interspecies interactions is particularly rich in tropical rainforests. Many tropical plants, for example, produce toxic compounds in order to evade the large number of animals (especially insects) that try to eat them. Several selections in this book discuss the economic implications of biodiversity for medicine, agriculture, and industries of various kinds.

Latin America's tropical rainforests also have a high degree of horizontal diversity, meaning that the assemblage of species found in one area may differ from those found only a few miles away. Sometimes called "patchiness," this adds further complexity to species diversity. There are also centers of particularly high diversity in various parts of the Amazon and along the Brazilian coast. Scientists have postulated that these might represent *Pleistocene refugia*—forested areas where large numbers of forest-dependent species concentrated during past dry periods (corresponding to glacial advances during the Ice Age), when grasslands expanded to cover much of Amazonia, leaving only islands of forest in favored spots. The forests that scientists would most like to see preserved in parks are these centers of diversity because they are especially vulnerable to species extinctions as a result of forest clearance.

Tropical rainforests interact with their physical environments in a number of ways that affect human well-being. They act as giant, solar-powered engines that pump water, nutrients, and gases such as carbon dioxide and oxygen through the earth's biosphere and atmosphere. Recent research indicates that by recycling water through the regional hydrological cycle, the Amazon rainforest generates about half of the rain that falls in the Amazon basin. Precipitation is captured by the forest and slowly returns by means of evaporation or transpiration as water vapor to the atmosphere, from which it can return to the forest as rain. Furthermore, the forest is like a giant sponge that holds a large amount of water not only in the vegetation but also in the leaf litter on the ground and in the soil. In this way it plays an important role in regional water cycles by helping to store a large percentage of the water from precipitation until it can be slowly released, either to the atmosphere (through the vegetation) or to feed streams and rivers from stored groundwater. When large-scale forest clearance occurs the ecosystem's ability to store water decreases, and a high proportion of precipitation runs off the unprotected land. Local climates and water cycles, therefore, may experience greater extremes in cleared regions. Of particular concern to humans, drought conditions may begin to occur regularly, often alternating with floods produced by the rapid runoff during rainy periods.

The warm, wet climate of tropical rainforest regions creates the seeming paradox of incredibly luxuriant vegetation rooted in infertile soil. Over 75 percent of Amazonia's soils are classified as acid, infertile, or poorly drained, and only 8 percent are moderately fertile, well-drained soils suitable for agriculture. Most soils occurring under tropical rainforest conditions, except on the floodplains or in certain volcanic areas, are deficient in nutrients because of the perpetually warm, rainy climate. The high temperatures of the tropics cause rapid decomposition of organic material—that is, downed trees, leaf litter, animal feces, or carcasses—as well as of the inorganic parent material of the soil. Frequent heavy rains quickly leach the decomposing materials out of the root zone. Tropical rainforest plants have adapted by quickly taking up nutrients as they become available, which explains why most of the nutrients in a tropical rainforest are stored in the vegetation and not in the soil as they are in the middle latitudes, such as North America and Europe. Thus, a thorny problem faces humans who seek to make a living in the tropical rainforest: clearing the forest for farming removes the nutrients necessary to sustain crops.

Destruction of the forest clearly disrupts various ecological services upon which humans depend, such as regulation of the water cycle and the climate, and protection of the soil. Often people remain unaware of that dependence until environmental disruption causes them problems. The current debate over how to manage Latin America's remaining tropical rainforest derives from differences in how these indirect services are perceived. Many scientists, environmentalists, and forest dwellers emphasize the importance of the forest's ecological services and the need to maintain them by protecting the integrity of the natural forest. But divergent economic interests and different degrees of dependence upon and familiarity with the tropical rainforest lead to different assessments of the value of its conservation versus the value of conversion to other kinds of production. Those who wish to preserve the tropical rainforest often live in it (at least part of the time) and know it intimately. Many depend on the forest and its ecological services for their livelihoods and therefore have a personal stake in rainforest conservation. On the other hand, proponents of economic development tend to focus on the economic resources (that is, material goods) produced by the forest or the land on which it grows and minimize the value of the indirect services provided by nature. Often living elsewhere, they seek to make money from logging and conversion of the forest to more profitable uses. They envision improving the economic status of the rural poor by providing paid employment in commercial ventures.

Perceptions of the realities and possibilities of the tropical rainforest have varied over Latin America's history and suggest considerable ambivalence toward rainforests. Since the inception of contact between Eurasia and the Americas, Westerners have viewed tropical rainforests as lucrative sources of raw materials. Beginning with the gold fever of the colonial period, the myth of potential wealth lying under or in the tropical forest has fueled its periodic exploration and exploitation in a long sequence of economic booms and busts. In addition to the extraction of minerals and petroleum lying underground, the tropical rainforest itself has been exploited for forest products such as dyewood, mahogany, rubber, and botanical specimens, a trend that continues today with the search for medicinal and industrial plants.

Europeans have also dreaded the tropical rainforest because of its plagues of insects and diseases as well as its sometimes fierce native inhabitants. Individuals, perhaps revealing more about themselves and their milieus than about the rainforest, reflect society's ambivalence in the variety of their perceptions of the forest. Contrast, for example, the views of Amazonia presented by José Eustasio Rivera and William H. Hudson in Part I. Rivera is probably more representative of the mainstream European perception of forests as wild, threatening, even evil places. Henry Walter Bates, although ostensibly providing an objective, scientific description of the Amazon rainforest, alludes to its melancholy silence and gloom. Perhaps the Westerner's dread of the tropical rainforest contributed to its persistence into the present by diverting development pressures to more promising environments.

The emotional connotations of the forest spill over into scholarly analyses of the tropical rainforest and its economic potential. In the past, anthropologists, geographers, and other scholars have viewed the tropical rainforest as a limiting environment, one that prevented the development of large populations and complex cultures. Recent research, undertaken in an era with a more positive—even romantic—perception of the rainforest and the people who live there, suggests that the tropical rainforest may have supported larger populations and more complex cultures in pre-Columbian times than previously realized. Furthermore, ethnographic fieldwork has revealed that contemporary Native American cultures utilize the tropical rainforest in complex and sophisticated ways, even though their material culture, or technology, tends to be simple.

The debate over the best way to develop the tropical rainforest centers on Amazonia (Map 2), which has become an arena where competing perspectives on development contest. (Similar processes, however, occur in other rainforest frontier zones, such as in Central America and southeastern Mexico.) The sparsely populated Amazon, like other tropical rainforest zones, has long been perceived as an "escape valve" for populations displaced by economic, social, political, and environmental problems in previously settled, more densely populated regions. Recently, though, scholarly research and activism by environmentalists and human rights advocates have encouraged new conceptualizations of the tropical rainforest, its environmental characteristics, and economic potential. The rainforest is now perceived as providing many "free" goods and services that can be managed and exploited in a sustainable way. In some cases, research suggests that conversion of tropical rainforest to other forms of land use, such as ranching or large-scale agriculture, may not produce as much income per hectare in the long run as natural forest managed sustainably. Extractive reserves—forests protected so that local inhabitants can exploit their renewable products such as rubber, nuts and fruits, and resins—are one way of promoting forest conservation and local economic development simultaneously.

A current, heated debate over the role of extractive reserves in the economic development of the Amazon illustrates the range of opinions regarding appropriate land use in the tropical rainforest. Powerful economic and political interests continue to favor opening up the Amazon, in spite of ecological arguments in favor of forest preservation and cost-benefit analyses that indicate that forest clearance may not be economically sensible in the long run. Large landholders and industrialists—foreign and national—seek personal and corporate profit, while the landless and the unemployed seek a way to support themselves and their families by acquiring land of their own on the frontier. Unequal land tenure and high unemployment in the more densely populated zones of Latin America have traditionally pushed migrants into sparsely populated frontier zones. High rates of population growth over the past thirty years, coupled with a development strategy that has further widened the gap between rich and poor, have increased the flow of migrants into the tropical rainforest.

Politicians try to maintain enough constituents to keep themselves in power by promoting the construction of roads into the Amazon wilderness, providing access to land without the necessity of implementing land reform elsewhere. With this they hope to simultaneously defuse popular unrest born of the misery and hopelessness of the underclass and curry favor with powerful economic interests with a personal stake in the development of the

Map 2. The Amazon Basin

Amazon. In some countries, such as Brazil, the politically powerful military wants to secure existing borders and protect the resources of the hinterland by promoting effective occupation of forested frontier zones.

The appropriate metaphor for the Amazon now appears to be not an escape valve, but a microcosm of the unresolved economic, political, social, and environmental problems that plague Latin America as a whole. As long as present conditions exist, the forces that fuel migration into the rainforest will continue. Concentration of land ownership and wealth, agricultural modernization, the need to make payments on large foreign debts, and the political goal of national integration (effective territorial occupation by members of the dominant culture) all increase the pressure to colonize remaining tropical rainforest zones—regardless of the environmental and social consequences for the people who have traditionally lived there. The selections that follow provide a sample of ideas about the nature of the tropical rainforest, the causes and consequences of tropical deforestation, and alternative approaches to developing Latin America's tropical rainforests on a more sustainable and equitable basis.

I

Perceptions of the Rainforest

Since their first encounters with Latin America, Europeans have expressed mixed feelings about the tropical rainforest. The lure of fabulous wealth and the hope of finding El Dorado have wrestled with the dread of mythical beings and horrible diseases in the *green hell*. Accounts of the tropical rainforest, whether novels, travel journals, or scientific reports, reveal at least as much about their authors as they do the forest. Every writer represents to a certain extent the prevailing worldview of his or her time and culture, but perceptions of the rainforest are also filtered through the lens of meanings created by the individual's experiences and beliefs.

The selections in Part I provide a sample of the variety of modern perceptions of the tropical rainforest. William H. Hudson and José Eustasio Rivera, writing in the early twentieth century, present romantic portrayals of the tropical rainforest, although from diametrically opposed viewpoints. In this extract from his novel *Green Mansions*, Hudson presents the rainforest as cathedral (Selection 1), while Rivera, in an excerpt from *The Vortex*, portrays it as the ultimate green hell (Selection 2). Henry Walter Bates, writing in the nineteenth century, represents the straightforward, objective approach of modern science (Selection 3). Excerpted from *The Naturalist on the River Amazons*, Bates's reading provides a factual description of the tropical rainforest environment where he collected specimens; it engages in relatively little editorializing.

Just as the tropical rainforest has been perceived in conflicting ways, so have its Native American inhabitants. Archaeologists and anthropologists frame their research in terms of the prevailing theories and conceptualizations of their times, and the past several decades have witnessed a marked shift in the way they perceive Native Americans. Betty J. Meggers and Clifford Evans (Selection 4) represent a previous generation of archaeologists and anthropologists who perceived Amazonia to be a difficult and limiting environment that prevented the development of advanced cultures. In more recent years, however, archaeologists have begun to consider the region more complex and culturally varied than previously supposed, containing some areas that once supported fairly dense populations and advanced cultures. Support for the contemporary perspective also derives from recent ethnographic research, which views tribal cultures as sophisticated managers of the tropical rainforest environments in which they live. Katherine Milton (Selection 5) exemplifies the current scholarly perspective on indigenous people, which emphasizes their intimate knowledge of and adaptation to the natural environment.

---

1 William H. Hudson ◆ from *Green Mansions*

William Henry Hudson developed a lifelong devotion to nature while grow-
ing up on his family's farm in Argentina. After moving to England in
adulthood he became popular for his interpretations of South American
nature, writing several romantic novels about Latin America. Green
Mansions, *first published in 1904, has proved the most enduring, although*
its first edition enjoyed only modest success. The book's subtitle, A Romance
of the Tropical Forest, *aptly describes Hudson's portrayal of the rainforest*
of Venezuela and Guyana. Although his language may sound somewhat
dated, his romantic view of the rainforest has resurfaced in some of the
recent popular enthusiasm for the tropical rainforest and its inhabitants.

I spent several hours in this wild paradise, which was so much more delightful than the extensive gloomier forests I had so often penetrated in Guayana: for here, if the trees did not attain to such majestic proportions, the variety of vegetable forms was even greater; as far as I went it was nowhere dark under the trees, and the number of lovely parasites everywhere illustrated the kindly influence of light and air. Even where the trees were largest the sunshine penetrated, subdued by the foliage to exquisite greenish-golden tints, filling the wide lower spaces with tender half-lights, and faint blue-and-grey shadows. Lying on my back and gazing up, I felt reluctant to rise and renew my ramble. For what a roof was that above my head! Roof I call it, just as the poets in their poverty sometimes describe the infinite ethereal sky by that word; but it was no more roof-like and hindering to the soaring spirit than the higher clouds that float in changing forms and tints, and like the foliage chasten the intolerable noonday beams. How far above me seemed that leafy cloudland into which I gazed! Nature, we know, first taught the architect to produce by long colonnades the illusion of distance; but the light-excluding roof prevents him from getting the same effect above. Here Nature is unapproachable with her green, airy canopy, a

From W. H. Hudson, *Green Mansions: A Romance of the Tropical Forest*
(London: Duckworth & Co., 1904).

sun-impregnated cloud—cloud above cloud; and though the highest may be unreached by the eye, the beams yet filter through, illuming the wide spaces beneath—chamber succeeded by chamber, each with its own special lights and shadows. Far above me, but not nearly so far as it seemed, the tender gloom of one such chamber or space is traversed now by a golden shaft of light falling through some break in the upper foliage, giving a strange glory to everything it touches—projecting leaves, and beard-like tuft of moss, and snaky bush-rope. And in the most open part of that most open space, suspended on nothing to the eye, the shaft reveals a tangle of shining silver threads—the web of some large tree-spider. These seemingly distant, yet distinctly visible threads, serve to remind me that the human artist is only able to get his horizontal distance by a monotonous reduplication of pillar and arch, placed at regular intervals, and that the least departure from this order would destroy the effect. But Nature produces her effects at random, and seems only to increase the beautiful illusion by that infinite variety of decoration in which she revels, binding tree to tree in a tangle of anaconda-like lianas, and dwindling down from these huge cables to airy webs and hair-like fibres that vibrate to the wind of the passing insect's wing.

Thus in idleness, with such thoughts for company, I spent my time, glad that no human being, savage or civilised, was with me. It was better to be alone to listen to the monkeys that chattered without offending; to watch them occupied with the unserious business of their lives. With that luxuriant tropical nature, its green clouds and illusive aerial spaces, full of mystery, they harmonised well in language, appearance, and motions;—mountebank angels, living their fantastic lives far above earth in a half-way heaven of their own.

---

2 José Eustasio Rivera ◆ from *The Vortex*

José Eustasio Rivera's powerful 1924 novel, La vorágine (The Vortex), *is today virtually unknown in North America. Yet Rivera's passionate protest against the exploitation of man and nature in the Amazon rainforest expresses surprisingly contemporary sentiments, however romantic and archaic the language. He talks of intergenerational equity—that overexploitation today defrauds future generations—and about how economic expansion exploits humans and nature, concerns that mainstream social scientists have only recently begun to articulate.*

Rivera is clearly outraged by the degradation of the rubber tappers and the inhumanity of the system of latex extraction that arose during the great

From José Eustasio Rivera, *The Vortex* (New York, 1935). Translated by Earle K. James.

Amazon rubber boom of the nineteenth and early twentieth centuries. Based on debt peonage that practically enslaved the rubber tappers, it trapped them in abject poverty and misery while enriching merchants and patrons, who claimed to own vast tracts of rainforest where the rubber trees grew. The system has continued to the present day in Brazil, although a movement began in the 1970s to free the rubber tappers from debt bondage (see Selection 20). Rivera foreshadows the Brazilian rural workers' movement of the late twentieth century.

Rivera's portrayal of the tropical rainforest as a vortex that sucks people into danger and degradation, however, seems an anachronism characteristic of his time and culture. The Vortex *belongs to a genre of novelas telúricas (Latin American novels of the land) of the early twentieth century in which the wilderness is conceptualized as barbaric, while urban life is regarded as civilized. Rivera likens the rainforest to a prison cell rather than a cathedral, as Hudson did in* Green Mansions. *A member of a Colombian commission to survey the country's boundary with Venezuela, Rivera actually experienced many of the dangers and hardships that the protagonist of the novel suffered. Indeed, Rivera's untimely death in 1928 was attributed to an attack of a tropical disease contracted during his time in the rainforest.*

No one knows what it is that upsets and confuses us when we travel through the jungles. Nevertheless, I think I've found the explanation: any of these trees would seem tame, friendly, even smiling in a park, along a road on a plain, where nobody would bleed it or persecute it; yet here they are all perverse, or aggressive, or hypnotizing. In these lonely places, under these shadows, they have their own way of fighting us: something scares us, something makes us shudder, something oppresses us, and then jungle giddiness turns our head, and we want to flee, and we get lost—and because of this thousands of rubber workers never emerge from the jungle.

"I, too, have felt its evil influence—especially in Yaguanarí."

For the first time I saw the inhuman jungle in all its horror, saw the pitiless struggle for existence. Deformed trees were held imprisoned by creepers. Lianas bound them together in a death grip. Stretched from tree to palm in long elastic curves, like carelessly hung nets, they caught falling leaves, branches, and fruits, held them for years until they sagged and burst like rotten bags, scattering blind reptiles, rusty salamanders, hairy spiders and decayed vegetable matter over the underbrush.

Everywhere the matapalo—the pulpy creeper of the forest— sticks its tentacles on the treetrunks, twisting and strangling them, injecting itself into them, and fusing with them in a painful metempsychosis. The bachaqueros vomit forth trillions of devastating ants. These mow down the mantle of the jungles and return to their tunnels over the wide swaths they cut, carrying

leaves aloft like the banners of an army of extinction. The comején grub
gnaws at the trees like quick-spreading syphilis, boring unseen from within,
rotting tissue and pulverizing bark, until the weight of branches that are still
living brings the giant crashing to the ground.

Meanwhile the earth continues its successive renovations: at the foot of
the colossus that falls, new germs are budding; pollen is flying in the midst
of miasmas; everywhere is the reek of fermentation, steaming shadows, the
sopor of death, the enervating process of procreation. Where is that solitude
poets sing of? Where are those butterflies like translucent flowers, the
magic birds, those singing streams? Poor phantasies of those who know
only domesticated retreat!

No cooing nightingales here, no Versaillian gardens or sentimental
vistas! Instead the croaking of dropsical frogs, the tangled misanthropic
undergrowth, the stagnant backwaters and swamps. Here the aphrodisiac
parasite that covers the ground with dead insects; the disgusting blooms that
throb with sensual palpitations, their sticky smell intoxicating as a drug; the
malignant liana, the hairs of which blind animals; the pringamosa that
irritates the skin; the berry of the curujú, a rainbow-hued globe that holds
only a caustic ash; the purging grape; the bitter nut of the corojo palm.

At night, unknown voices, phantasmagoric lights, funereal silences. It
is death that passes, giving life. Fruits fall, and on falling give promise of
new seed. Leaves come to earth with a faint sighing, to become fertilizer for
the roots of the parent tree. Crunching jaws are heard, devouring with the
fear of being devoured. Warning whistles, dying wails, beasts belching.
And when dawn showers its tragic glory over the jungles, the clamor of
survivors again begins: the zoom of the shrieking guan; the wild boar
crashing through the underbrush; the laughter of ridiculous monkeys. All
for the brief joy of a few more hours of life!

This sadistic and virgin jungle casts premonitions of coming danger
over one's spirit. Vegetable life is a sensitive thing, the psychology of
which we ignore. In these desolate places only our presentiments understand
the language it speaks. Under its influence man's nerves become taut and
ready to attack, are ready for treachery and ambush. Our senses confuse
their tasks: the eye feels, the back sees, the nose explores, the legs calculate,
and the blood cries out: "Flee! Flee!"

And yet, it is civilized man who is the champion of destruction. There is
something magnificent in the story of these pirates who enslave their peons,
exploit the environment, and struggle with the jungle. Buffeted by misfortune,
they leave the anonymity of cities to plunge into the wilderness, seeking a
purpose for their sterile life. Delirious from malaria, they loose themselves
of their conscience, and adapt themselves to the environment; and with no
arms but the rifle and the machete, they suffer the most atrocious needs,

while longing for pleasures and plenty. They live exposed to the elements, always ravenous, even naked, for here clothes rot on one's body.

Then some day, on the rock of some river, they build their thatched hut and appoint themselves "masters of the enterprise." Although the jungle is their enemy, they don't know whom to fight; so they fall upon one another and kill and subdue their own kind during intervals in their onslaught on the forests; and at times their trail is like that left by an avalanche. Every year the rubber workers in Colombia destroy millions of trees, while in Venezuela the balatá rubber tree has disappeared. In this way they defraud the coming generations. . . .

Dreams never realized, triumphs that were lost—why do you hover in my memory, as if trying to shame me? See what this visionary has come to: wounding an inert tree, in order to fatten the wealth of those who do not dream; enduring insults and tyranny just for a few crumbs at nightfall!

Slave, do not complain of your fatigue! Prisoner, do not regret your jail! You know nothing of the torture of wandering unfettered in a prison like the jungle, a green vault walled in by immense rivers. You don't know the torment of the shadows, when one may see a glimpse of sunshine on the opposite shore of a river, but a distant bank one can never reach. The chains that gnaw your ankles are more merciful than the leeches in these swamps. The keeper who torments you is not so cruel as these trees, who watch you without ever speaking.

I have three hundred trees to take care of, and it takes me nine days to lacerate them. I have cleaned them of creepers and lianas. I have opened a path toward each of them. On trudging through this army of giants, to fell the ones that don't shed latex, I often find tappers stealing my rubber. We tear each other with fists and machetes; and the disputed latex is splashed with red. But what does it matter if our veins increase the supply of sap? The overseer demands ten liters a day, and the lash is a usurer that never forgives.

And what if my neighbor dies of fever? I see him stretched out on the leafy mold, shaking himself, trying to rid himself of flies that will not let him die in peace. Tomorrow I shall move away, driven elsewhere by the stench. But I shall steal the latex he gathered. My work will be so much lighter. They'll do the same with me when I die. I who have never stolen, not even to help my parents, will steal when I can for my oppressors.

As I gash the dripping trunk, as I channel it so that its tears may flow into the tin cup, clouds of mosquitoes that protect it suck my blood, and the miasmas of the forests dim my eyes. Thus both the tree and I, suffering, are tearful in the face of death: and both of us struggle until we succumb.

Yet I cannot pity the organism that does not protest. Tremorous branches are not a sign of rebellion that will inspire me with affection. Why doesn't the entire jungle roar out and crush us, like reptiles, in order to punish this vile exploitation? I feel no sadness—only desperation. I would like to have somebody with whom to conspire! I'd like to start a gigantic battle of the species, die in cataclysmic struggles, see the cosmic forces inverted! If Satan would lead this rebellion. . . .

I have been a rubber worker, I am a rubber worker. And what my hand has done to trees, it can also do to men.

---

3 Henry Walter Bates ◆ from
The Naturalist on the River Amazons

Henry Walter Bates, a prominent nineteenth-century English naturalist, traveled to the Amazon in 1843 with Alfred Russel Wallace, cocreator with Charles Darwin of the theory of evolution by natural selection. This excerpt gives Bates's impressions from his first walk, with Wallace, in the tropical rainforest near Pará (now called Belém). He provides a good description of the sound and feel of the forest, as well as its appearance, and conveys a sense of the monotony of the tropical climate in his description of the daily routine of the two naturalists.

In this selection the modern reader can get some unintended insights into the midnineteenth-century world of the author—when vast herds of buffalo still roamed the great plains of North America and church domes towered over the other buildings of the great cities. Bates's passing reference to these as unremarkable facts highlights the rapidity with which humans can reshape their environments—often in unforeseen ways. Can we imagine what Amazonia might look like a century from now? Will there still be extensive tracts of natural forest where future naturalists and scientists can explore and make discoveries, as Bates did?

The two hours before breakfast were devoted to ornithology. At that early period of the day the sky was invariably cloudless (the thermometer marking 72 degrees or 73 degrees Fahrenheit): the heavy dew or the previous night's rain, which lay on the moist foliage, becoming quickly dissipated by the glowing sun, which rising straight out of the east, mounted rapidly towards the zenith. All nature was fresh, new leaf and flower-buds expanding rapidly. Some mornings a single tree would appear in flower amidst what was the preceding evening a uniform green mass of forest—a dome of blossom suddenly created as if by magic. The birds were all active;

From Henry Walter Bates, *The Naturalist on the River Amazon*. 1863. Reprint. New York: Dover, 1975.

from the wild-fruit trees, not far off, we often heard the shrill yelping of the Toucans. . . . Small flocks of parrots flew over on most mornings, at a great height, appearing in distinct relief against the blue sky, always two by two, chattering to each other, the pairs being separated by regular intervals; their bright colours, however, were not apparent at that height. After breakfast we devoted the hours from 10 a.m. to 2 or 3 p.m. to entomology; the best time for insects in the forest being a little before the greatest heat of the day.

The heat increased rapidly towards two o'clock (92 degrees and 93 degrees Fahrenheit), by which time every voice of bird or mammal was hushed; only in the trees was heard at intervals the harsh whirr of a cicada. The leaves, which were so moist and fresh in early morning, now become lax and drooping; the flowers shed their petals. Our neighbours, the Indian and Mulatto inhabitants of the open palm-thatched huts, as we returned home fatigued with our ramble, were either asleep in their hammocks or seated on mats in the shade, too languid even to talk. On most days in June and July a heavy shower would fall some time in the afternoon, producing a most welcome coolness. The approach of the rain-clouds was after a uniform fashion very interesting to observe. First, the cool sea-breeze, which commenced to blow about 10 o'clock, and which had increased in force with the increasing power of the sun, would flag and finally die away. The heat and electric tension of the atmosphere would then become almost insupportable. Languor and uneasiness would seize on every one; even the denizens of the forest betraying it by their motions. White clouds would appear in the east and gather into cumuli, with an increasing blackness along their lower portions. The whole eastern horizon would become almost suddenly black, and this would spread upwards, the sun at length become obscured. Then the rush of a mighty wind is heard through the forest, swaying the tree-tops; a vivid flash of lightning burst forth, then a crash of thunder, and down streams the deluging rain. Such storms soon cease, leaving bluish-black motionless clouds in the sky until night. Meantime all nature is refreshed; but heaps of flower-petals and fallen leaves are seen under the trees. Towards evening life revives again, and the ringing uproar is resumed from bush and tree. The following morning the sun again rises in a cloudless sky, and so the cycle is completed; spring, summer, and autumn, as it were, in one tropical day. The days are more or less like this throughout the year in this country. A little difference exists between the dry and wet seasons; but generally, the dry season, which lasts from July to December, is varied with showers, and the wet, from January to June, with sunny days. It results from this, that the periodical phenomena of plants and animals do not take place at about the same time in all species, or in the individuals of any given species, as they do in temperate countries. Of course, there is no hybernation; nor, as the dry season is not excessive, is there any summer torpidity as in some tropical countries. Plants do not flower or shed their leaves, nor do birds moult, pair, or breed simultaneously. In Europe, a woodland scene has its spring, its summer, its autumnal, and its winter aspects. In the equatorial forests the aspect is the same or nearly so every day in the year: budding, flowering, fruiting, and leaf-shedding are always going on in one species or other. The activity of birds and insects proceeds without interruption, each species having its own separate times. . . . It is never either spring, summer, or autumn, but each day is a combination of all three. With the day and night always of equal length, the atmospheric disturbances of each day neutralising themselves before each succeeding morn; with the sun in its course proceeding mid-way across the sky, and the daily temperature the same within two or three degrees throughout the year—how grand in its perfect equilibrium and simplicity is the march of Nature under the equator! . . .

The same unbroken forest extends all the way to Maranham and in other directions, as we were told, a distance of about three hundred miles southward and eastward of Pará. In almost every hollow part the road was crossed by a brook, whose cold, dark, leaf-stained waters were bridged over by tree trunks. The ground was carpeted, as usual, by Lycopodiums, but it was also encumbered with masses of vegetable debris and a thick coating of dead leaves. Fruits of many kinds were scattered about, amongst which were many sorts of beans, some of the pods a foot long, flat and leathery in texture, others hard as stone. . . .

What attracted us chiefly were the colossal trees. The general run of trees had not remarkably thick stems; the great and uniform height to which they grow without emitting a branch, was a much more noticeable feature than their thickness; but at intervals of a furlong or so a veritable giant towered up. Only one of these monstrous trees can grow within a given space; it monopolises the domain, and none but individuals of much inferior size can find a footing near it. The cylindrical trunks of these larger trees were generally about twenty to twenty-five feet in circumference. Von Martius mentions having measured trees in the Pará district, belonging to various species . . . which were fifty to sixty feet in girth at the point where they become cylindrical. The height of the vast column-like stems could not be less than one hundred feet from the ground to their lowest branch. Mr. Leavens, at the saw-mills, told me they frequently squared logs for sawing one hundred feet long. . . . The total height of these trees, stem and crown together, may be estimated at from 180 to 200 feet: where one of them stands, the vast dome of foliage rises above the other forest trees as a domed cathedral does above the other buildings in a city.

A very remarkable feature in these trees is the growth of buttress-shaped projections around the lower part of their stems. The spaces between these buttresses, which are generally thin walls of wood, form spacious chambers, and may be compared to stalls in a stable: some of them are large enough to hold half a dozen persons. The purpose of these structures is as obvious, at the first glance, as that of the similar props of brickwork which support a high wall. They are not peculiar to one species, but are common to most of the larger forest trees. Their nature and manner of growth are explained when a series of young trees of different ages is examined. It is then seen that they are the roots which have raised themselves ridge-like out of the earth; growing gradually upwards as the increasing height of the tree required augmented support. Thus they are plainly intended to sustain the massive crown and trunk in these crowded forests, where lateral growth of the roots in the earth is rendered difficult by the multitude of competitors. . . .

In some parts of the road ferns were conspicuous objects. But I afterwards found them much more numerous on the Maranham road, especially in one place where the whole forest glade formed a vast fernery; the ground was covered with terrestrial species, and the tree trunks clothed with climbing and epiphytous kinds. I saw no tree ferns in the Pará district; they belong to hilly regions; some occur, however, on the Upper Amazons.

Such were the principal features in the vegetation of the wilderness; but where were the flowers? To our great disappointment we saw none, or only such as were insignificant in appearance. Orchids are very rare in the dense forests of the low lands. I believe it is now tolerably well ascertained that the majority of forest trees in equatorial Brazil have small and inconspicuous flowers. Flower-frequenting insects are also rare in the forest. Of course they would not be found where their favourite food was wanting, but I always noticed that even where flowers occurred in the forest, few or no insects were seen upon them. In the open country or campos of Santarem, on the Lower Amazons, flowering trees and bushes are more abundant, and there a large number of floral insects are attracted. The forest bees of South America . . . are more frequently seen feeding on the sweet sap which exudes from the trees, or on the excrement of birds on leaves, than on flowers.

We were disappointed also in not meeting with any of the larger animals in the forest. There was no tumultuous movement, or sound of life. We did not see or hear monkeys, and no tapir or jaguar crossed our path. Birds, also, appeared to be exceedingly scarce. . . .

I afterwards saw reason to modify my opinion, founded on these first impressions, with regard to the amount and variety of animal life in this and other parts of the Amazonian forests. There is, in fact, a great variety of mammals, birds, and reptiles, but they are widely scattered, and all excessively shy of man. The region is so extensive, and uniform in the forest clothing of its surface, that it is only at long intervals that animals are seen in abundance, where some particular spot is found which is more attractive than others. Brazil, moreover, is throughout poor in terrestrial mammals, and the species are of small size; they do not, therefore, form a conspicuous feature in its forests. The huntsman would be disappointed who expected to find here flocks of animals similar to the buffalo herds of North America, or the swarms of antelopes and herds of ponderous pachyderms of Southern Africa. The largest and most interesting portion of the Brazilian mammal fauna is arboreal in its habits. . . . The most intensely arboreal animals in the world are the South American monkeys of the family Cebidae, many of which have a fifth hand for climbing in their prehensile tails, adapted for this function by their strong muscular development, and the naked palms under their tips. This seems to teach us that the South American fauna has been slowly adapted to a forest life, and therefore, that extensive forests must have always existed since the region was first peopled by mammalia. . . .

We often read, in books of travels, of the silence and gloom of the Brazilian forests. They are realities, and the impression deepens on a longer acquaintance. The few sounds of birds are of that pensive or mysterious character which intensifies the feeling of solitude rather than imparts a sense of life and cheerfulness. Sometimes, in the midst of the stillness, a sudden yell or scream will startle one; this comes from some defenceless fruit-eating animal, which is pounced upon by a tiger-cat or stealthy boa-constrictor. Morning and evening the howling monkeys make a most fearful and harrowing noise, under which it is difficult to keep up one's buoyancy of spirit. The feeling of inhospitable wildness which the forest is calculated to inspire, is increased tenfold under this fearful uproar. Often, even in the still hours of midday, a sudden crash will be heard resounding afar through the wilderness, as some great bough or entire tree falls to the ground. There are, besides, many sounds which it is impossible to account for.

---

4 Betty J. Meggers and Clifford Evans ◆ Environmental Limitations on Culture in the Tropical Forest

Betty Meggers and Clifford Evans's archaeological work has influenced our thinking about the Amazon for decades. Representing a perspective

From Betty J. Meggers and Clifford Evans, *Archaeological Investigations at the Mouth of the Amazon* (Washington, DC, 1957): 26–32. Smithsonian Institution Bureau of American Ethnology Bulletin 167.

called environmental determinism, they believed that infertile soils and extensive seasonal flooding placed severe limitations on the size of the human population and the development of advanced material cultures in Amazonia, as set forth in this 1957 article. A new generation of scholars is still debating their conclusions. Many seek to refute their hypotheses about the limitations of the Amazon basin as a home for human beings, and subsequent research has called into question the assumptions that they made about small, nomadic populations in Amazonia.

The geographer William Denevan, for example, using historical accounts from the period of initial European contact, as well as archaeological evidence, estimates a fairly large pre-Columbian population for Amazonia—from five to seven million. Apparently much of this population concentrated along the rivers, leaving sparsely populated areas in the infertile uplands, confirming Meggers's contention that the latter supported few people. Further research has supported her conclusions about the poverty of the majority of Amazonia's soils. But current theory favors the view that she underestimated the native population's complex adaptations to floodplains and management of the environment of the infertile uplands. Darrell A. Posey's article in Part III represents a perspective that is gaining ascendancy among modern ethnographers: native peoples, while lacking in material technology, manage their environments with sophisticated methods.

W e are familiar with the pattern of culture characteristic of the living tribes of the lowland tropical forest, and have noted some of the ways in which this type of culture is an adaptation to the environment in which it exists. In the present report, it will be shown that seven of the eight archeological Phases identified on Mexiana, Caviana, and Marajó Islands and in the Territory of Amapá fall within the Tropical Forest Pattern. They differ from one another in details of pottery type and decoration, in village size and composition, and in burial customs, but all of these variations come within the range exhibited among living Tropical Forest tribes.

The sites and ceramics of the eighth culture, the Marajoara Phase, are so outstanding that they previously completely overshadowed the less spectacular remains of the earlier archeological horizons on Marajó Island. Their exploitation is so obviously profitable, even in the eyes of the *caboclos*, that it is only with difficulty and persistence that one is able to secure information on Ananatuba, Mangueiras, and Formiga Phase sites within the limits of the Marajoara Phase area of distribution. The high degree of technical and artistic competence attained by the Marajoara Phase ceramicists caused early writers to suggest that the makers must have been descended from, or at least have had contact with, Egyptian or Oriental civilizations (Lisle du Dreneuc, 1889, p. 19). This evaluation cannot be given scientific credence today, but the observation on which it is based, namely, that Marajoara Phase culture is considerably more highly developed than other

living or extinct cultures in the area, receives the support of modern
archeological investigation. The quality and standardization of the ceramics,
the differential elaborateness of the burials, and the large earthworks are
material indications of a level of social and political organization more
comparable to that of Circum-Caribbean and Andean cultures than to Tropical Forest tribal society.

The appearance of this advanced culture on Marajó Island in the midst
of a succession of simpler ones throws the contrast between the two levels
of development into high relief and raises questions that otherwise might
not come to the attention of the archeologist. Why, for example, did none of
the other archeological cultures attain, or even begin to reach, such a high
level of development? Why did the Marajoara Phase undergo a cultural
decline on Marajó Island? Could it have originated elsewhere in the Tropical Forest area?

Seeking answers to these questions requires a study of anthropological
theory. Analysis of the forces contributing to the evolution of culture
elsewhere has shown that agriculture exercises a dominant role (White,
1949; Childe, 1951). Wherever it has been introduced, there is an almost
immediate and revolutionary change in the culture; where it has not penetrated, the culture never advances (except in special situations) beyond a
nomadic hunting and gathering level, with undifferentiated social
organization and simple technology. Agriculture is not a simple "open
sesame" to the unlimited vistas of civilization, however. Its effectiveness as
a subsistence base depends on two factors: the potentiality of the environment
and the agricultural technology of the culture. The variant combinations of
these extant in the world explain and in some cases determine the differences in level of development that can be described (Meggers, 1954).

The principle behind this conclusion can be summarized briefly. A
food-gathering type of economy is undependable and time consuming. The
return per man-hour of labor expended is small and sufficient only to satisfy
immediate needs. The supply of roots, fruits, and seeds is seasonal, and
game is unconcentrated. In order to maintain an adequate food supply,
constant activity is required by all the able-bodied members of the community,
which is limited to a small group typically composed of kin. This type of
cultural adjustment, characterized by a minimum of material goods and a
minimum of sociopolitical organization, was universal over the world until
the commencement of the Neolithic, which is marked by the introduction of
domesticated plants and animals. It has survived until the present in scattered
environments where agriculture cannot be introduced.

The adoption of agriculture as the basic food source meant that man
was able for the first time to devote a good part of his time and attention to
other things than the securing of food. As a result, the introduction of

agriculture everywhere transformed the typically nomadic life of hunters and gatherers with remarkable rapidity into a new pattern characterized by settled villages and by the acquisition of the ceramic and textile arts. This initial revolution brought little alteration in the social organization—no strong chiefs, social classes, occupational specialization—or in religious concepts or practices. These advances came later and depended upon the increasing productivity of agriculture; in other words, on the deflection of larger amounts of time and effort from food production to be expended instead on culture building.

Where the techniques are absent or the environment prohibits their use and agriculture does not increase in productivity, the culture is arrested temporarily or permanently after the consummation of the first stage of advance. In temperate regions like Europe and North America, the fertility of the soil can be permanently maintained and the yield often increased by scientific crop rotation, fertilization, and similar means. In desert regions like Coastal Peru or in fertile river valleys like that of the Nile, the soil is almost unlimited in its ability to produce abundant crops year after year, which selective plant breeding can augment. But there is no evidence from geographers, soil experts, agronomists, or botanists that such a thing is possible where tropical forest conditions require slash-and-burn agricultural exploitation, and anthropological data add confirmation. No culture deriving its subsistence from slash-and-burn agriculture is able to maintain any of the traits of advanced agricultural societies, such as well-developed leadership, class distinction, occupational specialization, priests, temples or high gods, large and permanent cities and towns, and empires. There are only small, scattered and semipermanent villages and a relatively simple development of some of the basic technologies, like ceramics, textiles, woodworking and basketry.

Much speculation has surrounded the promising potentialities of the American Tropics as the garden spot of the world. Observers of the densely populated areas in equatorial Asia have been led to view the Amazon drainage as equally capable of intense exploitation, lacking only in sufficient advertising. Anthropologists, seeing that the Amazon lagged behind tropical regions nearly everywhere else in the world in the level of cultural development, have been inclined to invoke the late start of the American Indians compared with cultures in the Old World, the constant state of hostility and warfare between the Amazon tribes, or simply to leave the question unanswered.

There is abundant evidence, both from geographers and ethnologists, however, that the limited productivity of slash-and-burn agriculture is the true cause. Robert Pendleton (1950, pp. 115–16), a leading authority on tropical land use, has recently put the situation in decisive language:

In higher latitudes, and particularly in the United States, a widespread opinion prevails that such humid regions as the enormous Amazon basin, now occupied by luxuriant and apparently limitless tropical high forests, must certainly have rich soils, and hence, great potentialities for the production of food, fiber, and other agricultural crops. . . . It is true that certain regions such as those with recently active volcanoes, and those recent alluvial soils in humid equatorial lowlands which are not deeply flooded, do have great crop growing potentialities; they are producing and can continue to produce much from the soil. Nevertheless, on the whole, the soils of the humid equatorial regions have distressingly limited possibilities for plant production. . . . This pessimistic attitude is no longer the result of mere opinion, for in a number of widely scattered regions in the humid low latitudes agricultural scientists have been and still are seriously at work.

The reason for this seeming contradiction in plant productivity is in the differential ability of the crops to utilize the resources of the soil:

The reason for the rapid decline in productivity is that practically all of the plant nutrients within reach of the roots of the forest trees have been taken up and are in the growing trees. Almost all the plant offal (dead leaves, twigs, fruit, fallen trees, etc.) which falls to the ground is quickly attacked by termites and decay organisms; as a consequence it rapidly disappears. Organic matter cannot persist long on the soil; leaf mold as it is known in the north temperate U. S. does not develop. However, the heartwood logs of certain very durable sorts of trees will last a couple of years or more. The nutrients thus released and washed into the soil by the frequent drenching rains are quickly taken up by the tree roots lying in wait just under the soil surface. All the nutrients within reach of the tree roots are in the vegetation, and are being cycled. When the forest is cut and burned the cycle is broken, the plant nutrients being released in soluble form in the ash. The soil itself is extremely acid, often being pH4. The burning slightly reduces the acidity and supplies available nutrients for the crop plants which may be planted in the clearing. But before the annual or biennial crop plants can develop extensive root systems sufficient to absorb any considerable proportion of these liberated nutrients, most of the soluble materials will have been washed down deep into the subsoil by the almost daily rains—thus quite out of reach of the roots.

The effects of this leaching process are dramatically reflected in differences in yield from the same field in successive years. [Charles] Wagley (1953, p. 67) reports that the second planting is only about half as productive as that of the first year after clearing. Re-use of the area before it has had sufficient time to return to tall secondary growth results in a less productive harvest than is achieved if the vegetation is allowed to reach this stage before another attempt at cultivation (op. cit., p. 68). Wasteful as it appears to be, slash-and-burn agriculture is the only method of exploitation that is adapted to the major portion of the Amazon area. The adverse conditions of high temperature and humidity, heavy rainfall, and low initial fertility of the soil make short intervals of cultivation separated by long periods of fallow and reforestation the only circumstance under which the long-range pursuit of agricultural return is feasible, given the plants available aboriginally.

In addition to the general poverty of the soil for agricultural purposes, there is a further factor that serves to reduce the utility of the land. This is its topography and elevation. Estimates of the possibilities of tropical agriculture often leave this out of consideration and as a result make the picture appear considerably brighter than it actually is. [Edward] Higbee (1948), for instance, has estimated that the land in a sixty-mile radius around the Maya site of Tikal could feed five hundred thousand people. This calculation is based on the observation that the production from one acre of land will feed one person for two years. After clearing, thirty years of fallow are required for the return of fertility, before reclearing is profitable. Under these conditions, an allotment of fifteen acres per person would insure a permanent food supply. Division of the area within a sixty-mile radius of Tikal into fifteen-acre plots gives Higbee his estimated population of five hundred thousand. However, this method of calculating subsistence potential fails to make allowances for irregularities in the terrain. To be usable for agriculture, the land must be above flood level and have a minimum of slope. In a region where rivers rise from ten to twenty or more feet in the rainy season, a substantial part of the land is submerged for several months each year. Hills often have steep banks and summits too small for a field. Our own estimate of agriculturally usable land in British Guiana, Brazilian Guiana (Territory of Amapá), and on the Islands of Mexiana, Caviana, and Marajó, is that it constitutes about one twenty-fifth of the total dry season extent. Since this is based on traveling over the countryside and along the rivers rather than on a specific survey, and in order to avoid an error on the conservative side, we increased this figure two and one half times, bringing it to 10 percent of the total land area.

Tropical areas with more favorable conditions for agriculture exist, but Marajó Island is not one of them. On the contrary, its potentiality is rather lower than average. The forested western part, poorly drained even during the dry months, is inundated during the rainy season. The campo dominating the eastern half is also hostile to agriculture. Unlike the fertile plains of temperate regions, the tropical grasslands are even lower in agricultural potential than the forests. It is only with extensive preparation of the soil with fertilizer and by careful nurturing that the modern ranchers succeed in bringing a rare fruit tree to maturity (Lage, 1944, pp. 244–245; Pendleton, 1950, pp. 119–120). Only in the limited area along the southeastern coast can the conditions be said to be all favorable to cultivation. Productivity can be judged on the basis of efforts to establish agricultural colonies on the opposite side of the Baia de Marajó, where the land is part of the same formation as on the Island (Pendleton, 1950, p. 116):

> The peasants who pioneered here soon found that while they could get a good crop of food the first year after cutting and burning the primeval forest and could get a following crop or two of mandioca, no further cropping was worthwhile for them, even though very little labor was needed to cut down and clear the second growth that came in after they abandoned their two or three years' cultivation of crops in the new clearing.

The inescapable effects of reliance on slash-and-burn agriculture have been recorded repeatedly by ethnographers: "The periodic exhaustion of the soil by manioc produces a seminomadic tribal life" among the Cubeo (Goldman, 1948, p. 770); "The Jívaro community is . . . moved at least every 6 years as new farm land is needed" (Steward and Métraux, 1948, p. 621), etc. The pattern of "shifting cultivation" requires that the rest of the culture remain simple enough to retain its mobility, to be capable of ready transferral from place to place, or become extinct as local food resources give out.

Examples of the degeneration or extinction of cultures that had become adjusted to permanently productive agriculture and were attracted or pushed into the tropical forest are also abundant. [Frederick] Johnson (1948, p. 196) summarizes the Central American situation:

> The few colonies which the Meso-Americans sent into the Tropical Forest were mere outposts, some of which succumbed to the environment, while others, probably under environmental influence, adopted the indigenous culture. The colonies which retained their Meso-American features were evidently not established long enough before the Conquest for local environmental and cultural influences to have changed them.

Students of the Andean cultures have commented that even the remarkably organized Inca system was unable to surmount the limitations of the lowland tropics. [Matthew] Stirling notes that "archeological sites . . . in the valleys of the Upano and Namangosa Rivers demonstrate that the material culture of the Jivaros in pre-Columbian times resembled that of the ancient cultures of the highlands much more closely than do present-day survivals" (1938, p. xi; also Steward, 1948, pp. 13–14).

This process of deculturation can be observed in progress in the changes that occurred in the culture of the Marajoara Phase during its habitation of Marajó Island. In this instance we have as complete possession of the facts as we are likely to have for the assessment of the causes of this decline. We have comparative material in the form of four other cultures of the Tropical Forest Pattern that occupied the same area at different times. These form a sharp contrast to the Marajoara Phase and emphasize its more advanced character, which can be paralleled only by cultures of the Circum-Caribbean and Sub-Andean levels of development. We have a detailed knowledge of the environment today, and the high probability that in the short time represented by the archeological sequence there was no notable ecological alteration. All of this evidence makes as clear a case as possible for the conclusion that this environment cannot support a culture more advanced than the Tropical Forest Pattern.

If this is true, then the Tropical Forest Pattern represents the maximum development of culture that could have been attained in the area where agricultural exploitation is limited to slash-and-burn. This limitation is first and foremost an environmental one, which operates in terms of restricting the subsistence resources, both in quantity and permanence. Some variation exists within the region, and this is correlated with larger or smaller communities, ranging from two or three families to a thousand or more individuals (Tupinambá). The upper limits of this range, however, resemble culturally the lower limits more closely than they do members of the more advanced Circum-Caribbean and Andean Areas. The cultural development of the Tropical Forest Area cannot be said to have been "arrested" by the advent of the Europeans as it might have been in other parts of the New World; it had already been arrested by the agricultural deficiencies of the environment in which it existed.

An understanding of this situation permits a more realistic interpretation and evaluation of the past and present cultures at the mouth of the Amazon than would otherwise be possible. The similarities between the archeological Phases and their comparability to living Tropical Forest cultures become the expected components of a total pattern of adaptation to and limitation by a particular type of environment. The deculturation suffered by the Marajoara Phase and its lack of influence on tribes in the nearby area become understandable and explainable. Knowing the limitations of the tropical forest for the development of culture makes it possible to conclude that some other part of the South American continent with greater subsistence potential must hold the key to the origin of the Marajoara Phase, and this clue can be pursued and verified by use of the comparative method.

That the ecological situation in the Tropical Forest Area can be so sharply defined is a fortunate and unusual circumstance. In most other types of environment, the limitations and possibilities for cultural development are less readily delimited, and differences in technological achievement, especially in the realm of agriculture, can play an important role in determining the productivity of the subsistence and through it the level to which the culture can attain. Hence the approach employed here may not turn out to be particularly useful to archeologists working in other parts of the New

World. This does not argue against making fullest use of it in the tropical forest, where the data recovered by archeology are so meager that all conceivable methods of analysis and interpretation must be explored.

Literature Cited

Childe, V. Gordon. 1951. *Social Evolution*. London.

Goldman, Irving. 1948. Tribes of the Uaupés-Caquetá Region. In *Handbook of South American Indians, Bureau of American Ethnology Bulletin* 143, vol. 3, pp. 763–798.

Higbee, Edward. 1948. Agriculture in the Maya Homeland. *Geogr. Rev.*, vol. 38, pp. 457–464.

Johnson, Frederick. 1948. The Post-Conquest Ethnology of Central America: An Introduction. In *Handbook of South American Indians, Bureau of American Ethnology Bulletin* 143, vol. 4, pp. 195–198.

Lage, Sandoval. 1944. *Quadros da Amazonia*. Rio de Janeiro.

Lisle du Dreneuc, P. de. 1889. *Nouvelles découvertes d'idoles de l'Amazone*. Paris.

Meggers, Betty J. 1954. Environmental Limitations on the Development of Culture. *Amer. Anthrop.*, vol. 56, pp. 801–824.

Pendleton, Robert L. 1950. Agricultural and Forestry Potentialities of the Tropics. *Agronomy Journ.*, vol. 42, pp. 115–123.

Steward, Julian H. 1948. The Circum-Caribbean Tribes: An Introduction. In *Handbook of South American Indians, Bureau of American Ethnology Bulletin* 143, vol. 4, pp. 1–41. 1949. South American Cultures: An Interpretive Summary. In *Handbook of South American Indians, Bureau of American Ethnology Bulletin* 143, vol. 5, pp. 669–772.

Steward, Julian H. and Métraux, Alfred. 1948. Tribes of the Peruvian and Ecuadorian Montana. In *Handbook of South American Indians, Bureau of American Ethnology Bulletin* 143, vol. 3, pp. 535–656.

Stirling, Matthew W. 1938. Historical and Ethnographical Material on the Jivaro Indians. *Bureau of American Ethnology Bulletin* 117.

Wagley, Charles. 1953. *Amazon Town: A Study of Man in the Tropics*. New York.

White, Leslie. 1949. *The Science of Culture*. New York.

5 Katherine Milton ◆ Civilization and Its Discontents

Until recently outsiders have remained ignorant of the vast storehouse of knowledge contained in the oral traditions, religious rituals, and other nonmaterial aspects of tribal cultures because their peoples are nonliterate and tend to devalue material possessions. Over the past several decades, however, ethnographers have begun to see indigenous cultures from within through the process of participant-observation—by living with these peoples as members of their communities. Westerners have gradually come to appreciate the wisdom encoded in indigenous cultures' adaptation to nature, and as this appreciation has grown, popular perception of native peoples has become more and more romantic.

The increasing awareness of the complex systems of tribal knowledge has led to a belated realization that modernization represents a great threat to the continued existence of these traditional cultures. The environments on which they depend are being destroyed, and new technologies and manufactured goods are changing their ways of life. Representative of the prevailing contemporary ethnographic views on tribal peoples, anthropologist Katherine Milton's 1992 perspective on the Indians of Amazonia derives from her extensive personal experience of living with them in their rainforest homes.

For more than a decade now, I have led a double life. I spend part of my time in the United States, living in an apartment in Berkeley and teaching anthropology classes at the University of California. The rest of my time is spent in the Amazon basin, where I live in the company of recently contacted Indian groups, studying their traditional ecology and features of their tropical forest environment. On returning to the United States after one of these extended stays in the jungle, I always experience culture shock as I strive to regain control of my possessions, which I have totally forgotten about.

Usually my first act is to retrieve my dust-covered car, which has languished for some six to eighteen months in a garage. The battery must be charged, and then I must wash and vacuum the car, fill it with gas, and check out its many parts. Once I am mobile, I rush to a large supermarket to stock up on cleaning supplies and food. My first few days are completely taken up with chores; there never seems to be a moment when I am not contemplating some type of home repair or new purchase.

Reprinted with permission from *Natural History* (March 1992): 36–43. © 1992 the American Museum of Natural History.

And then there is my body. What a job it is to live up to what is expected of the average American. I must visit the dentist—often more than one kind of dentist—to be sure my teeth are performing at top level. The doctor must be seen for a checkup; my eyes must be examined, glasses and contact lenses adjusted, and so on. I begin to wonder how my friends in Berkeley manage to have any free time at all, since I have fewer possessions than they do—I own no television set, no stereo or compact disc player, no video machine, home computer, food chopper, or any number of other items my friends seem to dote on. I don't even own my apartment.

Plunged back into life in Berkeley, I see myself as a slave of material possessions, and I notice that I deeply resent the time and energy required to maintain them. Nothing could be more different from the life I have been leading with hunter-gatherers deep in the rainforests of Brazil, where people have almost no possessions, and those that they do have are made from local forest materials and are entirely biodegradable.

The groups I have visited live far from any cities, towns, or commercial enterprises. They include the Mayoruna and Maku from Amazonas State; the Arara, Parakana, and Arawete from Pará State; and the Guaja from Maranhão State—peoples so remote and little known that few outside their immediate geographic area have heard of them. Often I am one of the first nonindigenous females many members of the group have ever seen. With my pale skin and hair I am a truly terrifying apparition to younger children, who sometimes scream with fear when they first see me.

All these peoples have been recently contacted: only a few months or, at most, years have passed since the Brazilian Indian Bureau (FUNAI) managed to establish a formal relationship with them. Previously, these groups avoided or were strongly hostile to outsiders, but with contact, they have permitted a few Indian Bureau employees to live with them, to assist them, and at times, protect them in dealings with other Indian groups or members of the wider Brazilian society. Living with these people has given me the chance to see how even modest changes in their traditional lifeways— the introduction of something as innocent in appearance as a metal cooking pot or ax, a box of matches or some salt—can be the thin edge of a wedge that will gradually alter the behavior and ecological practices of an entire society.

These people typically live in small villages of fewer than a hundred inhabitants, in some cases in groups of only fifteen or twenty. Most practice slash-and-burn agriculture on a small scale, complementing crop foods with wild game and fish, forest fruits and nuts, and occasionally, wild honey. For some months life may revolve around the village, but sooner or later every group I have worked with leaves, generally in small parties, and spends weeks or even months traveling through the forest and living on forest products.

Throughout the forest there are paths that the Indians know and have used for generations. They travel mainly when wild forest fruits and nuts are most abundant and game animals are fat, but families or small groups may go on expeditions at other times of year as well. They trek a few miles, make a temporary camp, and then hunt, gather, and eat several meals in the area before moving on to a new site. At certain times of year, many groups relocate to the borders of large rivers, where they obtain turtle eggs or other seasonal river foods.

The accumulation of possessions would be an impediment to this seminomadic life-style. Whenever individuals go on a trek, they carry everything they need. Leaving possessions behind in a thatch-and-pole hut, to be retrieved later, is not an option, since the humid climate and voracious insects would quickly destroy them. Great numbers of insects often live inside Indian dwellings, principally jungle cockroaches that hide in the roof thatch by day but come out by the thousands at night. Indians seem oblivious to them, letting them run about on their bodies and even crawl on the food so long as they are not perched on the next bite.

Granted, these are generally soft-bodied, small jungle cockroaches and not the tough, large roaches of our urban areas, but even so, I found it difficult to adjust to them. My frantic efforts to remove cockroaches from my body and clothes were regarded as strange by my Indian hosts. At one site, I resorted to storing my clothing each night in a heavy plastic bag, which I sealed shut and suspended from a piece of plastic fish line tied to a roof pole. Otherwise, at night, the roaches covered my shirt and pants so thoroughly that often the fabric could not be seen. Although the roaches would be gone the next morning, they would leave a musty smell; further, just the idea of wearing garments that I had seen coated with cockroaches gave me a squirmy, unclean feeling.

On the forest treks, the women are invariably the most burdened, something Western observers often find difficult to understand or accept. A woman will walk for hours carrying a toddler, a large palm basket containing fifty or more pounds of animal or plant foods, hammocks, a cooking utensil or two, a machete, and the family pets, such as parrots, monkeys, and young puppies. In all the groups I have observed, the women's legs and feet are deformed by the pigeon-toed walk they adopt to give them added traction and stability on the slippery, narrow forest trails. The feet of adult men turn in only slightly, because men usually carry nothing heavier than a bow and arrows (ostensibly to be free to take advantage of any hunting opportunities).

The most important possession the Indians carry with them, however, is knowledge. There is nothing coded in the genome of an Indian concerning how to make a living in a tropical forest—each individual must become a walking bank of information on the forest landscape, its plants and animals, and their habits and uses. This information must be taught anew to the members of each generation, without the benefit of books, manuals, or educational television. Indians have no stores in which to purchase the things they need for survival. Instead, each individual must learn to collect, manufacture, or produce all the things required for his or her entire lifetime.

Because people differ in their talents, the pool of community information and abilities is far greater than its component parts. Individual men and women have their own areas of expertise, as well as their share of general knowledge. Members of the group know whom to consult for special information on hunting practices, the habits of particular game animals, rituals, tool manufacture, crop varieties, and the like.

Tropical-forest Indians talk incessantly, a characteristic I believe reflects the importance of oral transmission of culture. When I lived with the Maku, I slept in a hammock inside a small communal palm shelter. If a Maku awoke in the middle of the night, he usually began to talk or sing in a very loud voice—apparently without any thought that anyone might object to this behavior. It was considered normal, what you do when you wake up in the middle of the night and aren't sleepy. Others learn, as I did, to sleep through it or, if they aren't sleepy, to listen to it. Vocal expression apparently is expected and tolerated in Maku culture, no matter what the hour, an indication to me of how much it is valued.

Unlike our economic system, in which each person typically tries to secure and control as large a share of the available resources as possible, the hunter-gatherer economic system rests on a set of highly formalized expectations regarding cooperation and sharing. This does not mean hunter-gatherers do not compete with one another for prestige, sexual partners, and the like. But individuals do not amass a surplus. For instance, no hunter fortunate enough to kill a large game animal assumes that all this food is his or belongs only to his immediate family.

Quite the reverse is true: among some forest peoples, the hunter cannot eat game he has killed or is restricted to eating only one specific portion of his kill. Game is cut up and distributed according to defined patterns particular to each group and based in large part on kinship and marriage obligations. A hunter may have amazing luck one day, moderate luck on another, and no luck at all on a third. But he can usually expect to eat meat every day because someone bound to him in this system of reciprocity may well make a kill and share the meat.

Despite the way their culture traditionally eschews possessions, forest-living peoples embrace manufactured goods with amazing enthusiasm. They seem to appreciate instantly the efficacy of a steel machete, ax, or cooking pot. It is love at first sight, and the desire to possess such objects is absolute. There are accounts of Indian groups or individuals who have turned their backs on manufactured trade goods, but such people are the exception.

When Cândido Rondon, the founder of the Indian Protection Service in Brazil, began his pacification efforts in the early 1900s, he used trade goods as bait to attract uncontacted Indians. Pots, machetes, axes, and steel knives were hung from trees or laid along trails that Indians frequented. This practice proved so successful that it is still employed (*see* "Overtures to the Nambiquara," by David Price, *Natural History*, October 1984).

Whether they have been formally contacted or not, forest-living groups in the Amazon Basin are probably well aware of steel tools and metal cooking pots. After all, such goods have been in circulation along trade routes in these regions for centuries, and an Indian does not have to have seen a non-Indian in order to acquire them. However, such manufactured goods are likely to be extremely scarce among uncontacted groups. When the Arara Indians were first approached in 1975, they fled their village to escape the pacification party. Examination of their hastily abandoned dwellings showed that stone tools were still being used, but a few steel fragments were also found.

Since they already appreciate the potential utility of manufactured goods, uncontacted Indians are strongly drawn to the new and abundant items offered to lure them from isolation. Once a group has been drawn into the pacification area, all its members are presented with various trade goods—standard gifts include metal cooking pots, salt, matches, machetes, knives, axes, cloth hammocks, T-shirts, and shorts. Not all members of the group get all of these items, but most get at least two or three of them, and in a family, the cumulative mass of new goods can be considerable.

The Indians initially are overwhelmed with delight—this is the honeymoon period when suddenly, from a position in which one or two old metal implements were shared by the entire group, a new situation prevails in which almost every adult individual has some of these wonderful new items. The honeymoon is short-lived, however. Once the Indians have grown accustomed to these new items, the next step is to teach them that these gifts will not be repeated. The Indians are now told that they must work to earn money or must manufacture goods for trade so that they can purchase new items.

Unable to contemplate returning to life without steel axes, the Indians begin to produce extra arrows or blowguns or hunt additional game or weave baskets beyond what they normally need so that this new surplus can be traded. Time that might, in the past, have been used for other tasks—subsistence activities, ceremonial events, or whatever—is now devoted to production of barter goods. In addition, actual settlement patterns may be altered so that the indigenous group is in closer, more immediate contact with sources of manufactured items. Neither of these things, in itself, is necessarily good or bad, but each does alter traditional behavior.

Thus, the newly contacted forest people are rapidly drawn into the wider economic sphere (even into the international economy: for example, the preferred glass beads for personal adornment come from Czechoslovakia). The intrusion of every item—mirrors, cloth, scissors, rice, machetes, axes, pots, bowls, needles, blankets, even bicycles and radios—not only adds to the pressure on individuals to produce trade goods but also disrupts some facet of traditional production.

Anthropologist Paul Henley, who worked with the Panare, a forest-based people in Venezuela, points out that with the introduction of steel tools, particularly axes, indigenous groups suffer a breakdown in the web of cooperative interdependence. In the past, when stone axes were used, various individuals came together and worked communally to fell trees for a new garden. With the introduction of the steel ax, however, one man can clear a garden by himself. As Henley notes, collaboration is no longer mandatory nor particularly frequent.

Indians often begin to cultivate new crops, such as coffee, that they feel can be traded or sold easily. Another is rice, which the Indian Bureau encourages forest people to plant because, of course, all "real" Brazilians eat rice every day. Rice is an introduced crop both to Brazil and to forest Indians. Traditional crop foods, the successful cultivation of which has been worked out over generations in the forest environment and which are well suited to the soil conditions in particular regions, may become scarce, with the result that the Indian diet becomes unbalanced.

Indians who traditionally plant manioc as a staple crop may be encouraged to increase the size of their fields and plant more manioc, which can then be transformed into farinha, a type of cereal that can be sold in the markets. Larger fields mean more intensive agricultural work and less time to hunt—which also affects the diet. The purchase of a shotgun may temporarily improve hunting returns, but it also tends to eliminate game in the area. In addition, shotgun shells are very expensive in Brazil, costing more than $1 U.S. apiece. Dependence on the shotgun undermines a hunter's skill with traditional hunting weapons, such as blowguns and bows and arrows, as well as the ability required to manufacture them.

Clearing larger areas for fields can also lead to increased risk from diseases such as malaria and leishmaniasis, because cleared areas with standing water of low acidity permit proliferation of disease-bearing mosquitoes and flies. New diseases also appear. Anthropologist-epidemiologist Carlos Coimbra, Jr., for example, has shown that Chagas disease, which is transmitted to humans by trypanosome-carrying assassin bugs, apparently does not yet affect Indian populations in lowland areas of the Amazon basin. Only when Indians cease their seminomadic way of life and begin to live for prolonged periods in the same dwellings can Chagas-carrying bugs adjust their feeding behavior and begin to depend on human hosts rather than small rodents for their blood meals.

The moment manufactured foods begin to intrude on the indigenous diet, health takes a downward turn. The liberal use of table salt (sodium chloride), one of the first things that Indians are given, is probably no more healthful for them than it is for Westerners. Most Indians do not have table salt; they manufacture small quantities of potassium salts by burning certain types of leaves and collecting the ash. Anthropologist Darrell Posey reports that the Kayapo Indians of Brazil make salt ash from various palm species and use each type for specific foods.

Sweets and other foods containing refined sugar (sucrose) are also given to Indians, whose wild fruits, according to research by botanists Irene and Herbert Baker, contain primarily other sugars, such as fructose. Indians find that foods containing sucrose taste exceptionally sweet, and they tend to crave them once sampled. While a strong, sugary taste in the natural environment might signal a rare, rich energy source, the indiscriminate consumption of canned foods, candies, and gums containing large amounts of refined sugar contributes to tooth decay and can lead to obesity and even health problems such as diabetes.

Results of dietary change are often difficult to anticipate. Anthropologist Dennis Werner found that the Mekranoti of central Brazil, who did not make pottery, traditionally roasted most of their food. But the introduction of metal cooking pots allowed them to switch to boiled foods. This, in turn, allowed nursing mothers to provide supplemental foods to their infants at an earlier age. Werner found that the average nursing period in the Mekranoti had dropped steadily from 19.7 months prior to 1955 to 16 months in recent years, which corresponded to the period of steady increase in the use of metal cooking pots in the village.

One of the first things the Indian Bureau doctors generally do after contact is try to protect the Indians from the Western diseases that may be communicated to them during their first prolonged interaction with outsiders. The doctors give them immunizations and may also hand out drugs to prevent or eradicate dangerous malarias. Pregnant women, infants, and preadolescents often receive massive doses of antibiotics. Antibiotics and antimalarial drugs, although helpful in some respects, may also have detrimental effects. For example, individuals exposed to antibiotics in utero or when young generally have teeth that are abnormally dark and discolored. Some drugs are reputed to interfere with fertility among women in recently contacted groups. If this lack of fertility combines with a drop in population size due to deaths from new diseases, a population can fall to a precarious low.

Perhaps the most critical disruption suffered by these groups, however, concerns how detailed information on features of the forest environment is diluted and forgotten. This is the pool of shared knowledge that traditionally has been the bedrock, the economic currency, the patrimony of each of these nontechnological forest societies. Manuel Lizarralde, a doctoral student at the University of California, Berkeley, who has done ethnobotanical work with the Bari of Venezuela, reports that in just a single generation there was a staggering loss of information about the identity of forest trees and their uses.

Despite this tale of disruption, disease, and destruction, many of the indigenous forest cultures are proving to be far more resilient than might be expected. The indigenous peoples remaining today in the Amazon basin are true survivors who have successfully resisted the diseases, explorers, missionaries, soldiers, slave traders, rubber tappers, loggers, gold miners, fur traders, and colonists who have persistently encroached on them during the past five centuries.

Anthropologist Bill Balée, for example, had found that the Ka'apor Indians of Maranhão State, in peaceful contact with outsiders since 1928, still maintain many features of their traditional economy, social organization, and ritual life. He attributes this to the continued integrity of the nuclear family and the persistence of specific ritual duties between husband and wife that prohibit certain foods at different seasons or life stages. Such ritual practices have not only spared red-legged tortoises and other wild resources from being overharvested but have also diffused hunting pressures over a large area, thereby contributing to the persistence of the traditional economy.

Unfortunately, cultural persistence will do indigenous peoples no good if their tropical forest habitat is destroyed. Deforestation is primarily the result of outside influences, such as lumbering, cattle ranching, and colonization, that are permitted by government policies. Some estimates suggest that all remaining tropical forests will be destroyed by the year 2045.

Once the technological roller coaster gets moving, it's hard to jump off or even pause to consider the situation. Some say, so what? We can't all go back to the jungle, we can't all become forest-living Indians. No, we can't.

But as I stand in my apartment in Berkeley, listening to my telephone's insistent ring and contemplating my unanswered mail, dusty curtains, dripping faucets, and stacks of newspapers for recycling, I'm not sure we wouldn't be far happier if we could.

II

Explanations for Deforestation in Latin America

The tropical rainforest has become a major arena for the conflicts arising out of the dominant development strategy in Latin America. Based on modernization and the encouragement of rapid economic growth, this approach fuels a stream of people and capital into the ever more remote reaches of Latin America's rainforests. The moving frontier represents both a continuation and an intensification of the historical processes set in motion by the arrival of the Iberians five hundred years ago.

The economic and political systems established by the Spanish and Portuguese gave rise to a society of extreme concentration of resources and wealth in the hands of a few, exemplified by the latifundia system. (Latifundia—great estates—traditionally included a work force tied to the estate by debt to the owner.) Today, one of the legacies of colonialism in Latin America is a land-tenure system in which the majority of arable land is controlled by only a few landowners. Many of the latifundia are dedicated to extensive and inefficient cattle production, which has continued to expand since the 1960s, contributing to the destruction of vast areas of tropical rainforest (Selection 7). Most of the rural population is either landless or relegated to *minifundia*, farms too small to support a family.

The contemporary approach to development in Latin America has created social conditions that encourage migration to frontier zones. Agricultural modernization during the past two or three decades has caused a decrease in employment opportunities on the latifundia, a "squeezing out" of small independent farms, and the emigration of landless peasants searching for a way to support their families. Until recently, the underdeveloped economies of Latin America had relatively few industries, and even now there are not enough industrial jobs to employ all potential workers. This, added to an unprecedentedly high rate of population growth since the 1950s (Selection 6), has created a large reserve of un- or underemployed workers that has kept wages low. The resulting poverty and misery is widespread and motivates migration to the frontier.

Government policy encourages this population shift because the settlement of the forested frontier serves the needs of the state in various ways. Powerful politicians generally come from, or are allied with, the landholding class and therefore tend to seek solutions to agrarian problems without having to undertake land reforms opposed by the landed elite. Opening up frontier zones to colonization by the landless, usually by building roads, serves two important purposes: it protects the interests of the politically powerful landed elite, and it defuses potential unrest by the poor and landless. In addition, state concerns over effective control of remote frontier areas and fears of neighbors' designs on land and resources have led governments to encourage the settlement of the hinterlands by members of the dominant culture.

Crushing foreign debts also have forced many Latin American countries to exploit their natural resources—such as petroleum, gold, iron ore, or tropical hardwoods—in order to earn foreign exchange for debt repayment (Selection 8). Pursuit of economic development along the lines of the United States model encourages the construction of large hydroelectric dams to promote industrial growth. This strategy has been encouraged by the lending policies of multi-lateral banks (the World Bank and the Inter-American Development Bank), which historically have supported megaprojects, such as the Grande Carajás project in Brazil (Selection 9).

In Central America and the Caribbean, the military, in conjunction with U.S. foreign policy, has affected the region's remaining tropical rainforests. During the contra war against the Sandinista government of Nicaragua, for instance, the United States built airstrips in both Honduras and Costa Rica to help supply contra forces. These airfields, and roads to them, resulted in the deforestation of these previously isolated zones. Of greater long-term importance is U.S. policy regarding development in the region. The United States has fostered an approach to development that has widened economic disparities and fueled civil unrest. Many of the region's military governments have responded with internal repression, and this has led to guerrilla activity or civil war, which have environmental as well as social consequences.

Proponents of rainforest conservation face powerful obstacles. Urban populations, often divorced from and unaware of the problems caused by deforestation, have more political power than do rural populations, which are more directly interested in forest issues. In particular, Latin America's elites are often opposed to paying for policies from which they derive little, if any, benefits. On the contrary, forest conservation generally will penalize the elites, who lose the potential profits from developing the land, but benefit others such as indigenous people, rubber tappers, and, in some cases, peasants. Another obstacle derives from the widespread perception that economic growth and environmental protection are mutually exclusive. These obstacles prevent effective implementation of the conservation programs proposed by environmentalists and supported by scientific research over the past several decades. Selection 10 analyzes the environmental and social consequences of this approach to development.

In conclusion, a number of social, economic, and political factors contribute to government policies that promote settlement in rainforest regions (Selection 11) and their conversion to other, more "productive" uses (Selection 12). Many observers emphasize one factor over others in their explanations of the causes of deforestation. The selections in Part II provide a sample of the various perspectives on tropical deforestation. Taken together, they reveal the complex dynamics involved in forest clearance in Latin America. And an understanding of the various factors is not just an academic exercise; it is a necessary foundation for the formulation of effective policies to control deforestation and environmental degradation. Policy based on simplistic, one-dimensional explanations of deforestation will inevitably fail.

---

6 John Terborgh ◆ The Whys and Wherefores of Deforestation

In his book Where Have All the Birds Gone? (1989), *John Terborgh writes about the declining populations of migrant birds that breed in North America and winter in Latin America. Like that of the proverbial canary in the coal mine, the fate of these birds is an indicator of the health of the environment. The passages chosen for this selection represent a summary of Terborgh's analysis of the principal causes of deforestation in Latin America and are representative of a viewpoint commonly presented in the scientific literature about tropical deforestation. Drawing upon the Malthusian perspective, Terborgh stresses population pressure as the primary factor in the environmental degradation of the tropics. Technological changes during the second half of the twentieth century, especially in medicine and public health, have allowed a "population bomb" to explode in less developed regions, such as Latin America, and this, in turn, has caused environmental degradation.*

Terborgh tempers his Malthusian argument with some consideration of the historical differences in the colonization and economic development processes of North and Latin America. He points out the importance of the stratified and rigid rural society of Latin America and the use of Latin

From John Terborgh, *Where Have All the Birds Gone?* 114–42. © 1989 by Princeton University Press. Reprinted by permission of Princeton University Press.

*America's resources by North American and European countries to fuel
their own industrialization and the growing consumer demands of their
increasingly affluent populations. Because Latin America's economies are
underdeveloped, conservation values are just beginning to emerge, and the
region's major preoccupation continues to be economic development.
Terborgh stresses that, under present conditions, the key to conservation of
forests is job creation and control of population growth.*

In a dynamic society, change is inevitable. We should, however, be aware
that changes in the environment entail costs as well as benefits. As a
society, we have historically focused almost exclusively on benefits, while
ignoring the costs. It is time we began tallying the costs, because they have
been considerable.

As for the future, it is important to keep in touch with the rates and
directions of ongoing change. We cannot reverse the past, but we can in
principle control the future. If we care about the future, then we should do
everything rationally possible to learn about it in advance. Herein lies the
value of science. It is the business of science to make predictions.

The process of rational analysis begins with the gathering of facts. It
continues by putting the facts to use in making predictions. In the simplest
case, the predictions are mere linear extrapolations of current trends. Once
predictions have been made, the process ends with evaluation. Are the
projected changes desirable or undesirable? How are anticipated benefits to
be weighed against calculated costs? These are value judgments that only
society can make. It is the job of the scientist to provide the facts and
projections from which society can arrive at its judgments. . . . An uninformed
public cannot make reasoned judgments. Hence as a scientist, I have felt
compelled to speak out.

Conservation is essentially a debate over land-use policy, because land-
use patterns determine the blend of habitats available to support wildlife. If
we were ever to arrive at a state in which the entire landscape of the United
States was taken over by urban development or cornfields, we would
obviously have no wildlife left at all. A few densely populated nations are
already close to reaching this condition. To maintain wildlife there must be
some compromise between the needs of nature and the needs of humans.
The conservation movement has vigorously sought to establish a national
consensus on where the balance between these two needs should lie. Although
there is as yet no general agreement, few Americans would assert that
nature deserves no place at all. We are clearly evolving toward a national
compromise, even though no one can say just where it will eventually lie.

Many tropical countries have only barely begun their own national
debates. If we were to take the creation of Yellowstone National Park in
1872 as the starting point in our national debate, it can be appreciated that

we have made progress, but that it has taken a long time. The concern we must have for birds that migrate to the tropics is that they spend half the year or more in countries where the equivalent landmark conservation legislation was enacted much closer to 1972 than to 1872. It is clear that there is a long way to go in achieving national conservation consensuses in these countries too, but given the rapid pace of environmental change, there does not seem to be enough time. . . .

Development has taken a different course in Latin America and has been propelled by different forces. The earliest European settlements, in Santo Domingo, Panama, and Mexico, began one hundred years before the Pilgrims landed at Plymouth Rock.

At first the impetus was gold, not freedom from persecution, and a gold rush seldom leaves culture, enlightenment, and prosperity in its wake. Settlers did trickle in after the gold frenzy abated, but at a much slower rate than in North America.

In Mexico, Guatemala, Peru, and Bolivia, a landed gentry gained wealth and status through ruthless exploitation of native populations, creating a rigid caste system that endures even today in forms both subtle and overt. Elsewhere, as in Hispaniola, Jamaica, Brazil, and Venezuela, in the absence of sufficiently numerous or tractable native peoples, black slaves from Africa were the instrument of enrichment. In both cases, the result was similar—a stratified, rural-based society whose captains lived in indolent luxury as absentee landlords in the capital cities. In this stagnant and viscous milieu, upward mobility depended more on having the right genes and social connections than on hard work and ingenuity, and opportunity did not exactly beckon. Immigrants poured into North America by the millions, while the countries to the south lay dormant.

This dormancy persisted for nearly four hundred years and was finally broken by forces from the outside. The industrialization of the north created a demand for primary materials—copper, tin, and later petroleum—at the lowest possible cost. Along with rising prosperity in Europe and North America came burgeoning markets for tropical agricultural products— sugar, coffee, cocoa, and bananas. It was the stimulus of this economic pull that attracted new blood and investment to the region and that began to rouse it from its somnolence.

Meanwhile, there had been no impetus to propel the colonization of the rainforest, the great frontier of tropical America. The climate was uncomfortable and the soils were poor. And beyond these deterrents, the land did not yield products that appealed to palates conditioned in Europe. Diseases such as malaria and yellow fever were rampant and essentially untreatable. Under these conditions, the reward for colonizing the jungle was the likely loss of thirty years from one's life span. The European population of Latin America consequently looked only to mountains or semiarid coastal regions for their livelihoods, and the vast evergreen forests of Central and South America lay practically untouched.

The period since World War II has seen the overturning of this status quo. Two related factors were decisive in bringing about the changes. First, a global antimalaria campaign, spearheaded by the World Health Organization, plus the advent of an effective yellow fever vaccine, lifted the pall of fear and suffering that had inhibited the settlement of vast forested hinterlands. And second, the population bomb exploded in the Third World. Millions of penniless and illiterate peasants failed to find jobs in the cities or land in the comfortable highlands that had for so long been the bastion of the region's landed gentry. Faced with no other alternatives, they flooded into wilderness that no one had previously wanted and began to hack out pitiful little plots such as the ragged Ecuadorean cattle pasture described in Chapter 11.* Mountain slopes and fertile valleys in the foothills region of Central America and the Andes drew the first waves of settlers. The steamy Caribbean lowlands of Central America and the Amazon basin have held out as the last frontier. But even these are disappearing fast. Ours was a frontier of opportunity; this is a frontier of desperation.

Ironically, the people of Latin America do not want to colonize the humid tropical forest. To be sure, there are a few rugged individualists, as there are in any society, whose psyches compel them to a life of self-reliance in remote outposts where no man is their master. But such people are a tiny minority, and the wilderness is big enough to accommodate them. The great majority of the immigrant peasants who are felling the region's forests would far rather have steady jobs and live in the city. But the cities are crowded with thousands of others who, like themselves, cannot find work. Most of the peasants I have met in the region's jungles have tried life in the city and failed to become established. With all other avenues closed, the forest beckoned as the last resort.

The life of a peasant settler in the rainforest is not an enviable one. To find unclaimed land, he is often forced to travel far from existing roads and settlements. Great hardships are consequently forced upon him. There is often no school for his children and no doctor, should someone in the family fall ill. The chances are that he will try to produce a cash crop such as coffee or cacao, but he is obliged to proceed without adequate knowledge of how to care for a plantation and with no capital to buy fertilizers, pesticides, or genetically improved stock.

---

*See John Terborgh, "A Glimpse at Some Tropical Habitats," in this volume.—Ed.

Vicissitudes are commonplace. An epidemic can sweep through his plants and wipe out the accumulated capital of several years' labor. And markets for export commodities are notoriously unstable. The choice of what to plant is usually based on market values of the day, but several years later when a plantation begins to bear, the economic conditions have often changed. Finally, should all these hazards be overcome, and our farmer succeeds in harvesting a crop, to sell it he must then carry the sacks for many miles, on his back or on the backs of burros, to reach the nearest roadhead. A middleman and his truck will meet him there, offering the lowest possible price. Not being able to walk the many additional miles to the city, the farmer has no alternative to accepting what he is offered.

This is not a life you or I, or any sane person, would aspire to. Those who enter upon it are not mindless of its drawbacks. That is why most would prefer to live in the city with steady jobs and access to schools and doctors for their children. But to be in a city without a job, in a country where social welfare programs are unknown, is to starve. Life may be harsh in the forest, but at least one can plant a garden, raise some chickens, and go to bed every night with a full stomach. The keys to conservation in Latin America are thus jobs and people—more of the former and fewer of the latter. The present trends are leading to disaster.

In traveling through the Neotropics one can hardly fail to notice that there is a close relationship between human population density and the state of the countryside. The most lightly populated countries, such as Surinam and Guyana, are cloaked in primary forest, whereas at the opposite extreme are impoverished nations such as Haiti and El Salvador, where hardly an acre of natural habitat remains. As population densities approach and exceed one hundred persons per square kilometer, people begin, in desperation, to spread into the farthest and least desirable corners of the landscape—cold, mist-shrouded mountaintops, hot, impenetrable thorn scrub. No place is too forbidding or remote to escape the pressure of the landless unemployed. . . .

These two countries [Haiti and El Salvador] have come to the end of the road as far as their natural environments are concerned. Can other countries be far behind? If we take the hundred-persons-per-square-kilometer criterion as our guide, we see that the answer is no. The Dominican Republic, Jamaica, and Trinidad-Tobago are already over the threshold. At current rates of increase, Cuba, Guatemala, Costa Rica, and Honduras have less than thirty years remaining. . . .

For the short term, the outlook for these countries is a continuation of current trends. In spite of migration to the cities, the absolute number of rural peasants continues to increase, putting ever greater pressure on undeveloped land. Although birth rates are beginning to show hopeful signs of decline in several nations, the demographic profiles of nearly all tropical American countries are so bottom heavy (half the population under sixteen), that one or more doublings in population size are inevitable, even if, beginning tomorrow, all new mothers refrained from having more than two children. Given these harsh realities, nothing short of a miracle could prevent one country after another from going over the hundred-persons-per-square-kilometer threshold. When this happens, the remaining natural habitat is doomed, and along with it the essential requirement for overwinter survival of many songbird species.

---

7 James J. Parsons ◆ The Scourge of Cows

Geographer James Parsons pioneered the study of the impact of cattle on tropical America when he began to raise questions in the 1960s about Latin America's "beef boom." In "The Scourge of Cows" (1988), a comprehensive overview of scholarly research on cattle and deforestation, Parsons illustrates the international linkages that affect the cattle industry in the region. He reveals clearly the complexity of the relationship between society and nature, focusing in this case on the export beef boom and its role in the destruction of tropical forests in Latin America.

My interest in livestock in Third World development was initially spurred less by any concern for Third World economic development as such (and I here direct my attention primarily towards the tropical parts of Latin America) than by an interest in landscapes and landscape change—especially vegetation change resulting from human activity. The advance of pasture (grassland) at the expense of lowland rainforest and dry tropical forest in the Americas first attracted my attention some thirty-five years ago on the Caribbean coast of Colombia inland from Cartagena in the Magdalena and Sinu river valleys. Not long after, during a visit to Costa Rica, my attention focused on the Pan-American Highway, which was pushing southward toward the Panama border, opening up the richly forested Valle General and the Pacific lowlands of that country to pioneer settlement. The process was just beginning to be dominated by cattlemen. The destruction of Amazonia was to come later.

As a geographer I was interested in the fact that most of these newly forming *potreros* (pastures) were composed not of native American species

Reprinted from the *Whole Earth Review* (Spring 1988): 40–47, by permission of the author.

but of grasses of African origin. They were palatable to cattle and they were aggressive colonizers. They were here to stay. Several of them, like pangola and kikuyu, had only recently been introduced to the New World tropics. A couple of them dated back to the eighteenth century, having moved gradually from points of introduction in Brazil or the West Indies to other parts of tropical America. These Old World grasses or their cultivars are still arriving, now more often through experimental introductions than by chance. The "Columbian Exchange," as Alfred Crosby terms it—the transfer of economically valuable plants that began in 1492—is still going strong.

Grass, of course, was of singularly little interest or utility to Native American populations. They had no cattle, really no domesticated grazing animals with the exception of the high-Andean pastoralists with their llamas and alpacas. There were, of course, natural grasslands or "savannahs" (the Arawak term) in the American tropics—the most extensive being the llanos or plains of the Orinoco in the interior of Venezuela and Colombia—but even these lacked the big game, the grazers, of the African plateau. It is in association with such creatures that the more palatable native grasses of that continent seem to have evolved over millions of years. We know little of how or why.

In America, grass only came to be seen as useful or desirable after Columbus' second voyage, on which the first cattle were introduced to the New World. When the Spaniards saw the savannahs of Santo Domingo and Cuba and, later on, the mainland, all they could think of was cattle. The savannahs were successional stages of abandoned Indian gardens. As Indian populations were decimated their abandoned fields grew up with second-growth scrub and weedy native grasses. Spanish livestock, in effect, replaced native peoples. Alexander Skutch, the ornithologist, who holds the tropical forest and its ecological diversity in reverence, speaks of "the scourge" of the cow and the grass its introduction has generated, and how it had been the great good fortune of the Indian cultures that domestic livestock had been unknown to them, thus providing no incentive to convert forest to grass.

Cattle-keeping, of course, is a cultural thing. The original domestication of wild cattle in the Middle East, according to Eduard Hahn, was probably for ritual or ceremonial purposes. Their use for milk and meat came later and even today is hedged in on all sides by taboos and prejudices and, in the case of milk, by genetically based digestive barriers associated with lactase deficiency. Most of the world's beef is consumed by the better-off members of Western cultures. The United States alone produces one fourth of the world's red meat but is still an importer. Throughout the Far East hundreds of millions of people have never tasted beef and have not the slightest desire to try it. In Hindu India, steak is as unthinkable as dog chops in America. Most Chinese find the idea of slaughtering cattle to make steaks appalling. It is pork, a much more efficient converter of energy, that they are addicted to and seek out when they can afford it.

There are, of course, other reasons for keeping cattle besides their value as food processors—for draft or transport, for their hides, their horns, bones or dung (for fertilizer) and often as a form of wealth, a kind of mobile bank account that can be driven on foot to market or, in case of drought, flood or war, to other areas. The very word "capital," which comes to us from the Latin, may be derived from "cattle." The Spanish *ganado* originally meant that which has been gained = property (*ganadería*). Keeping cattle is still considered an especially prestigious activity in some cultures, including that of Latin America. As the proportion of animal products in the diet of Western nations has increased, modern governments have seen beef exports as an irresistible source of much-needed foreign exchange. This has been the root of the aggressive promotion of pasture expansion for stockraising as a part of Third World governments' development programs.

Beef is seen especially as a source of protein, symbol of the mass middle-class "good life" in America. But it is an expensive one. Its preeminence in our diet is of recent origin. Before 1875 pork was our preferred daily meat; ham was the choice for honored guests. For the English in earlier times it had been mutton and even rabbit. As late as 1950 more pork than beef was consumed in the United States. Today we consume nearly twice as much of the latter as of the former. But we still talk of "living high off the hog" and "bringing home the bacon" and we accuse politicians of "pork barrel" rather than "beef barrel" legislation. But a change is in the wind again. Per-capita beef consumption has begun to drop after a long uphill climb. Medical warnings of cholesterol and the role of saturated fats in cardiovascular problems have contributed. So have cheaper pork and (especially) poultry. But worldwide the upward spiral of beef consumption continues as population soars and American middle-class values spread.

Before World War II most beef in America, as in other developed countries, was from grass-fed animals. Recently our cattle, which still grow up eating grass, have been spending the last month or two of their lives in feedlots being stuffed with grain and by-products of agricultural processing (cottonseed or soybean cake, sugar-beet pulp, molasses). Such "finishing" produces a fat-marbled beef that draws a premium price but is inefficient in energy terms. It involves transforming edible protein in the form of grain or soybeans into fat simply to make the meat taste better. It takes six to eight pounds of grain or the by-products of food and fiber processing to produce one pound of weight gain in cattle. For pigs and poultry the conversion ratio is at least three times more efficient. They also lend themselves far more readily to production by small-scale farmers and they thrive on waste products and garbage.

The World Bank says that some 600 million tons of cereals, half the world's production, are annually fed to animals, an amount that could feed the world's hungry three times over. Two thirds of our U.S.-tilled cropland produces animal feed, with corn, sorghum, and soybeans, along with alfalfa and other hay, leading the way. Significant amounts of these crops are exported to developing countries to feed livestock and poultry. Grain converted to meat loses 75 to 90 percent of its protein value so it is woefully inefficient in these terms. In the wake of a world food crisis (a crisis in distribution, not production) the use of grains to feed animals has come under close scrutiny. But here as elsewhere, the market rules. To shift consumption of grain from animals to people would require a massive transfer of purchasing power from rich countries to poor ones. Even if this unlikely prospect were realized the longer-term consequences would be problematic. Most of the world's hungry are farmers or live in farm areas where basic cereals are grown. It would be difficult if not impossible to inject large amounts of additional cereal into these areas without sharply reducing incomes and production in the very regions where increased income is most needed.

So where's the beef? The world has some 1.2 billion cattle, together with a billion sheep and half that many hogs. There are close to five billion people; our numbers and theirs are growing equally rapidly. The United States, with less than 5 percent of the world population, has 10 percent of the cattle. The number of cattle equal or exceed the number of people in a few countries; especially the southern-hemisphere meat exporters such as Australia and Argentina, but also surprisingly in some of the fastest-growing Latin American countries—Brazil, Colombia, Nicaragua, Costa Rica, Honduras. Even Cuba comes close to the one-to-one ratio.

Through the microbiological flora in their second stomach (rumen), cattle can convert to food otherwise unusable cellulose. That means grass, something that our gastric systems can't handle. So the world's vast open lands, its unused two-thirds that are too steep, too rocky, too dry, too wet, too salty, too infertile to permit cultivation for crops, can be and often are used to produce protein by grazing animals. Unfortunately there has been a long history of overdoing it. Overstocking of cattle, especially on the drier margins, has led repeatedly to soil erosion, deterioration of the plant cover, and the process popularly if improperly termed "desertification."

The pressure to provide more food for cattle recently has posed an increasingly ominous threat to the world's tropical forests, or at least the 57 percent of them in the Americas. Suddenly, and largely because of the acceleration of clearing for pasture (and wood products), we have become sensitized to a looming global crisis—the threat that the world's most complex and massive ecosystem may be on its way to extinction.

Four fifths of the soils of the humid tropics of the New World are acid and infertile. The lushness of the forests that they support is misleading. Where there is forest cover, nutrients are almost entirely locked up in the biomass of the trees and their roots and are continuously recycled through leaf fall and root uptake. When the forest is cleared to make way for short-rooted crops and grasses, bases and essential plant nutrients are rapidly leached from the soil due to continuously high temperatures and high rainfall.

The forest creates its own environment. Once removed it is not readily reestablished; there is some question whether it may ever be, in anything less than very large tracts. For a year or two after clearing, the ashes and decaying leaves and branches support reasonable crop yields but the rapidly weathering exposed soil may soon be impoverished. Eventually it is abandoned to secondary weedy growth unless major inputs are made of fertilizers, pesticides and herbicides, the means for which are seldom at hand. Interior South America has been described by Georg Borgstrom as "a great fertility desert." Except for the narrow river floodplains and restricted outcrops of basalt (terra rosa) or other volcanic parent materials, the soils are unfit for permanent cropping. And markets are almost always far away.

The traditional American Indian land-use system was a kind of forest-fallow or shifting cultivation (slash-burn or swidden) where, after two or three years, the land is abandoned to secondary growth for fifteen or twenty years before another cycle of clearing and cultivation is initiated. The modern colonists who are making clearings (*rozas*) in the high forests, attracted by new penetration roads and sometimes by government credits, tend to be as interested in cash returns as in subsistence. After a crop or two the *roza*, increasingly infested with noxious insects and weeds, is likely to be directly planted to jaragua or Guinea grass and sold to the small capitalists who follow behind. The *caboclo* or campesino may go on to clear another patch of *monte* somewhere ahead, but where a road or a nascent commercial center is close at hand, his hard-earned money is often quickly squandered. He frequently ends up as a wage earner on the same property that was once his own.

An alternative scenario, depending on the land-tenure situation, is when large landowners who have obtained title to tracts of forest pay *colonos* to clear a few hectares or contract them to do so in return for the privilege of taking two or three crops of maize or manioc from the cleared land, at the end of which time they must leave it in pasture. Then they move on to repeat the process. In such a fashion men with capital or influence become the permanent benefactors of the sweat of those who have gone before them with axe or machete. Agriculture becomes merely an intermediate step in the conversion of forest to pasture. It's all reminiscent of how the Argentine pampas years ago were converted to alfalfa and clover by Italian immigrants contracted by large landowners anxious to improve the carrying capacity of their stock-raising haciendas.

Concern for the future of the world's tropical forests and the possible consequences of their destruction has led to a recent outpouring of popular and scientific writing. For a world-view one can scarcely do better than Catherine Caufield's *In the Rainforest*, which gives appropriate attention to the unique role of cattle-raising and the "pasture revolution" in the case of the Americas. Widely contrasting figures are offered as to the rate and extent of tropical forest destruction. Two thirds of the Central American forest are believed to have gone, mostly converted to pasture. The Caribbean coastal plains of Colombia have been converted into a largely man-made grassland in one generation; the boundaries of the grasslands of the Llanos are being expanded at a quickening pace. The great Amazon rainforest (*selva*) appears more and more like a green, motheaten carpet frayed at its edges and increasingly pocked with holes as access roads have been pushed down from the crowded Andes and the Brazilian highway system has been extended to crisscross virtually the entire Brazilian portion of the river's drainage basin. Along with improved technologies for roadbuilding and forest clearing (enter the chainsaw) has come the revolution in public health and most importantly, at least for the moment, the successful suppression of the dreaded malaria, which for so long put the brakes on the settlement of these lands.

In the Amazon basin *la marcha* against the *selva* has been fueled by the rising tide of nationalism, which demands the incorporation of sparsely settled areas into the political and economic life of each country. It is a popularly held belief that "to govern is to people." Any aboriginal tribes that may stand in the way of such colonization activities are generally either eliminated or driven deeper into the forest. In conflicts between Indian and *colono* the latter always wins. Grandiose schemes for *la conquista de la selva*, however ecologically disruptive they may be, are likely to be seen as providing a unifying cause, a common purpose or rallying point to which all factions may subscribe. At the same time they provide a distraction from the more intractable social and political issues of the day.

The promotion of cattle ranching as a development strategy seems to be almost entirely a Latin American phenomenon. In Africa tsetse fly and trypanosomiasis, as well as several other diseases (rinderpest, hoof-and-mouth), severely limit cattle numbers and their distribution. In any case they are chiefly found on the dry margins, kept by semi-nomadic herdsmen in small, noncommercial herds and prized as much as a symbol of status as a source of food. Desertification is an overriding concern, and mobility a principal mechanism for countering it. In most of Asia cultural considerations and high human population densities make development via livestock all but unthinkable. Australia, especially tropical Queensland where major advances in tropical grass selection and range management have occurred, offers the closest parallel to the Americas, but here cattle ranching is a high-tech business, well capitalized and increasingly oriented toward the export market. The U.S.S.R., facing high and growing demands for meat, has given priority in recent years to importing feeds, especially from the huge U.S. surpluses.

In Brazil, with more than half of the great Amazon rainforest, it was the military coup of 1964 and the subsequent "revolution from above" that made the development of the Amazon a cornerstone of that country's program. It was called "the moral equivalent of war," and it put huge blocks of state forest lands in the north into the hands of Big Business, corporations both from Sao Paulo and from overseas. The Belém-Brasília highway had been completed by 1960 and others soon thereafter, including the much-publicized "Trans-Amazon" (now all but abandoned). The most recent and most destructive such development seems to be the new road system that has opened up Rondônia state along the once-remote Bolivian border.

As new roads were built, colonists flooded in and so did corporate interests, attracted by generous fiscal incentives. In Brazil, Amazonia was seen as a new farming and stock-raising frontier that was to serve as a safety valve for the drought-ravaged northeast, blunting demands for land reform. It was an idea that fit neatly with military ideology, including the securing of national sovereignty by establishing a substantial civilian presence in the vast northern forest. At the same time the economy was to be stimulated and jobs provided by an unprecedented road-construction program. Cattle were to provide a new source of cheap meat, first for growing Brazilian markets and later for export.

Cattle raising was to be given special priority, taking advantage of new Australian pasture technologies and the availability of improved breeds of Brahma-type animals and their crosses, which are resistant to tropical conditions. From the beginning, entrepreneurial interests were given special consideration in the form of cheap credit, tax exemptions and generous land concessions. A 1966 tax law permitted 50 percent of corporate tax liabilities to be canceled by an equivalent investment in what came to be defined as "Amazonia Legal." A land market developed where none had existed before, and enormous speculative gains were there for the asking. Attracted by government largesse and promises of favorable tax treatment, numerous transnational corporations jumped in—some, like the King Ranch and a

Swift-Armour consortium, experienced with cattle; others, like several European firms, not. A favorable FAO [U.N. Food and Agriculture Organization] report on prospects for livestock in Latin America and another a few years later by the World Bank encouraged international development agencies to become involved, citing their mandates to promote "the downward redistribution of wealth and income for the betterment of the poor and landless." Between 1960 and 1980 the World Bank funded 123 livestock development projects, two thirds of them in Latin America but more especially in Brazil. The Inter-American Development Bank (IDB) and Agency for International Development (AID) were also active in the area. One Brazilian government report estimated that between 1960 and 1975, 38 percent of all the rainforest destroyed in that country could be attributed to large-scale cattle development. Today there may be some eight million cattle in the Brazilian Amazon, about the same number as in Nebraska, "The Beef State."

In the last few years the golden flow has slowed, in part because of the foreign debt crisis facing Brazil and other Latin American countries. More importantly, experience has shown that stock-raising in the tropical forest, at least in Amazonia, is not the panacea it was once thought to be, that the soils under grass lack staying power, and that soil compaction from trampling and brush invasion are intractable problems, not to mention diseases, biting insects and poisonous weedy plants. The paucity of information and experience remains an overwhelming obstacle to successful ranching in the tropics. Geographer Susanna Hecht reports that nine out of ten of the new ranches along the Belém-Brasília went out of business within eight years of their establishment. Today this well-traveled highway passes through hundreds of miles of abandoned secondary scrub. Only with costly fertilizer and pesticide use, coupled with lower stocking rates and aggressive hand weeding, does there seem to be much hope for a sustainable ranching industry on these upland (*terra firme*) soils.

The invading brush, usually seen as a major problem, may yet be converted into a valued resource. At least there may be potential for palatable browse in the few nitrogen-fixing legumes among the many invading species here (one introduced browse plant, a *Stylosanthes* from Australia, has given outstanding results), but as yet little advantage has been taken of them. In part it is a cultural problem, linked to the deeply rooted perception of an ideal stock-raising environment as composed of lovely, smooth European-type pastures. In fact animals that live in invaded, deteriorated pastures are sometimes fatter and glossier than those on clear pasture. Deeper root penetration gives brush species an advantage in nutrient cycling. So the search for those that nodulate continues. Fertilization of these acid soils is not only costly but of uncertain effectiveness. It often backfires, destroying microrrhiza in the soil, locking up phosphorus and promoting the leaching of other essential nutrients such as calcium and potash.

As ranching the Amazon loses some of its gloss, Brazil has been turning to a family of industrial megaprojects that promise even greater environmental impact, such as the damming of some of the region's major rivers, beginning with the Tucurí hydroelectric project on the Tocantins and the Grande Carajás mining development in which bauxite, iron ore, copper and the precious metals are all involved. The infrastructure of cities, railroads and highways promises to be on a Chicago-like scale. Most startling in the view of environmental groups would be the recently proposed construction of at least twenty iron smelters that would use wood in the form of charcoal as the main source of energy with the inevitable destruction of primary forest. Blast furnaces at last in the Amazon!

The conversion to pasture continues. It not only increases land values; it is the best way to secure land title, because here as elsewhere land unused (i.e., in forest) is always a potential target for squatter invasions or for expropriation under government land reform programs. So the visitor to Rondônia (recently opened to a new land rush as a result of the asphalting of a new 800-mile highway from Cuiabá north to Pôrto Velho) sees large areas in pasture but few cattle. Such is the logic of Amazonian development. Subsidies, fiscal incentives, new roads and speculation in an inflationary economy produce enormous untaxed capital gains for the few. Land has been a vehicle for the capture of subsidies just as it has on the irrigation projects of the arid west of the United States.

When the land itself has been of minimal importance, cautious management of it has seemed irrelevant and environmental degradation inevitable. It is ironic, as my colleague Hilgard Sternberg pointed out years ago, that even accepting the dubious hypothesis that the best way to meet the protein needs of the country is to increase beef production, this goal could be much more easily reached by using existing pasture in southern and central Brazil in a more rational, intensive way. The trade-off of the tropical rainforest, with its unique genetic diversity and potential, habitat of half the world's known species of living things, for the short-lived returns of the "pasture revolution," seems a singularly bad deal. And this takes no account of possible eventual impacts of forest removal on regional and global climates or the annihilation of surviving Indian peoples who are so thoroughly integrated into this great tropical ecosystem.

Colombia and Venezuela present a rather different picture. In the north the dry season may last for five months. Deforestation has been most conspicuous in more humid interior locations against the mountains. Irrigated crops have competed successfully with the traditional cattle culture for the best land. As long ago as 1915, a packing house was built at Covenas near the mouth of the Sinu river in anticipation of the development of a major meat-export trade. Until the recent sharp devaluation of its currency, Venezuela had been a traditional importer of Colombian beef cattle, up to 200,000 a year moving across the border on the hoof. The doubling of cattle numbers and improved pasture area since 1950 in Colombia have been largely to supply the market demands of a population growing at more than 3 percent annually. Because of hoof-and-mouth disease, fresh and frozen beef from Colombia, as from the rest of South America, continues to be excluded from the United States.

In Colombia, where the "bull cult" is strong and where cattle numbers exceed humans, beef cattle utilize more than half the developed land, even in the mountains. In neither of the major commercial ranching areas, the Llanos (with 15 percent of the national herd) and the North Coast (with three times that number), have international assistance programs been of much significance in the continued expansion of the industry and the pastures supporting it. A semi-official Cattle Bank has been the principal source of credit. The old cattle culture of the North Coast (Costeno) has a traditional latifundia structure with large haciendas worked by a landless campesino class in a clientele relationship with the landholders. In the Colombian Amazon (Caquetá, Putumayo) where forest removal following the completion of roads from the upper Magdalena Valley created a quarter-million hectares of improved fenced pasture, political violence and the turmoil associated with clandestine coca-growing has put the brakes on development. For the rest of the country the carrying of herds through the long dry season (*verano*) is a major problem. Seasonal drives, a kind of transhumance, are the rule between the higher *sabanas* and the seasonally inundated floodplain of the Magdalena, where even at the height of dry season there is water and green grass. It is an area that in pre-Columbian times was intensively cultivated around the calendar under a unique system of chinampa-like raised garden beds.

In Ecuador and Peru, with much smaller populations, the cattle industry and thus the extension of man-made grasslands are less well developed, though petroleum discoveries on the Andean piedmont east of the Andes have led to the construction of several access roads that are attracting growing numbers of colonists with aspirations to become stockmen.

It is Central America that has of late been the focal point of much of the forest-to-pasture controversy. Here, where the political units are much smaller and the volcanic-derived soils often much better, deforestation has tended to be less destructive of the productive capability of the land. The explosion of cattle ranching has been promoted by superior transportation (the Pan-American Highway) and proximity to the open U.S. market.

Although coffee remains the top export, two thirds of Central America's farmland is devoted to cattle raising. Most of this is on the drier Pacific side of the isthmus. Stanley Heckadon suggests that the land-hungry peasants of Panama's Azuero district actively "hate" the forest. It stands in their way as an unfriendly barrier. But their neighbors, the Guaymi Indians on the other side of the isthmus, consider it a friendly home.

In Central America, too, the best way to establish land title has been to cut down the trees. Unless institutional brakes are placed on the *potreroismo* that has been sweeping these countries, it is projected that Central America may be completely denuded, except for national parks and reserves, within a decade. Yet per-capita consumption of beef may be lower today than when the rapid growth of the industry began twenty-five years ago. A new cattle-ranching elite, politically powerful, has tended to replace the coffee elite as the ruling class. The Somozas of Nicaragua were a conspicuous example. The absence of hoof-and-mouth disease and the new demand for lean, grass-fed beef in the United States have especially favored the development of the export trade.

In 1984 the United States imported 44,000 tons of frozen boneless beef from the five Central American countries, down from a peak of more than twice that five years earlier. This represented between 10 and 15 percent of all U.S. frozen beef imports (New Zealand and Australia are the principal suppliers), between 1 and 2 percent of all U.S. consumption.

The conversion of forest to pasture in Central America, as in Amazonia, may have peaked. Political unrest has contributed its share, encouraging herd liquidation and on-the-hoof exports to non-U.S. markets such as Mexico and Venezuela. But there has also been a growing recognition of the negative consequences of continued forest destruction—soil erosion, reservoir siltation, losses of gene pool, wildlife, tourist attractions, etc. Resulting social ills are no less obvious, including an increased migrant flow from countryside to city and declining production of traditional food crops. Small farmers tend to be driven off the land wherever cattle raising becomes dominant because cattle require little manpower. Ironically, rural unrest may work in favor of wildlife and discourage land clearing. It seems to be doing so on the east coast of Nicaragua, where there has been continuing conflict between the Miskito Indians and the government. In Panama the threat of continued clearing on the upper drainage of the Canal's Gatun Lake is a matter of widening public concern. Quick action may have thwarted an AID plan to bulldoze a military access road through a pristine rainforest in eastern Honduras. In Costa Rica, too, conservation groups and scientists associated with the Organization for Tropical Studies have been exceptionally active, supported by enlightened local political leadership and a substantial grant for land purchase for a tropical forest reserve by at least one major foreign foundation. There are signs that a new land ethic may be forming in which, as the late Archie Carr suggested, a quetzal or a condor may one day be prized above a cow. But change comes slowly. Joseph Tosi's charge that "the innocent-looking beef cow is at the center of a destructive ecologic cycle that is strangling Central America" has yet to be refuted.

There has been much talk of late about "the hamburger connection," suggesting that the U.S. appetite for Big Macs or Whoppers might be responsible for the almost exponential rate of deforestation in Central America. But with this area's population growing at close to 3 percent a year, only twelve years will be needed to add another eight million people. Tom Vale, University of Wisconsin geographer, has calculated that a decade of growth at these rates is all that is needed to absorb the productive potential of all the land currently devoted to export beef production. Even if Central America were to end exports, feeding the population growth would soon require all the land now used for maintaining livestock. Forest clearance would then resume. And if diets are to improve, still more land would be required. Cessation of beef exports would buy a little time but would hardly solve the problem. In the long run population growth will make equivalent demands on the forest.

Development is inevitably a destructive process. Production means pollution, breaking down, spreading out, using up. The best we can do is to minimize its harmful effects. The principal harmful effect of livestock development in the Third World is long-term environmental degradation, especially the destruction of tropical forests whose recovery even under the best of circumstances may require some hundreds of years. Things have gone as they have in good part because the land has been cheap or free and labor abundant, so that there has been little incentive for intensification or efficiency. The potential of existing pastures is far from being reached. "Even the sad yields that pastures do produce," writes James Nations, "carry no benefits for the local population, either Indians or immigrant colonists. . . . Food production systems practiced by traditional rainforest people are, without exception, more productive than the pasturelands that are replacing these systems." He cites his own work among the forest Lacandons of Chiapas, who are being displaced by immigrants from the highlands inexperienced in rainforest ways. They are laying waste to a previously productive *selva* for short-term gains.

Livestock production in developing countries is currently among the world's most inefficient industries. One report suggests that the present beef-cattle population of existing grassland areas of tropical America could probably be increased four to five times through application of available knowledge to existing pasture and animal resources. The cow, itself a product of the tropics, is a magnificent converter of cellulose, the best there is. With perseverance, a scaled-down but sustainable grassland economy based on sound ecological principles and the new findings of animal industry research centers in places like Australia, Puerto Rico and the International Center for Tropical Agriculture in Colombia may be within reach. But only if future population growth can be held within check. More than enough of the forest has already been cleared to make room for the cow. It is time to pause in this mindless assault upon nature, time to think more in terms of saving what is left. We are rapidly running out of time and forest.

---

8 Koy Thomson and Nigel Dudley ◆ Transnationals and Oil in Amazonia

Reprinted from the British journal The Ecologist, *this 1989 article focuses on the cultural and environmental threats posed by oil production in the Amazon. Among the most ubiquitous of problems is that the production and transport of oil in Latin America is usually accompanied by leaks and spills that cause serious environmental contamination. Koy Thomson and Nigel Dudley point out that the penetration of roads, first for exploration and later for the production of oil, causes the inevitable destruction of rainforests. Wherever roads are built in Latin America, colonists follow, clearing forests throughout surrounding areas regardless of the impact on Native American inhabitants and the environment.*

The authors emphasize the role of environmental ("green") rhetoric promoted by the public relations departments of oil companies in obscuring their substantial negative impacts on Latin America's environments and peoples. The governments of oil-exporting countries, such as Ecuador, also have an incentive for underplaying the negative impacts of oil production— their economic reliance on foreign earnings from oil. There is another dimension in the pattern of denial about the true cost of oil that Thomson and Dudley have chosen not to address. (It is, however, discussed in Selection 25.) The demand for oil is driven by high rates of consumption in the industrialized world, especially in the United States. Recognition of this fact obliges us to confront our own patterns of consumption and their roles in tropical deforestation.

During the 1980s, oil concessions have been granted throughout Amazonia, setting in place a process of destruction beginning with exploration and ending in extraction. In September 1988, Occidental Petro-

From *The Ecologist* (November-December 1989): 219–24. Reprinted by permission of *The Ecologist*, Agriculture House, Bath Road, Sturminster Newton, Dorset DT10 1DU, England.

leum Company reached an agreement with the government of Peru to increase its production from rainforest areas by twenty thousand barrels a day. It currently has at least thirty wells in the rainforests, and plans twenty-four more.[1] In Colombia, Amoco has agreed to a three-year technical evaluation program with Ecopetrol for an area of seventy-four million acres of rainforest in the southeast of the country. Texaco has acquired rights in four areas of Colombian rainforest. In Ecuador, Texaco, Gulf, Conoco, Shell, British Petroleum, and Esso Hispanol are all involved in exploration.[2]

Direct destruction is caused by numerous activities, including clearance for seismic lines, access for exploration teams, helicopter landing areas, settlements for workers, drilling operations, drainage pits, and roads.

The Impact on Tribal People

In 1982, the chief of the Amazonian Satere-Mawe group in Brazil wrote that exploration crews from the French transnational Elf Aquitaine "came into the reservation like an illness" after they had explored supposedly "protected" tribal lands. He accused Elf employees of polluting waterways with refuse, thoughtless deforestation, landing their helicopter in the middle of a village, distributing alcohol, and showing pornographic films to villagers.[3]

By May 1986, prospecting rights to a third of the entire area of the seventy-seven Indian Reserves in the greater Amazon basin had been requisitioned by mining companies—seventeen million hectares out of a total of fifty-two million. Approximately 40 percent of the companies involved are transnational companies (TNC), including the Canadian TNC Brascan, British Petroleum, General Electric, and Rhodia. If development goes ahead, both the native peoples and the environment will suffer irreversible damage.

Road Building

Oil companies build roads into oil sites primarily because it is cheaper than flying workers by plane or by helicopter, although it is sometimes claimed that governments insist on roads being built. Far more important than the actual area of forest cleared for the roads, is the role that roads play in allowing access to settlers and land speculators into previously impenetrable rainforest.

The impact of colonization is increased by the oil companies bringing workers into the drilling area, many of whom are on short-term contracts. Workers are currently flooding into the oil drilling areas of the Carajás region of Brazil. When their contracts are finished, a proportion of the workers will stay to swell the ranks of the migrant farmers and miners. Oil workers also frequently hunt game in the forest, endangering birds and larger animals. Employees of oil exploration teams in Peru hunt illegally for meat and skins to sell in urban markets.[4]

The Contamination of Waterways

Oil spills and routine leakages pollute waterways and coastal areas whenever oil is drilled in or near water, or is transported by ship. Damage to fish stocks from oil pollution is one of the problems identified by tribal groups living in drilling areas.

Much of the concern over water pollution has been focused on its impact on the vast Amazon basin river system. In June 1988, it was revealed that Texaco had discovered a potentially huge oil field on Marajó Island in the mouth of the Amazon River. Brazilian President José Sarney claimed that it was equivalent to a North Sea oil field, but experts believe the optimism to be premature.[5] However, there have been some additional strikes off the coast of Brazil, and it is possible that a large strike will soon result.[6]

In the Oriente region of Ecuador, there have been at least thirty major oil spills from the Trans-Ecuadorean pipeline, with an estimated loss of sixteen million gallons of petroleum. Two spills in 1987 and 1989 caused extensive damage to flora and fauna along hundreds of miles of river.[7]

Threats to Protected Areas

It is usual in most countries for oil drilling to take precedence over designated national parks or wildlife conservation areas. In Ecuador, the oil companies are drilling in the Cayambe Coca Ecological Reserve, in the north of the country near the Colombian border. The Manglares-Churute Ecological Reserve (Ecuadorian dry forest), in the west, is (or was) also in an area under consideration for oil drilling.[8]

The Yasuní National Park

A major controversy is presently centered on plans to construct a 175-kilometer, $22 million road through the 680,000 hectare Yasuní National Park in Ecuador, one of the largest and most important reserves in the Amazon and home to the Waorani Indians, some of whom have never been contacted by outsiders.[9] The park is perhaps the richest area in the entire region, containing fifty species of fish, five hundred bird species and over one hundred mammal species, including jaguar, ocelot, giant otter, freshwater dolphins, and at least ten species of primates. The Ecuadorian government has overturned its own legislation in giving permission (and encouragement) for the road to be built.

The Yasuní Park is especially vulnerable as it lies within the Oriente region, where Ecuador's best reserves of oil (the country's principal foreign exchange earner) are located. Occidental, the U.S. transnational, started drilling near the boundary of the park in mid-1987, and already exploration by Occidental and others in and around the park has visibly reduced the number of large mammals in the area. Drilling is expected to damage irreversibly the area's river system.[10] Several companies have been ceded blocks for exploration and exploitation within the park, including Occidental, Consortium Elf Aquitaine of France, Petrobrás of Brazil, YPF of Argentina, Consortium Conoco Ecuador, and British Petroleum.

The proposed road through Yasuní is supported by the Ecuadorian State Oil Corporation (CEPE), although its actual construction will be carried out by Conoco Ecuador Ltd. (Conoco is a subsidiary of the chemical giant, Du Pont). CEPE will reimburse Conoco for the cost of the road once the Yasuní oilfield is commercially active, partly through a proposed $80 million loan from the World Bank. The deal with CEPE is part of a standard service contract which permits oil companies to explore for oil, drill wells, bulldoze roads, create infrastructure for workers and subcontractors, and construct pipelines. Since April 1986, Conoco has invested approximately $45 million in the exploration of the block containing the Yasuní National Park.[11]

Surveying for construction of the road is almost complete, and Conoco has already discovered oil in four of its wells, three of which are commercially productive. Construction of the Yasuní road could begin any time between March and November 1989.

Colonization

Conoco claims that it will leave the area "in a condition comparable to that in which we found it," but this is extremely unlikely. There is already evidence from Ecuador of what happens after oil-drilling roads are constructed. The construction of oil pipeline roads by CEPE in the Cuyabeno Wildlife Reserve, led to its colonization by more than a thousand people.[12] Although the Oriente region is being increasingly logged, timber exploitation is hampered to some extent by a lack of infrastructure.[13] This may not be the case for much longer, however, and according to one environmentalist in Ecuador, "the pipelines (Quito to Esmeraldas) and their accompanying roads now criss cross the Oriente in a crazy mosaic of environmental and cultural destruction."[14]

It is almost inevitable that if the road is built there will be a massive colonization of the Yasuní National Park by farmers, ranchers, land speculators and timber cutters.

The struggle against this destruction is being led by the Indian Federations of Ecuador, who are pressing for an accord with the Ecuadorian government to protect Waorani territory. Fundación Natura, the Ecuadorian Foundation for Conservation, has expressed grave concern about the future of all the sixty-three thousand Indians thought to be living in the Ecuadorian rainforest.[15] In July 1987, a bishop and a nun were speared to death after entering Waorani territory to establish peaceful contact and soften the impact between them and a consortium of oil exploration teams, including Petrobrás, Elf Aquitaine, and BP. In consequence, oil exploration temporarily stopped in that area, but has been resumed by Petrobrás this year.

Conoco's Environmental Promises

Conoco is extremely sensitive about its environmental image, and in a memorandum from senior management, dated March 1987, employees, contractors, and visitors were given a series of "rules and courtesies which must be observed" in the Yasuní Park. They were instructed that:

> Conoco has a worldwide reputation as an environmentally concerned company and your cooperation in maintaining our record would be appreciated. Repeated violations of these instructions will be grounds for dismissal.
>   Conoco's activities have an impact on the environment in which it operates—on the land, air, water, and the life forms found there. We will conduct all operations in a lawful and environmentally responsible manner. Specifically, Conoco will: (1) Comply fully with all pertinent environmental laws and regulations.

In a letter to Friends of the Earth, in March 1989, it gave further assurances about its work in the Yasuní National Park:

> To date, we have drilled seven wells, and each drill site covers no more than four acres. Equipment, materials, and personnel for drilling have been airlifted by helicopter so no roads have been built into the drill sites . . . we have issued mandates to our employees and contractors not to hunt wildlife or disturb the flora and fauna of the park. . . . If the oil is to be produced, the construction of an access road would be necessary and would constitute the primary potential impact on the rainforest. This would come from the oil operations as much as from potential agricultural colonization and logging operations by local people who typically move in if unregulated."[16]

At present, the Ecuadorian government is breaking its own laws, and Conoco is apparently only too happy to follow suit.

Exploration in National Parks

A key policy element for any environmentally responsible oil company must be to refuse contracts which involve exploration in national parks. Conoco has not only refused to leave the park, but has refused to take the second most preferable option, that of constructing the pipeline by air. Conoco admits that this is feasible, but rejects it as too costly. James Nations, of the Center for Human Ecology at the U.S. Embassy in Guatemala, claims that:

> At a Yasuní Park planning workshop held in Quito during May, 1988, conservationists pointed out that when ecological and social costs are included in the oil companies calculations—rather than externalized as at present—a pipeline built by air would be cheaper than a pipeline built by road through the Yasuní National Park. While the Yasuní area is expected to produce petroleum for only twenty years, the park could last forever. . . . In the long term, income generated by tourism and germ plasm protection in the Yasuní National Park would be worth more to Ecuador than twenty years of oil production. [17]

Conoco officials say that the possibilities of not building the road are "slim-to-none."[18] They claim that CEPE is responsible for the project, and as a service company, they only work for CEPE. But as Nations points out, "ultimately, it makes little difference how much money they spend on the Yasuní pipeline, because CEPE will reimburse the company's investment. CEPE in turn could use the World Bank loan to cover these costs."[19] Nations suggests that the World Bank should request that the pipeline be built by air, citing "the World Bank's new policies on the protection of wildlands and biological diversity," as the reason why it should do so. In fact, if the World Bank stuck to its environmental policies, it would not give the loan to CEPE in the first place. The $800,000 being offered by the World Bank for conservation measures is merely a gesture and is small recompense for the harm which will be caused by the larger loan.

Oil and Gas in the Brazilian Amazon

Exploration for oil and gas in the Brazilian Amazon has increased sharply over the last few years and the exploitation of fossil fuel reserves now threatens to open up even the most remote areas of the rainforest. There is no reason to believe that the effects of oil industry infrastructure development in previously remote regions will be any less destructive than those already seen elsewhere in the east.

Both Brazilian and foreign TNCs, including Petrobrás, Elf, Pecten (Shell U.S.), BP, and Idemitsu, have been involved in oil and gas exploration in the western Amazon since the late 1970s. The first major infrastructure project was not announced until 1983, when Brazil declared its intention to build a $5 billion, three thousand-kilometer pipeline right across the Amazon from Caraurai in the northwest to São Paulo. The start of the pipeline is currently only accessible by boat or by air.

In January 1983, discussions started about the possibility of building another three thousand-kilometer pipeline from the Juruá gasfield in western Amazonas to São Paulo.[20] Petrobrás had been drilling in Juruá for several years and estimated the gasfield to be some three hundred miles long and forty miles wide.

Limiting the Transnationals

During 1987, Brazil tried to stop foreign TNCs from distributing petrol and oil products in Brazil. The plan collapsed after intense lobbying and a nationwide advertising campaign, only to be replaced by a new constitutional clause requiring all foreign mining and minerals exploration companies to hand over control and majority ownership to Brazilian nationals over a five-year period.[21] In addition, the constitutional assembly approved a clause halting the licensing of any new contracts for oil exploration by foreigners. From October 1988, oil drilling, prospecting, and minerals extraction were forbidden to companies not controlled by Brazilians.

One effect of the constitutional clause will be to make an already complex system of subsidiaries and "paper" companies even more opaque, thus dimming the chain of ownership and therefore responsibility. For example, in 1987, BP, in association with Brascan, had 197 separate companies in Brazil, 112 of which had requested concessions. The great majority of these companies had an insignificant capital, some as low as one cruzeiro, and were, in effect, paper companies.[22]

Some transnationals will no doubt find a way around the constitutional definition of "a Brazilian company of national capital," and maintain their control while ostensibly operating through legitimate Brazilian companies.

Brazilian TNC Exploration

Brazilian exploration, meanwhile, is accelerating and building on the first major oil discoveries within the Amazon basin itself in 1986.[23] In that year a well was discovered in the Urucú river basin, halfway between Manaus and the Peruvian border, which produced 950 barrels per day. Extraction costs were estimated at $3 a barrel, a quarter of those for offshore production. The strike was the largest so far made onshore in Brazil.[24] Subsequent strikes in the Urucú area, have led Petrobrás to estimate that the field encompasses an area of 150,000 square kilometers, three-and-a-half times the size of Switzerland.

According to Petrobrás, a "Master Plan for Managing the Amazon's Environment"

> is in the final development phase, and will guide Petrobrás operations in the region. The initiative is being undertaken for the first time in Brazil, and seeks to transform the company into an agent for promoting self-sustaining local development, assuring that industrial activity harmonizes with conservation of nature. . . . Petrobrás's guidelines for the Amazon also include environmental education: programs will be prepared together with the company's and contracted firms' employees and with local communities to develop an environmental consciousness aiming at a nonpredatory use of natural resources.[25]

It would take a heroic leap of the imagination to suppose that Petrobrás could meet these objectives in a single operation, let alone in an area of 150,000 square kilometers.

Mercifully, development of these fields has been slowed by financial constraints, but Petrobrás hopes to begin barging five thousand barrels per day of Urucú oil to Manaus by late 1989.[26] The refinery at Manaus is expected to produce 20 percent of Brazil's national consumption. Proposals have recently been made for an 800-kilometer gas pipeline to supply the city of Manaus which might continue to Carajás, over 500 kilometers further east.

British Petroleum's Environmental Record

In 1987, BP was exploring in eight tropical rainforest countries, including Brazil, Colombia, and Ecuador.

Its record in Brazil has come under scathing attack in the past, notably from Roberto Gama e Silva, a retired admiral who directed mining interests in Brazil during the last military government. In a book detailing the environmental and social impact of TNCs in the Amazon, he claimed that BP had built up a network of over one hundred companies in collaboration with Brascan, and two Brazilian affiliates. Between them these companies owned over six thousand prospecting licenses, covering twenty-two million hectares.[27]

The latest attack has come from the London *Sunday Times*, which in April 1989 investigated the company's role in an open-cast cassiterite mine (used for tin manufacture) deep inside the Jamari National Forest in Rondônia. The mine is operated by the Companhia de Mineração Jacunda, which is jointly run by BP and Brascan.

Initially, BP claimed that 5,467 hectares of forest have so far been lost in the process, while the Brazilian forest service estimates that the true figure is nearer 97,208 hectares, some 40 percent of the total "protected" area. Following a full BP inquiry into the Jamari operation, BP admitted that the total forest cleared amounted to 5,720 hectares, 1,694 hectares of which was due to the mine itself, and 3,228 hectares due to a BP dam built to serve the mine.[28]

According to the *Sunday Times*, despite BP's claims of sensitive road building, up to two hundred meters of forest had been cleared on either side of the road serving the mine. Brazil nut trees, which are protected under Brazilian law, had been burned, and nearby rivers were clogged with silt. Almost six hundred workers and their families have been moved into the area.[29]

BP Elsewhere in Amazonia

BP ceased oil exploration in Brazil in 1988, but it is still involved in exploration in other areas of Amazonia.

BP claims to have a constantly updated, detailed set of environmental guidelines for oil exploration and drilling in tropical forests, complying with twenty-one principles of environmental protection. However, in discussions with Friends of the Earth U.K., the company was not prepared to release details of the twenty-one underlying principles, so it is impossible to judge how comprehensive the codes are in practice.[30]

Environmental impact assessments (EIA) are theoretically carried out before starting any project, but it is known that this does not always occur in practice. Internal BP documents demonstrate a marked lack of attention to environmental procedure in rainforest areas compared with operations in developed countries. For example in 1987, in the U.K., BP prepared twenty-two environmental impact assessments, forty baseline environmental surveys and eighteen environmental monitoring surveys. In tropical areas, the record was dismal; only one preliminary EIA, one incomplete EIA, no baseline surveys, and no environmental monitoring.

Migration Along Seismic Lines

BP has stated that it takes great care when undertaking seismic exploration. Guidelines limit the width of the path to two meters during exploration and BP claims that LANDSAT images and ground-level exploration suggest that all signs of seismic lines have disappeared after ten to twenty years.

In Ecuador, this is clearly not the case. Mass migration up exploration routes and seismic lines is a serious problem, with seismic lines showing up clearly as migration routes in LANDSAT imagery. This problem is now severe in Ecuador, despite official assurances from BP to Friends of the

Earth that road building in the areas of oil exploration are strictly controlled and that settlements and subsidiary roads are not causing an environmental problem. Oil company maps obtained by Friends of the Earth show extensive development of side roads in some areas, and of settlements alongside the roads.

Observers who have traveled into BP blocks in the area south of Coco near the river Napo, in the central Ecuadorean Amazon, report seeing additional road building, subcontracted from BP, which does not show up on any maps. Settlements are springing up almost continuously along this stretch. These developments are directly related to oil exploration in the region.

Blocks held by Texaco and Conoco in Ecuador show similar problems with migration up seismic lines and paths to exploratory sites. The scale of the problem can be immense; Conoco alone has laid 2,307 kilometers of seismic lines.

Action by BP

BP is an active member, perhaps the most active member, of the International Petroleum Environmental Conservation Association (IPIECA), a voluntary coordinating body for the petroleum industry set up with the United Nations Environment Program (UNEP). BP has submitted its own environmental code to UNEP, through the IPIECA forum.

As a result of the *Sunday Times* exposé, BP has "fast-tracked" its audit of tropical forest operations, which is now complete, and will be using the findings to produce a new set of operational guidelines, including a checklist (as produced for onshore operations in the U.K.), for use by field operators.[31]

Shell in Latin America

Shell is involved in numerous operations in Latin America, and has been in long and delicate negotiations with the government of Peru over a vast natural gas find in the southern Amazon region.

The company also has a number of oil exploration blocks in Peru in the Madre de Dios basin, in the southern forests, near other Shell exploration areas over the border in Bolivia.[32] If Shell finds large enough reserves, it aims to construct a trans-Andean pipeline from the rainforest to the southern coast at an estimated cost of $700 million.[33] Shell is to put up about half the investment for the project, with the balance from the Inter-American Development Bank (IDB). So far, Shell has completed 3,400 kilometers of seismic lines and drilled six exploratory wells.[34]

In Brazil, Shell is best known for its involvement in two bauxite projects, a six hundred million-ton reserve by the Trombetas river jointly owned with the U.S. Alcoa, and a smelter on the island of São Luis, again with Alcoa, through Shell's sister company Billiton.[35]

Local environmentalists claim that the aluminum smelter on São Luís has resulted in the loss of thousands of hectares of rainforest and mangrove swamp due to the construction of roads and settlements linked to the development.

Double Standards

Both Shell and BP have long maintained a high public profile on environmental issues in the U.K. Both sponsor conservation awards, and both have high profile "green" advertising campaigns.

The 1986 Shell Information Handbook highlights the company's projected attitudes towards the environment:

> The potential environmental impacts of Shell products, processes and operations must be fully assessed and appropriate measures adopted to ensure environmental acceptability. . . . New processes are considered through the mechanism of an environmental impact assessment, so that environmental acceptability is built in from the beginning during the planning of major operations such as those connected with exploring for and producing oil and gas. . . .
> It is sometimes necessary to go beyond specific studies and consider general topics of overall relevance to group activities. This special attention has been paid to such topics as acid rain, waste management, and oil pollution in the marine environment.

Exploration in tropical rainforests certainly qualifies as a case for special attention.

Shell U.K. Ltd., is now involved in prospecting for oil in rural Hampshire and Dorset in southern England. Facing protests from influential local authorities and the frequently well-off inhabitants of the area, Shell has mounted a large-scale public relations exercise and has published a one hundred-page report from Aberdeen University which shows that current controls over onshore drilling in countries like Britain, with a vociferous middle class to defend their rural homes, are already tight.[36] Shell and other oil companies are being forced to adopt extensive strategies for minimizing environmental damage, to the extent of choosing sub-optimal sites to preserve woods and hedges, carrying out complete rehabilitation of any natural areas, and so on. The British government has pledged that onshore oil and gas developments will not go ahead unless they conform to strict environmental standards.[37]

There is little evidence to suggest that Shell is as concerned about the infinitely richer and more biologically diverse forests of the tropics. Unlike BP, it has no comprehensive set of guidelines for operations in tropical rainforests.

Future Threats

In the wake of the *Exxon Valdez* disaster, oil companies worried about expensive curbs on their activities in the rich nations are now increasingly looking to the Third World.

The magazine *Business Week* reported in May 1989 that "left with scant funds and fewer prospects, the handful of drillers and service companies that can afford to are following the majors overseas to North Yemen, Colombia, Brazil, Malaysia, and India, where finding costs are lower and tax incentives are offered."

There are a number of important reasons why, for example, BP, which has one of the best environmental divisions of any oil company, will continue to damage tropical forests in which they operate.

First, there is neither the institutional will, structure, nor staffing to ensure that policy emanating from the London headquarters will be adopted and implemented by the two thousand or so diverse subsidiaries overseas. This situation is made worse when BP is a minority partner. Effectively, although an environmental obligation clearly exists, the operations of these companies are beyond the control of the central group. Although sources within BP claim that when the environmental performance of partners has been poor, the company has withdrawn from partnerships, this is difficult to confirm.

Second, guidelines are still inadequate, particularly with regard to tribal peoples.

Third, in the absence of either an effective government, a vocal middle class, or active nongovernmental organizations to scrutinize the activities of the TNCs, environmental and social guidelines are simply ignored.

Conclusion

An ocean of green rhetorical froth has spewed forth from the oil transnationals, obscuring pipeline leakages and detracting from the tidal wave of social calamity and deforestation which is bearing down upon Amazonia. Genuine action, though, is ankle deep, and even sincere attempts to minimize the impact of oil extraction can divert attention from more profound questions of equity and sustainability.

It may well be that Conoco deliberately minimizes the area of operations in the Yasuní National Park, and forbids hunting on pain of dismissal, but such gestures are a sham. Although national park workers in Ecuador favor foreign oil companies over Ecuador's CEPE because of the foreigners' greater concern for environmental and human rights issues (CEPE has an appalling environmental record, including the direct discharge of oil into watercourses),[38] a truly responsible oil company would refuse to explore in a national park in the first place.

BP, as has been shown, may have an excellent series of new and field-tested operational guidelines for rainforests, but creation of access is inherent in its present style of operations. It is the oil companies who are slicing Ecuador into bite-size chunks for the colonists. In other parts of Amazonia, drug smuggling and illegal mining operations are aided and facilitated by the construction of roads.

In Brazil, environmentalists face huge problems with their own transnational, Petrobrás, whose global reach extends, through its subsidiary Brasoil, to the North Sea. It is highly unlikely that Petrobrás's operations in the Urucú river basin, covering an area of remote and delicate rainforest three-and-a-half times the size of Switzerland, will be anything less than disastrous, despite the Green Master Plan.

Clearly, oil transnationals are a vital link in a chain of development which is unplanned, unsupervised, unpoliced, and unsustainable. Their impact lends strength to an increasing call within Brazil to halt road building in Amazonia, close existing access roads, and fell bridges, until such time as an effective institutional structure is in place to deal with the problems of land tenure, corruption, and maldevelopment.

If the oil companies are to live up to their own green rhetoric, they face little choice but to pull out of rainforests altogether.

Notes

1. Kendall, S., "Peru to Step Up Jungle Oil Production," *Financial Times*, 29 Sept. 1988.

2. Petroconsultants, Foreign Briefing Service, Map of Ecuador, Geneva, 1987.

3. Survival International, *Survival International Review* 7, 3–4, London, 1982.

4. International Union for the Conservation of Nature, *Peru, Conservation of Biological Diversity*, Conservation Monitoring Centre, Cambridge, 1988.

5. Barham, J. and Butler, S., "Experts Cautious about Texaco 'N. Sea size Oil Find' in Brazil," *Financial Times*, 2 Jun. 1988.

6. Charters, A., "Brazil Finds Deep Water Field," *Financial Times*, 18 Aug. 1987.

7. Kimmerling, J., *Petroleum Development in Amazonian Ecuador: Environmental and Social Impact*, National Resources Defense Council, Washington, 1989.

8. International Union for the Conservation of Nature, *Directory of Neotropical Protected Areas*, Conservation Monitoring Centre, Cambridge, 1984.

9. Dunphy, M. and Hayes, R., "Beautiful Ecuadorian Rainforest: Update on Oil Exploration," *Rainforest Action Network Alert* 16, San Francisco, 1987.

10. Nations, J. D., *Road Construction and Oil Production in Ecuador's Yasuní National Park*, Center for Human Ecology, Texas, 1988.

11. Ibid.

12. Ibid.

13. IUCN, Ecuador, *Conservation of Biological Diversity*, Conservation Monitoring Centre. Cambridge, 1988.

14. Friends of the Earth, pers. comm., 1989.

15. Ibid.

16. Chapman, A., letter to Koy Thomson of Friends of the Earth U.K., 20 Mar. 1989.

17. Nations, J. D., *Road Construction*.

18. Ibid.

19. Ibid.

20. *Petroleum Economist*, Jan. 1984.

21. Dawnay, I., *Financial Times*, 29 Apr. 1988; ibid., 30 Apr. 1988.

22. Fernandes, F. R. C., *Quem e Quem no Subsolo Brasileiro*, MCT/CNPq. 1987.

23. *Financial Times*, 16 Nov. 1986.

24. *Lloyds List*, 11 Nov. 1986.

25. *Petrobrás News*, Jun. 1989.

26. *Petroleum Economist*, May 1989.

27. Charters, A., *Financial Times*, 3 Dec. 1986.

28. Pers. comm. from BP, Aug. 1989.

29. *Sunday Times*, 18 Jul. 1989.

30. Cowell, E., pers. comm., 1988.

31. Pers. comm. from BP, Aug. 1989.

32. Graham, R., "Hopes and Fears of Peru's Oil Industry," *Financial Times*, 16 Jan. 1985.

33. Gillespie, "Shell in 710 Million Pound Deal to Develop Big Peruvian Gas Find," *Financial Times*, 11 Mar. 1988.

34. Ibid.

35. Branford, S. and Glock, O., *The Last Frontier: Fighting over Land in the Amazon*, Zed Press, London, 1985.

36. Tomlinson, *Environmental Planning Regulatory Background to Onshore Exploration and Production*, Centre for Environmental Planning and Management, Aberdeen University, 1987.

37. Brown, K., "Environment Warning over Onshore Oil," *Financial Times*, 25 Oct. 1984.

38. Nations, J. D., *Road Construction*.

9 Dave Treece ◆ The Militarization and Industrialization of Amazonia: The Calha Norte and Grande Carajás Programs

In this article, originally published in 1989 in The Ecologist, *Dave Treece explores the impact that the Brazilian government's approach to developing the Amazon has had on the tropical rainforest and its indigenous inhabitants. Because of its need to service its enormous foreign debt, Brazil is pursuing a strategy to open up the Amazon and use its resources to promote large-scale industrial development, as the United States did earlier in its history. Part of the government's concern has also been to secure Brazil's frontier against the perceived threat of incursions by neighboring countries or the appropriation of natural resources by foreign entities.* Integrar para não entregar *(integrate in order not to forfeit) was the slogan that accompanied these nationalistic goals.*

Two major programs exemplify the Brazilian development strategy: Calha Norte and Grande Carajás. These projects place a large proportion of the Amazon under the control of the central government and promote development of the region's natural resources at the expense of the remaining unacculturated Indians and the rainforest on which they depend. Treece concludes that the Amazon's integration into the global economy—not its isolation or marginalization—is the cause of the emiseration of its native inhabitants and the degradation of its environment. In other words, he perceives that what is generally considered to be the solution to the problems of underdevelopment—economic growth through industrialization— actually exacerbates these problems.

B etween 50,000 and 60,000 Indians, from 51 territories, will be directly affected by a major program of military occupation, colonization, and development of lands along Brazil's 6,500-kilometer frontier with Colombia, Venezuela, Guyana, Suriname, and French Guyana. Representing 24 percent of Legal Amazonia and 14 percent of Brazil's entire territory, the Calha Norte program embraces some of the country's largest tribal communities, many of which are already threatened by petroleum prospecting, mining activities, and other developments. Among the tribal groups affected are the 3,000 Indians of the Javari valley and the 20,000 Tikuna of the Upper Solimões, the 18,000 Indians of the Upper Río Negro, and the 9,000 Yanomani of Roraima.

From *The Ecologist* (November-December 1989): 225–28. Reprinted by permission of the author and *The Ecologist*, Agriculture House, Bath Road, Sturminster Newton, Dorset DT10 1DU, England.

The project is the brainchild of General Rubens Bayma Denys, secretary-general of the former National Security Council who, in a statement in June 1985, justified his proposals by arguing that the existence of a "demographic void" in the region, the "susceptibility of Guyana and Suriname to Marxist ideological influence," and the possibility of border conflicts between neighboring countries, could render Brazil's national sovereignty vulnerable, and even "project East-West antagonisms onto the northern region of South America."

Not surprisingly, given the alarming implications of the program both for the Brazilian and Indian population of the region and for the neighboring countries, General Bayma Denys recommended that the plans should not immediately be made public knowledge: "It should be observed that many of the themes dealt with, such as the reformulation of indigenist policies, the re-demarcation of frontiers or the localization of military installations, require secret handling, at least in the early stages of their analysis, by virtue of their high political sensitivity."

The military authorities have assumed a policy of economic integration for the tribal communities affected. For General Leônidas Pires Gonçalves, "there is not a Yanomani nation, there are 'Yanomani' tribes," and Calha Norte is a logical means of reconciling the development of the region with the integration of its population. Another army officer made even fewer concessions to the rights of the Indians: "The most important thing at the moment is to occupy the great empty spaces of the frontier region of the northern watershed of the Solimões, where there is a predominance of pockets characterized by a total absence of Brazilians, white men, or *civilizados*. The presence of the Indian, alone, is insufficient to guarantee the defense of regions such as we have in Amazonas and Roraima."

It is not coincidental that some of the largest tribal communities to be affected by the Calha Norte project inhabit lands containing valuable mineral and fossil fuel reserves. Gold is already being mined on Tukano and Baniwa lands on the Upper Río Negro, and further south-west petroleum prospecting has led to violent conflicts with the Korubo of the Javari valley. In a key area of northern Roraima, 27 concessions have been granted to companies including BP and Anglo-American for mining operations on Yanomani territory, which contains gold, diamonds and cassiterite. A further 363 applications have been lodged, representing a direct threat to one third of the Indian's land.

The central objective of the indigenist policy for Calha Norte is to ensure unrestricted access to the mineral reserves located on tribal territories, and to incorporate the Indians into the colonization and development program planned for the region. It is stated policy that all indigenous communities inhabiting territories within 150 kilometers of the frontier are to be denied their constitutional right to legal and effective protection or demarcation of their lands. In their place, Fundaçao Nacional do Indio (FUNAI), the government Indian agency, is being allocated resources for the creation of "indigenous colonies" in which Indians are to participate in "community development projects" and agricultural schemes. In addition, missionary and health workers fighting to provide medical protection for the Indians against introduced disease, and to monitor and publicize their plight, have been expelled on the orders of FUNAI and the National Security Council. In total, up to 60,000 Indians from eighty-three areas face the loss of their right to territorial security, the devastation of their forests, and the shattering of their society and culture by the labor and commodity markets.

The Assault on the Yanomani

The Yanomani, who for more than ten years have been campaigning for the creation of a park in northern Roraima, have been particularly brutally affected by such policies. The absence of effective legal protection for their lands has opened the door to successive invasions by free-lance gold diggers and commercial mining companies.

Announcements in 1987 and early 1988 of a demarcation decree for the territory were dramatically overtaken by one of the largest spontaneous movements of people to be witnessed in Amazonia. Within four months from the end of 1987, twenty thousand gold diggers had entered the Yanomani lands in the Couto de Magalhães area, arriving from all over the country at a rate of one hundred to two hundred every day, by river, on foot, and in small planes which were able to take advantage of the new enlarged airstrip installed under the Calha Norte project. Precipitated by the announcements of the area's demarcation, the gold rush had brought forty thousand miners into Roraima by the middle of 1988, in the knowledge that FUNAI had no adequate structure to deal with the invasion and that the efforts of the federal and military police to stem the flood would be ineffective. Official estimates of the numbers occupying the Yanomani lands by the end of 1988 were of the order of one hundred thousand.

The latest government response to this critical situation, far from seeking to restore to the Indians their constitutional right to the exclusive occupation and use of their traditional lands, serves on the contrary to legalize the presence of the gold diggers, to pave the way for the entry of large-scale commercial activities, and to accelerate the physical, social, and cultural disintegration of the Yanomani people.

Thus, two thirds of the eight million acres to be set aside as "Yanomani Indian land" are to be categorized as forest or national park and therefore subject to laws which do not take Indian land rights into consideration, allowing their economic development under the administration of FUNAI and the Brazilian Institute for Forest Development (IBDF). In effect, the Yanomani's territorial rights are to be limited to an archipelago of nineteen separate zones hedged in by the areas of forest and national park and by areas designated for mineral prospecting, commercial mechanized mining and timber extraction.

The invasion of the Yanomani lands, effectively condoned and institutionalized by the government, has already taken its toll on the tribal communities. By March 1988, more than 50 Indians had already died from influenza and malaria introduced by the miners; in just one area north of Paa-Piu, 280 out of 320 Indians had flu, 84 of them with pulmonary complications. Numerous violent confrontations have been reported since the killing of four Indians and one miner in an incident in August 1987. The numbers killed by disease and violence during 1988 may be as many as 500. Only a serious operation to ensure the peaceful removal of the gold diggers and the effective demarcation of the Yanomani's traditional lands as a continuous area can prevent the tragedy which has already begun from engulfing an entire people.

Grande Carajás

Mining and industrial development projects are also causing ecological degradation and severe social impoverishment in the areas affected by the Grande Carajás project. All told, the project, which is intended to open up eastern Amazonia to industry and industrialized agriculture, is to occupy 900,000 square kilometers—an area the size of France and Britain combined.

The centerpiece of the project is the Serra dos Carajás open-cast iron ore mine. The iron ore project, which consists of the mine itself, railway, and port, is being part funded by the World Bank and the European Commission. Other projects include a bauxite mine capable of producing 8 million tons of bauxite a year, and an aluminium smelter that will produce 800,000 tons of aluminium and 20,000 tons of aluminium oxide a year for sale to Japan. In addition, some 55,000 square kilometers will be cleared to make way for export-oriented plantations and biomass fuel farms. A further 30,000 square kilometers will be given over to ranches.

Approximately half of the Grande Carajás region, 450,000 square kilometers or 5 percent of the area of Brazil, is forest, ranging from true rainforest to seasonal evergreen forest and open savannah. The immediate threat is from the iron smelters and charcoal plants being set up along the railway from the Carajás mountains in Pará to the deep-sea port at São Luís, and from the mining operations in and around the main Carajás mineral province. Currently four smelters are in operation. Some twenty-five charcoal-based smelters have been planned for the area close to the railway.

The aim is to produce 2 million tons of pig iron per annum by 1991, rising to 16 million tons per annum by 2010. Charcoal production for pig-iron smelting will destroy 3.1 cubic meters of wood for each ton of pig iron produced. Annual production of 2.5 million tons of pig iron will therefore lead to 610,000 hectares of forest destruction a year—a figure which would double current official figures of deforestation in Brazilian Amazonia.

In addition, a 3-million-tons-per-annum steel plant is being considered near São Luís, at an estimated cost of U.S. $2-3 billion. For this, the Brazilian government is negotiating to import coal by sea from Colombia. According to the national steel plan, some 8 million tons per annum of steel are to be produced in the Carajás region by the year 2010.

Since Brazilian companies are allowed to deduct 25 percent from their annual taxes if this is invested in Amazonia, most of the furnaces are being built by subsidiaries of steel or mining companies from the central Brazilian state of Minas Gerais. Many are also being built with government loans from FINAM—the Fund for Investment in Amazonia. Once built, they are exempt from income tax for ten years.

The Responsibility of the World Bank and EC

While the pace of destructive development in the region has quickened, none of the institutions involved in funding the projects has taken any serious action to ensure that even minimum safeguards are employed in defense of the Indians and their environment. The European Community (EC) has failed to carry out any independent monitoring of the iron ore project. Indeed, a meeting with the community's director of credits and investments revealed that the EC has relied upon the annual missions of the German banking consortium, KfW, which is entirely lacking in the technical competence necessary to assess environmental and social matters.

The construction of charcoal-fired pig-iron furnaces along the Carajás railway continues apace, despite the warnings of the chief environmental officer for the state mining company, Companhía Vale do Rio Doce (CVRD), about the disastrous environmental and economic consequences. CVRD, the World Bank, and the EC still hold to the now rather hollow argument that no responsibility can be accepted for environmental or social problems outside the arbitrary "area of influence" of the iron ore project. This is despite the clear infrastructural role of the iron ore mine, railway, and port (which comprise the iron ore project) as an export corridor for the region, and despite admissions from within CVRD itself of its responsibility for the pig iron/charcoal projects given its monopoly on the supply of iron ore and rail transport (*see* B. Rich, "The Greening of the Development Banks," *The Ecologist*, Vol. 19, No. 2, 1989).

As far as the tribal communities of the region are concerned, the same authorities claim great successes. But the extension of the official "support program" introduced in 1982, has done nothing to advance the situation of the sixteen territories out of twenty-seven (only twenty-five are included in the program) which still lack full legal and physical protection. Contrary to the claims of CVRD, the World Bank, and others, figures from the Brazilian nongovernment organization, CEDI, indicate that the demarcation process has been completed for less than 37 percent of the area traditionally occupied by Indian lands. Demarcation processes may have begun in many cases, and even been completed in some instances; however, the problem remains largely one of nonprogress or of incorrect demarcation (too small, or nontraditional, useless areas), and of land invasions. The reassurances of World Bank and EC representatives about continued funding for the Amerindian project ignore the central problem of FUNAI's institutional incompetence to administer such funding, as demonstrated not only by the experience in Carajás but also by the legal investigations into an ex-president of the agency's involvement in illicit timber contracts on Indian lands.

CVRD has now declared that it has no intention of renewing funding for the Amerindian project after the present budget has run out. The fifteen thousand Indians of the region are therefore to receive no further support to withstand the continuing impact of a development program that is expected to run for several centuries.

The Expropriation of Guajá Land

In perhaps the most urgent case, that of the 250 or so nomadic Guajá of Maranhão, two thirds of the Indians' territory has been expropriated for cattle ranching.

On 6 May 1988, the Awá Indian area was officially demarcated by FUNAI. This was to have been ratified by the Brazilian president. On 29 August 1988, however, the minister of the Federal Resources Tribunal suspended the demarcation at the request of thirty-six cattle ranchers who have claims totaling 111,000 hectares in the Indian area. Granting this land to the ranchers will reduce the area of territory earlier declared for demarcation by 60 percent, from 147,500 hectares to 65,700 hectares. A demarcation study and proposal made by the anthropologist Mércio Gomes (contracted by CVRD) in 1985 had recommended that 276,000 hectares be demarcated.

The dispossession of the Guajá not only leaves them exposed to the depredation of the cattle ranchers, it also gives the green light to those seeking new sources of timber for the charcoal-burning smelters rapidly being installed alongside the Carajás railway.

Alternatives to Charcoal?

Official policy is that charcoal from natural forests will be the principal energy source for at least the first eight years until charcoal from plantations becomes available. Since the charcoal will have to be supplied from ever-increasing distances, the financial viability of the projects is likely to be jeopardized. The experience of iron and steel production in the state of Minas Gerais, where over one half of charcoal consumption is from natural forests, has been of widespread deforestation. Transport costs from sites up to 800 kilometers from the plants now amount to up to two thirds of total delivery costs. Furthermore, given the low international prices of pig iron, production using charcoal from natural forests is only financially viable if the economic and environmental costs of deforestation are ignored.

In addition to objections from the local state governments of Pará and Maranhão to the environmental consequences and the lack of economic benefit to the region itself, CVRD considers that charcoal is too valuable to be used for pig-iron production, and should be reserved for production of higher-value goods such as specialty steel. CVRD is collaborating with the São Paulo-based company Prometal in a project to set up a steel plant near the Carajás mine.

Meanwhile, CVRD's own environment department has expressed its clear opposition to the pursuit of the program of charcoal-powered iron smelters. In an internal document dated April 1987, CVRD's superintendent for the environment, F. F. de Assis Fonseca, has pointed out that, not only are the projects economically unviable unless native forests are used, but no measures are being taken, nor have they been contemplated, by the companies setting up the smelters to reforest the region. Even if they were, agro-forestry knowledge is insufficient to start large-scale reafforestation in the short term. At the same time, even the viability of projects using native timber is threatened by falling steel prices and rising charcoal prices. At present, it is only the fiscal incentives offered to the companies under the Grande Carajás program which make investment in these projects attractive. According to the viability study carried out for CVRD, optimistic predictions are that timber production capacity in the region will be exhausted within twenty years.

In September 1988, a number of Brazilian nongovernment organizations (NGO) brought a civil prosecution against the Brazilian government and the companies responsible for the pig-iron smelters for violating environmental and forestry law, and for failing to observe the constitutional requirement to carry out environmental impact studies in advance of such projects. The NGOs are calling for a halt to iron smelting until thorough studies into alternative energy sources to charcoal have been completed and acted upon. . . . The case may already have succeeded in preventing the installation of the new pig-iron plants planned for the region. Meanwhile, for the past twelve months, the World Bank (with financial and technical support from the European Community) has been ready with a proposed study into energy alternatives for Carajás. Only the intransigent opposition of the Brazilian government has prevented the study from going ahead.

Social Impact

In the state of Maranhão alone, there are 450,000 landless families out of a total population of just over 4.5 million. The concentration of land ownership (26 million hectares out of the total 32 million hectares are big estates, but only 37 percent of this area is actually occupied) is being intensified by charcoal production and other projects. As more forest is given over to charcoal, more peasant farmers will be thrown off their land. Those who are not, like the Indian communities of the region, will be pressured into selling their own timber and producing charcoal for the furnaces.

Pollution is a serious problem, given that the pig-iron plants do not have pollution controls. Disease, too, is on the increase: tuberculosis is now amongst the chief diseases suffered by residents of Piquiá, Açailándia, which is surrounded by smoke from the charcoal furnaces. The full extent of associated respiratory problems will only become apparent after a number of years, but already those working in the furnaces themselves are coughing up black bile. The majority of small farmers in the area are now employed by the new industrial firms, their land swallowed up by speculation.

Immigration into the region has also led to a severe reduction in the availability of fish on the island of São Luís, where in one locality production dropped from 1,000 kilograms per week in 1986 to 600 kilogram in 1987 and 50 kilograms by this year. In Marabá, at the center of the scheme, family incomes are calculated at 5 percent of the amount necessary for the minimum requirements of food, health, transport and housing.

Responsibility for Destruction

Most important perhaps, for those campaigning on the issue, is the question of CVRD's responsibility for the environmental and social impact of developments in the region beyond its own iron ore project, a responsibility which, along with the other funders of the project, it has so far denied. However, as Fonseca puts it, "CVRD's responsibility is greatly increased by the fact that it holds the monopoly on the mineral and on the rail transport. Any iron and steel project in the northern region can only exist with the support of CVRD." Under pressure from both the iron and steel lobby and from ecologists and the Forestry Institute, "it will be difficult for the company to defend itself from accusations of being the chief party responsible for the devastation." The same must apply to the EC, the World Bank and the other financial institutions supporting the iron ore project, yet which have attempted to disassociate themselves from the environmental and social disruption produced by the project.

Conclusion

Today, the last isolated communities of Amazonian Indians are being swiftly and brutally taught the laws of world economics. The fragile boundaries of a world which seemed closed have been irrevocably opened up—a process that will continue regardless of what steps are now taken (and must be taken) to provide the Indians with the territorial security that can enable them to withstand and resist the onslaught on their ways of life. For it is their very integration into the world economy, rather than their marginalization, which explains the increasingly intolerable conditions of life they are forced to endure.

Whatever the individual victories of isolated communities (and they are few and far between), Brazil's distorted structure of land ownership can only continue to exert pressure to "open up" Amazonia for ranching and settlement; the burden of foreign debt and the irrational dynamic of the development process are accelerating the industrialization of the region at a dizzying pace. Ultimately, therefore, any real advance in the control exerted by Indian groups over development on their lands will depend upon the balance of political forces in society at large.

The task ahead must be to build upon the incipient links being forged between various forest peoples' groups and those seeking to defend their environments and working and living conditions elsewhere in the country, in order to challenge those mining companies, government agencies, and military forces which are violating the rights of tribal peoples. Only the advance of this movement can guarantee the Indians the possibility of genuine control over their lives.

10 Joshua Karliner ◆ Central America:
Political Ecology and U.S. Foreign Policy

Joshua Karliner explores a little-known dimension of the international causes of deforestation—U.S. foreign policy—in 1990 this essay. He suggests that the United States has mistaken its true interests by pursuing a development strategy that has exacerbated the traditional economic and social inequalities of the region. By promoting economic growth at the expense of the basic needs of most Central Americans, this strategy has led to political instability and environmental degradation. Karliner contends that environmental problems are symptoms, not causes, of an underlying structural crisis that is the result of five hundred years of domination and exploitation by foreign powers. U.S. environmentalists, Karliner claims, need to move beyond their fixation on narrow issues, such as population growth or the "hamburger connection," to ally themselves with movements that address the fundamental power relationships in Central America.

The United States government sees Central America as a strategic bridge between two oceans and two continents. These geographic characteristics, which have contributed historically to deep U.S. involvement in the region, also account for the extraordinary biological diversity on the isthmus. A wide variety of life forms from both North and South America, including migratory birds and rare, often unidentified plant species, meet in Central America's lush tropical forests. But since World War II, U.S. security and development imperatives have been the primary force behind the rapid deterioration of this biological wealth. And since the early 1980s, the steep escalation of U.S. military involvement in the region has threatened to irreversibly destroy Central America's ecological equilibrium.

The region's biologically rich and fertile yet fragile natural resource base, upon which its economies depend, is suffering from decades of development policies that have promoted export agriculture over basic human needs, creating a pattern of unequal land distribution. This has enriched local elites and foreign corporations while forcing the majority of the population off the prime agricultural land. When the Central American people rebel against these unjust conditions, the region's governments and the U.S. government respond with repression and militarization, fueling a downward spiral of poverty, war, and environmental destruction.

From *Lessons of the Rainforest*, ed. Suzanne Head and Robert Heinzman (San Francisco, 1990), 144–45, by permission of Sierra Club Books.

More than two thirds of Central America's original forests have been felled, with most of the destruction occurring since 1960. Deforestation continues today at a rapid rate of more than four thousand square kilometers a year. Deforestation of the region's rainy, steep-sloped uplands has caused the siltation of downstream potable water sources, hydroelectric dams, irrigation projects, and coastal fisheries. Soil erosion has impoverished more than half of all the agricultural land, causing farm productivity to decline sharply.[1]

In Costa Rica, deforestation is so bad that the government, once an exporter of timber, is beginning to import wood. The Choluteca region of Honduras, almost completely deforested by cattle ranchers and cotton growers between 1950 and 1980, has been undergoing a process of desertification, which contributes to increasing hunger. In El Salvador, the most ecologically deteriorated nation in Latin America, every major watershed and river basin suffers siltation, droughts, and floods. Only a tiny percent of the original forest remains.

Yet despite environmental deterioration and its dynamic, spiraling relationship to socioeconomic deterioration, few policy makers or activists make the connection between the interwoven issues of poverty, ecological destruction, and war in Central America. Those debating U.S. policy in the region have not only failed to recognize that there are environmental dimensions to the region's deepening crisis, but have also neglected the widespread environmental impacts of U.S. foreign policy itself.

Many mainstream environmental organizations have also failed to see the relationships between these issues, singling out rapid population growth as the "underlying problem" in Central America.[2] Although population, likely to double in the next twenty-five years, does contribute to crisis in the region, it is not the root cause. Neither is deforestation, although almost all the region's rainforests will disappear in roughly the same amount of time. Both population growth and deforestation are rather symptoms of a much deeper, underlying structural crisis. This crisis has roots in Spanish colonialism, a highly stratified class structure, a myopic U.S. foreign policy, and an unjust international economic order that treats the Third World as a gigantic resource reserve.

The Roots of Destruction

Since the Spanish Conquest, Central America's natural resources have helped fuel the development of the North's economies. Wood, minerals, and luxury crops have been extracted or cultivated and shipped to colonial Spain, England, and later, the United States. Early efforts by Central

Americans to control this exploitation of natural resources ran into strong resistance from the Northern powers. During the first half of this century, U.S. troops intervened repeatedly to defend strategic and corporate interests in the region.

In the 1950s the United States began pursuing a more sophisticated strategy that used multilateral and bilateral aid agencies to consolidate its political and economic grip on the region. This "new and improved" development model was designed to increase production of agricultural crops for sale to transnational corporations on the world market. This agro-export strategy promoted economic growth by intensifying banana and coffee production, and diversifying agricultural exports to include nontraditional products such as cotton, beef, sugar, timber, rice and later, fruits and flowers.

This agro-export development focus has increasingly skewed what was already an unequal land-tenure system by further concentrating fertile land in the hands of a few Central American families and multinational corporations. By the mid 1970s, 4 percent of the population owned 73 percent of the land, and the poorest 77 percent of the region's people owned just 7 percent of the land.[3] Impoverished Central Americans have been forced into farming forested hillsides and colonizing the region's rainforests, where they have no option but to cut down the forest to grow corn and beans for survival.

Such inequity has inevitably led to widespread movements for land redistribution and other economic reforms. The U.S. response to these reform movements has been to bolster its alliances with the local militaries and the export growers in order to defend the status quo. The result has been increased poverty and environmental destruction, as well as the emergence of repressive, military-dominated governments that fortify the agro-export model.

Ecological Destabilization Policies

Perhaps the single most environmentally destructive policy the United States ever implemented in Central America was the Latin America-wide Alliance for Progress. In the name of development and economic growth, the Alliance pushed wave after wave of agricultural export crops from Central America's fertile Pacific shores eastward across its diverse terrain. The Alliance did promote agrarian reforms, but in reality these reforms turned out to be rainforest colonization schemes, designed to make room for more export crops while easing pressures for redistribution of the most fertile lands. While these export crops were booming, food production in Central America sank and malnutrition soared. Militarization, aimed at assuring "stability and security," enforced these social and economic policies.[4]

The two most destructive commodities promoted by the Alliance were cotton and cattle. By the mid-1960s, pesticide-drenched cotton covered most of the region's fertile Pacific plain, where corn and forestland had dominated just ten years earlier. Throughout the 1960s and 1970s a cattle boom, financed by multilateral and bilateral loans, stampeded Central America, pushing more peasants off their land and overrunning the region's rainforests. By 1980, 22 percent of the land mass, more land than was utilized by all other agricultural commodities combined, was in permanent pasture.[5]

Once again, movements for social change, which threatened the stability of the agro-export model, grew out of these economic inequities. In response, the Alliance fostered militarization to keep these movements down. Gruesome stories abound of peasant communities that were literally blown away for organizing resistance to cattle ranchers who were evicting them from their lands and pushing them deeper into the rainforest.

In the mid-1960s, for example, Guatemalan peasants organized to keep their land. An armed guerrilla movement emerged at the edge of the rainforest to challenge both the government and the ranchers. In response, a U.S. Special Forces team directed a Guatemalan counterinsurgency campaign that used helicopter gunships, fighter bombers, and napalm to destroy a five hundred-person guerrilla insurgency. It is estimated that the army killed an additional six thousand to eight thousand people in the process. Once the resistance was virtually eliminated, military officers were rewarded with huge cattle ranches, the rainforest continued to disappear, and multinationals began to exploit mineral and oil resources. Similar conflicts occurred in Nicaragua and Honduras, and—with less violence—in Costa Rica.[6]

In this context the "hamburger connection" (the import of Central American beef by the U.S. fast-food industry), a frequent target of U.S. environmental activists, can clearly be seen as merely another symptom of the larger Central American nightmare of export agriculture, unequal land distribution, repression, and U.S. military intervention. U.S. environmentalists would be wise to move beyond their current fast-food fixation and consider allying themselves with movements that address fundamental power relations in Central America.

Peasant movements fighting for land redistribution are challenging these power relations and may become the fundamental force that can reverse the surging tide of rainforest destruction in Central America. For while they are not driven strictly by ecological considerations, genuine land reform movements are inherently environmental movements in that they seek to bring food production out of the forests and off the hillsides.

Ya Seen One Rainforest, Ya Seen 'Em All

The U.S. government response to Central American movements for social change during the late 1970s and 1980s has been to increase intervention in the region. U.S. policy in the Reagan years was dominated by a campaign to roll back the socialist-oriented Nicaraguan revolution through a combination of the contra war and economic pressure. At the same time, the United States has spent billions of dollars in military and economic aid on a policy aimed at containing revolutionary movements in the rest of the region and building a "military shield" to provide a stable environment for "development" and "democracy."[7] "Development" of course means maintaining the agro-export formula; "democracy" is the name in which any challenges to this export formula, and ultimately to U.S. power in the region, are squelched.

Annual U.S. foreign assistance to El Salvador, Honduras, Guatemala, and Costa Rica increased nearly sixfold between 1980 and 1987, jumping from $150 million to $895 million a year. The United States spent two thirds of the aid it gave Central America and the Caribbean on direct military and "security" assistance, and roughly 1 percent went to environmental protection.[8] This pattern of escalating military spending in Central America, combined with nearly total neglect of environmental problems and their root causes, is foreclosing future options for sustainable economic development in the region. In its effort to save the region from supposed communism, the United States is literally destroying Central America.

Nowhere is this clearer than in El Salvador.[9] Its economy has all but collapsed, and is being sustained only by the $1.3 million that the United States pumps in daily—more than 50 percent of the country's national budget. According to a report by the U.S. Congress Arms Control and Foreign Policy Caucus, 75 percent of U.S. aid to El Salvador is directly related to the war, even though the majority is called funds for "economic support." This military-oriented spending overwhelms the $1.5 million—or .005 percent—of aid annually spent on environmental and natural resource management. In fact, in 1988 the United States spent almost two hundred times as much on war-related aid in El Salvador as it did to protect and restore the environment.[10] Rather than addressing the roots of crisis in El Salvador, U.S. tax dollars have brought about more than one million refugees and seventy thousand Salvadoran deaths (many were killed by right-wing death squads).

The U.S. war in El Salvador has also claimed a direct ecological toll. For example, El Pital, El Salvador's only lower montane forest, has been reduced to a series of charred remnants. Once targeted as a national park, El Pital was more recently the target of a U.S.-backed counterinsurgency bombing campaign. Counterinsurgency has also turned vast areas of Morazán and northern Chalatenango provinces into virtual wastelands—crops destroyed, forests charred, and landscapes scarred with bomb craters. In 1982 the paramilitary death squad Organización Democrática Nacionalista (ORDEN) killed four park rangers at the Montecristo Cloud Forest National Park and assassinated thirty other community members who were cooperating with the park service.

A similar situation exists in Guatemala, where the army has carried out a scorched-earth counterinsurgency campaign destroying forests, fields, livestock, and at least 440 villages. Between 1982 and 1987 more than one million Guatemalans were displaced from their land. Many of these refugees have fled to the lowland rainforests of neighboring Mexico, where they practice slash-and-burn agriculture.

In Honduras, the second poorest nation in the Western Hemisphere, a massive infusion of U.S. aid made the country a staging ground for the contra war as well as a command post for counterinsurgency in El Salvador and Guatemala, earning it the nickname "Pentagon Republic." Honduras' share of development assistance actually declined in the 1980s, while military aid and environmental destruction increased. In 1986, for example, according to the government-run Honduran Forestry Corporation (CORFOP), Honduras lost more than one thousand square kilometers of forest. This was due to U.S. military maneuvers and construction, the flight of Nicaraguan refugees from the contra war, and the presence of more than ten thousand contras themselves. This military-induced deforestation more than doubled Honduras' normal deforestation rate.[11] According to information obtained by the Environmental Policy Institute, a United Nations and Honduran government report charges that these activities have caused more than $125 million in damages to Honduran forests. According to the director of CORFOP, "The contras are changing the whole ecology of the zone—the vegetation, wildlife, soils, and water sources are being damaged."

In Nicaragua, international attention has focused on contra atrocities against doctors, teachers, and agricultural extension workers. However, the war dealt a series of blows to Nicaragua's innovative environmental policies as well. For example, the contras assassinated more than thirty employees working in the environmental and forestry sectors between 1983 and 1987, and kidnapped at least another seventy-five. Sandinista efforts to fight back are also causing some environmental damage; the army's ground-based mobile rocket launchers and MI-24 helicopters, for example, have destroyed patches of forestland.[12]

Perhaps the most devastating impact of the conflict was the indirect economic effect. Nicaragua's huge per capita foreign debt, the U.S. economic embargo, U.S. economic pressure to halt all multilateral loans to Nicaragua, and the contra war combined with internal mismanagement to create a severe economic crisis that crippled the country's social and environmental programs. A 1987 World Wildlife Fund report noted that "the drain on the economy from the continued conflict has had a far-reaching negative impact. Government conservation programs are severely reduced and local people are increasingly tempted to exploit natural resources for fast, hard currency."[13]

The U.S. rollback policy in Nicaragua and its containment policy in the rest of Central America have effectively blocked some of the fundamental changes that are necessary if Central Americans are to begin building environmentally sustainable, socially just societies. Nevertheless, the Sandinista revolution has taken some significant steps toward creating this ideal.

Revolution in the Rainforest

The Sandinista revolution succeeded in 1979 by violently overthrowing the 42-year-old, U.S.-created and -supported Somoza dictatorship. Since then the government has pursued some environmentally destructive policies such as promoting agricultural development on forestry land. Overall, however, the revolution's structural reforms and efforts to break with the traditional agro-export patterns have given the Sandinistas unprecedented potential for implementing comprehensive environmental reforms. Since 1979, Nicaragua has moved toward a more ecologically sustainable style of development that could save its rainforests—the largest remaining in Central America.[14]

During their first month in power, the Sandinistas nationalized all of Nicaragua's forests, which Somoza had previously doled out in concessions to multinational timber corporations. They also quickly moved to implement a program of land reform, which within five years had successfully halted all rainforest colonization projects and redistributed more than one fifth of the nation's productive farmland.

During their second month in power, Sandinistas created the Nicaraguan Institute of Natural Resources and the Environment (IRENA), the first environmental agency ever in Nicaragua. In addition to implementing a broad spectrum of other programs, by 1982 IRENA had targeted 18 percent of Nicaraguan territory for national parks and reserves, including the largest pristine rainforest north of the Amazon basin, the ten thousand-square-kilometer Bosawas forest on the Honduran border. It was in Bosawas that IRENA began managing the country's first rainforest national park, Saslaya, in 1981.

In 1982, however, in one of the opening salvos in their war against the environment, the contras kidnapped Saslaya's administrator and two rangers, forcing the closure of the park. Further contra attacks burned numerous reforestation projects, destroyed vehicles and buildings, and made it unsafe for environmentalists to work in many rainforested areas.

Nevertheless, Nicaragua continues to maintain some of its innovative environmental programs—including environmental restoration, development of alternatives to pesticides, and a sea turtle conservation program. These programs and others, along with a small but vocal nongovernmental environmental movement, receive support from international environmental organizations as well as some Western European governments. One of the outstanding programs is an effort to create a rainforested "peace park" on the border with Costa Rica which, on the Nicaraguan side, combines land reform, forestry, and rainforest conservation. U.S. support for this kind of "long-range conservation and development program," writes John B. Oakes in the *New York Times*, is "the surest way to help the Central American people restore their economy and stabilize their politics." Yet, despite broad international support for the project, he notes, "our government is conspicuously absent."[15]

A Role for U.S. Environmentalists

When we consider the U.S. role in Central America, it becomes clear that environmentalists who want to save the region's rainforests must work to shift Washington's policies away from supporting militarization and export agriculture and toward peace, social justice, and ecologically sound development in the region.

If we are serious about saving the rainforests of Mesoamerica we must go beyond supporting national parks and tiny environmental groups. We must not merely join consumer campaigns to boycott beef, or efforts to make multilateral development banks' loans more environmentally sound. We can no longer afford to be single-issue environmentalists.

These specific efforts are important. But if the World Bank continues to direct 80 percent of its loans to the export sector—with or without environmental safeguards—farmers will be pushed off their land and rainforests will fall. If the global debt crisis is not resolved, Central American nations will continue to ravage Nature in order to service their loans. If the United States does not reverse its promotion of militarization and agro-exports, any environmental programs that the U.S. Agency for International Development may introduce are in effect a smoke-and-mirrors distraction from the real damage U.S. policy is causing.

The bottom line is that if the basic needs of Central America's population are not met, if there is not enough land to grow food, the rainforest will continue to disappear. If the demands of the subordinated for land and social change continue to run up against brutal repression, people will fight back. If the United States continues to undermine all efforts at structural change that might allow a more socially just, economically viable, and ecologically sound development model to emerge in Central America, the United States will also continue to undermine the very stability it claims to be seeking in Central America.

Although it is important for environmentalists to organize consumer boycotts, keep pressure on the multilateral development banks, and support parks and environmental organizations in the region, it is imperative to build a broader environmental movement, one that supports social change in Central America and allies itself with movements throughout this hemisphere that are working for such change. A broader environmentalism must address such issues as peace and equity, while also contributing an environmental perspective to both land reform movements in Central America and the growing U.S. movement to change our government's policies in the region. It is through this broader environmentalism that we may ultimately be able to save the rainforests.

Notes

1. For the best statistical overview of environmental conditions in Central America, see H. Jeffrey Leonard, *Natural Resources and Economic Development in Central America* (Washington, DC: International Institute for Environment and Development, 1987).

2. Robert Cahn, ed., *An Environmental Agenda for the Future, by Leaders of America's Foremost Environmental Organizations* (Washington, DC: Agenda Press, 1985).

3. Kevin Danaher et al., *Help or Hindrance? United States Economic Aid in Central America* (San Francisco: Institute for Food and Development Policy, 1987), p. 15.

4. Walter LaFeber, *Inevitable Revolutions: The United States in Central America* (New York: W. W. Norton and Company, 1984). Also Walter LaFeber, "The Alliances in Retrospect," in Andrew Maguire and Janet Welsh Brown, eds., *Bordering on Trouble: Resources and Politics in Latin America* (Washington, DC: World Resources Institute, 1986).

5. Leonard, *Natural Resources*, p. 99. Also Robert Williams, *Export Agriculture and the Crisis in Central America* (Durham, NC: University of North Carolina Press, 1986), p. 113.

6. Williams, *Export Agriculture*, pp. 129–51.

7. For a clear articulation of this ideology and policy, see Henry Kissinger et al., *Report of the National Bipartisan Commission on Central America* (Washington, DC: U.S. Government Printing Office, 1984). For an analysis, see *Changing Course: Blueprint for Peace in Central America and the Caribbean* (Washington, DC: Institute for Policy Studies, 1984).

8. Lawrence Mosher, "At Sea in the Caribbean," in Maguire and Brown, *Bordering on Trouble*.

9. Most information in this chapter on El Salvador comes from Daniel Faber and Bill Hall, *El Salvador: Ecology of Conflict*, Green Paper Number Four (San Francisco: Environmental Project on Central America [EPOCA], 1989). Also see Jenny Pearce, *Promised Land: Peasant Rebellion in Chalatenango, El Salvador* (London: Latin America Bureau, 1986).

10. Arms Control and Foreign Policy Caucus of the U.S. Congress, "Bankrolling Failure: U.S. Policy in El Salvador and the Urgent Need for Reform" (Washington, DC: U.S. Congress, November 1987), p. 24; and "Environment and Natural Resources: A Strategy for Central America" (U.S. Agency for International Development, March 1989).

11. Robert A. Rice and Joshua Karliner, *Militarization: The Environmental Impact*, Green Paper Number Three (San Francisco: EPOCA, 1986). See also *Environment Under Fire: Ecology and Politics in Central America*, a video documentary by EPOCA and Moving Images (San Francisco, 1988).

12. Gustavo Adolfo Ruiz, *The Environmental Impacts of the Contra War*, a paper presented at the First Central American Environmental Action Conference (Managua, 1987).

13. World Wildlife Fund country report: *Nicaragua* (Washington, DC: WWF, 1987).

14. Peter Rosset and John Vandermeer, eds., *Nicaragua: Unfinished Revolution* (New York: Grove Press, 1986).

15. John B. Oakes, "Greening Central America," *New York Times* (April 22, 1988).

---

11 José A. Lutzenberger ◆ from
Who Is Destroying the Amazon Rainforest?

José A. Lutzenberger is a prominent Brazilian environmentalist. In the years since 1987, when his article was published in The Ecologist, *the environmental movement has gained strength in Brazil, truly coming of age in 1990 when President Collor de Mello named Lutzenberger to head the newly created National Secretariat of the Environment. Following Lutzenberger's lead, Brazilian environmentalists have begun to challenge their government's conceptualization of "development," which is presented in Selection 12.*

In this article, Lutzenberger outlines how the Brazilian state's drive for capital accumulation and power underlies the current approach to developing the Amazon. The state has allied itself with large corporations—both multinational and Brazilian—to accomplish its program. This technocratic view of "progress," Lutzenberger asserts, is destroying the ecology of the Amazon and societies and people that have adapted to living sustainably in

From *The Ecologist* (July-November 1987): 155–60. Reprinted by permission of the author and *The Ecologist*, Agriculture House, Bath Road, Sturminster Newton, Dorset DT10 1DU, England.

the rainforest. He concludes that it is not peasants who are ultimately responsible for the destruction of the rainforest; they are, in fact, victims of an economic and political system that drives them to the Amazon frontier where they are forced to destroy the forest. Lutzenberger identifies the fundamental assumptions of Brazil's development strategy as the major cause of deforestation and environmental degradation in Amazonia.

We are witnessing today in Brazil and in much of Latin America the biggest holocaust in the history of life. Never in the course of three-and-a-half thousand million years, since the first stirrings of life on this planet, has there been such a wholesale, accelerated, violent and irreversible demolition of all living systems as today. We have passed the point where we only desecrate this or that scenic landscape, this or that ecosystem. We are now in the process of demolishing whole biomes. Now we are getting ready to finish off the last large, more or less intact and contiguous jungle on earth, the Hylaea, or tropical rainforest in Amazonia.

This systematic destruction is being carried out in the name of "progress." The Brazilian government, the military dictatorship which set itself up in 1964, set a course for "development" at any cost. Its definition of development is a technocratic one—an economic model geared to fast industrialization, where the highest aim is megatechnological concentration and a cash crop agriculture, with vast monocultures, to feed industry and the export market.

The Role of Multinationals

Large-scale devastation of the tropical rainforest and its surrounding transitional forests takes several forms. At one extreme we have gigantic projects. Multinational or Brazilian corporations or powerful individuals go to Amazonia to make large sums of money. Among them are such giants as Anderson Clayton, Goodyear, Volkswagen, Nixdorf Computer, Nestlé, Liquigás, Borden, Kennecott Copper, and the American multibillionaire Daniel Ludwig, or even farmers' cooperatives from the south of Brazil, such as Cotrijui. This is a very small fraction of the list which runs into hundreds. These organizations set up enormous projects—cattle ranches, paper mills, single species monocultures of exotic trees for pulp, immense rice plantations, sugarcane plantations for the "gasahol" program, timber mills, mining operations.

More often than not, these operations are financed with state subsidies—tax rebates. That is why they are extremely wasteful and can accept scandalously low rates of productivity. On the extensive cattle ranches, the production of meat hardly reaches fifty kilograms per hectare per year, and it rapidly declines after a couple of years as the soils are leached of the scarce nutrients remaining after deforestation. The grasses and legumes sowed for pasture give way to scrub unpalatable to cattle. The scrub is then kept down with heavy machinery, annual burning, or herbicides. This contributes still more to the destruction of the soil and to still lower production. In northern Europe, on organic farms not using imported feed, meat production is closer to six hundred kilograms per hectare per year plus between four thousand and six thousand liters of milk per hectare. No milk is produced on the Amazonian cattle ranches. We must remind ourselves that the intact forest, obliterated to give way to pasture, can produce at least ten times as much food in the form of tropical fruit, game, and fish. Every single adult Brazil nut tree left standing can produce hundreds of kilos of precious food, every pupunha [pejibaye] palm tree or many of the innumerable other species of palm trees occurring in the forest can produce dozens of kilos of food, feed, and construction material. For the inhabitants of the forest there also is no shortage of firewood, a problem that is becoming extremely serious in other parts of the world.

A devastating social effect of those schemes is that they employ an average of one worker per two thousand cattle, that is, one person on at least three thousand hectares! The same area of forest could easily feed and house several hundred people if left intact. The traditional life-style of the Indian, *caboclo* [backwoodsman], and the *seringueiro* (rubber tapper) is also much more pleasant, easier, independent, and secure than the life-style of the ranch worker. The irony is that the little meat produced is meat for export. The Amazonian *caboclo* wisely says, "Where cattle move in, we move out, cattle mean hunger." The only beneficiaries are the corporations who do not even spend money in the areas they devastate. But they keep saying that they are in the business of feeding starving humanity.

The social devastation caused by the other schemes—the extensive monoculture of trees, open-pit mining, gigantic dams, timber mills, logging on an industrial scale, commercial fishing for export—are just as bad. They are all geared to the enrichment of the powerful groups outside the region. There is no concern for the needs of the local population, much less for their life-style and culture. The local people are uprooted, marginalized, alienated, and they go either to the slums or escape even deeper into the jungle, as long as there is jungle. The Indians are already reaching the end of the line.

The Brazilian government is now selling off whole mountains, as in the Carajás Project (see *The Ecologist*, vol. 17, no. 2/3). Recently the minister of planning boasted of having received the first down payment of a few hundred million dollars from Japan for ore to be mined in the Carajás mountains. What will future generations say?

Colonization Schemes

At the other extreme we have large-scale demolition of the forest by small settlers, but this is also due to outside forces. The State of Rondônia, in the west of Brazilian Amazonia, about the size of Great Britain, is being systematically cleared by settlers at a rate that, if continued, will leave it without forest within but a few years. The small settlers are more efficient destroyers of the forest than the big companies, who usually abide by the law that requires them to leave half the forest intact. The settler cannot stop, he must go on clearing until nothing is left. Rondônia was chosen as an escape valve. Brazil's colonization agency, Instituto Nacional de Colonizaçao e Reforma Agraria (INCRA), circulates whole-page ads showing aerial views of forest being cleared by settlers. The legend says, "Brazil is making the largest agrarian reform in the world." But these settlement schemes are conceived precisely in order not to have to face agrarian reform in other regions. The settlers come from the northeast where landlords have always prevented a healthy peasant culture from developing and from the south, where soybean monoculture, producing feed for the cows that produce the "butter mountain" of the [European] Common Market, also drives thousands of people off their land. Farther north, in central Brazil, the gasahol program is also displacing masses of people.

The migrants from the south often form the third wave of migration in a century. German and Italian immigrants came to the old colonies in Rio Grande do Sul and Santa Catarina in the last century. Their descendants first moved to the Uruguay river valley [in southeast Brazil]. In the 1950s, they moved to West Paraná, then on to southern Mato Grosso. The frequency of migration waves is becoming shorter. Some families are now moving for the second time. They will probably not stay long in Rondônia.

Hundreds of migrants arrive in Rondônia every day in addition to those unhappy people, much more numerous, who can only escape to the slums of the big cities. Some of the migrants try to settle on their own. They simply move to jungle areas as they become accessible through the new penetration roads that are constantly being opened by the road authorities. If they are lucky, they eventually get title to the land they settle on. For this they have to prove that they have made "improvements" on it. INCRA accepts as improvement the clearing of forest. Hence every settler cuts down as much forest as he can, often much more than the area he can cultivate. Some clear hundreds or thousands of hectares. Many of the settlers go from one clearing to another. As soon as they get title or sufficient proof of property they sell to the bigger estates and move on. We have met settlers who make a living out of such land speculation.

More generally, not so much in Rondônia, but in other remote regions of Brazil, the wild settler is soon displaced by someone who comes with "legal" title to enormous tracts of land. The settler is then considered a squatter and driven off by the *jagunco* or hired gunman. No records are kept of the names and numbers of those who disappear.

Where the migrants settle legally, they end up in the settlement schemes of INCRA. These schemes are another example of the total disregard for the Amazonian landscape and its people. The division of the land is conceived on the drawing board. A checkerboard-like pattern is imposed on the land without the slightest concern whatever for topography, steep slopes, rock outcroppings, little rivers or brooks, much less ecosystems—a concept that does not exist in the heads of INCRA planners. The lots are 250 meters by 1000 meters or 500 meters by 2000 meters or even 4000 meters. Thus, the farmer actually gets a long strip of land. In some cases his strip cuts across the same waterway several times as it meanders through the forest. He will have to build several bridges. Another farmer may have no access whatever to water, or his land may cut across two steep slopes with two high plateaus and some lowland in between or vice versa. Inevitably he will cut down the forest on the slope. The soil will be eroded away after the first harvest, if there is a first harvest. Even the areas officially left as forest reserves are marked on the map as geometric shapes, somewhere in a corner of the project, without reference to landscape. There is absolutely no provision for the preservation of these areas. The INCRA people say it is the responsibility of the Instituto Brasileiro de Desenvolvimento Florestal (IBDF)—the forestry agency; IBDF says it has no means to take care of the reserves. In no time they are destroyed by illegal settlers. It often seems as if the whole scheme is deliberately set up so as to guarantee maximum devastation.

The farmers are left to themselves. There is no agricultural extension service worthy of the name. Government extension agencies promote cash crops and the credit system is geared to monoculture. Most credit plans include a certain percentage of the money for pesticides and chemical fertilizer, regardless of need. Cash crop monoculture is controlled by specialized agencies such as CEPLAC for cocoa, IBC for coffee, and SUDHEVEA for rubber tree plantations. Each agency insists on pure monoculture. Where farmers, out of their own wisdom, make mixed stands of coffee, cocoa, rubber, and citrus trees, the agencies threaten to cut credit unless the farmers turn to pure monoculture of the respective crop. But practice has shown that mixed stands make for healthier plants, require less or no pesticides, and produce more on a more sustainable basis.

Socially, too, the settlement schemes are very disruptive. First, they help to prevent the necessary reforms in the regions where the migrants come from; second, they destroy the existing social fabric in the settlement areas; and third, the new settlers soon run into serious trouble when their soils become degraded and there is no more virgin forest to move into. We have seen settlers on soil so poor that even in the ashes of the clearing, their harvests were not enough for survival.

Local Indians are pitilessly liquidated, the survivors being driven even deeper into the remaining jungle, until they meet colonists advancing in the other direction. Moreover, the rainforest Indians are extremely vulnerable to western diseases, such as the common cold, measles, and venereal disease. As soon as a tribe makes contact with the "civilized" invaders, they face lethal epidemics. Often as many as 90 percent of a group die within a few years. For the few survivors, it is the end of their culture. It is sad to see the total demoralization of the so-called civilized Indian.

The disappearance of the rainforest Indian cultures is perhaps one of the greatest tragedies of our time. The rainforest Indian is a true ecologist. He knows the forest as no modern ecologist can possibly know it. He reveres it. Yet we are exterminating the Indians before we can even learn from them.

Our indecent life-style seems to be trying to make sure that, when it collapses, there will be no alternative life-styles left to take its place.

Traditional Industries Destroyed

The new settlements also displace the *caboclo* and the *seringueiro*. The *caboclo*, the successor of the Indian, is usually of mixed stock, white and Indian, sometimes Negro. He lives in the forest, surviving on shifting agriculture and as a hunter/gatherer. His life-style is quite compatible with the survival of the forest, as long as his population does not increase too much. But we are still very far from that. He has no reverence for the forest and its animal life but he keeps much of Indian wisdom.

There is also the small logger. His life-style is compatible with the survival of the rainforest. He logs only on the floodplains from where he can take his logs out when the water is high, making rafts for transportation to small lumber mills. Felling is selective with little harm to other trees. The floodplains represent the only really fertile soils in the rainforest, being fertilized every year by the annual flood. . . . Trees grow fast on the floodplains. Old loggers often resume logging where they started in their youth. In twenty to thirty years enormous trees grow back, of a size it would take two centuries to grow in Europe.

Where the big multinational logging companies or the large timber companies from the south of Brazil move in, the situation is quite different.

They do not limit their activities to the floodplains but operate mostly on the highlands, where soils are extremely poor and regeneration is therefore much more difficult. They also use heavy machinery, causing tremendous degradation, often destroying the whole ecosystem. They are required by law to "reforest." But reforestation consists only of commercial monocultures. This reforestation is often done by specialized companies. The law does not require reforestation to be made in the place where the forest was logged; it is often done somewhere else, even thousands of kilometers away. The reforestation companies often destroy natural ecosystems, other forests, for their plantations. This is so because it is easier to get large tracts of contiguous land in the remaining wilderness areas. The "reforested" area is also almost always much smaller than the area of forest destroyed by logging. There is no supervision and bribing is easy.

Local fishermen, who until recently provided 60 percent of Amazonia's protein, are also being driven off by commercial fishing boats. It is often said . . . that the Amazon can feed the world with fish protein. That is another illusion. There is enough fish for a growing local population but not for a large-scale export business. The Amazonian rivers are incredibly rich in fish. There are more than one thousand different species. Many have not even been classified by zoologists. But there is very little primary production [growth of aquatic plants] in most of the Amazonian rivers. Fish life is mostly dependent on the forest, especially the forest on the floodplains. Many species feed on fruit or forest residues only during the high water season when they leave the river bed and spread out into the plain. The rest of the year they live off their fat reserves. The destruction of the floodplain forests and of the forests along the smaller waterways in the highlands contributes directly to the diminution of water fauna. Even today there is overfishing. Some important species such as the pirarucu and the tambaqui are nearing extinction and the manatee is very close to extinction. Commerical fishing is also extremely wasteful. It is now common practice for fishing boats to throw overboard whole loads of commercially less valuable fish when they hit upon a school of more valuable species. The commercial fishing fleets have autonomy over thousands of kilometers. In many areas the local population already complains that it is becoming difficult to catch the fish it needs.

Finally, there is the *seringueiro*, or rubber tapper. Like the Indian, he has no sense of land ownership but he has a sense of territory! Each *seringueiro* has his *estrada* or road. He may walk as much as thirty kilometers a day collecting the latex. Today he is no more the slave laborer he was in the past. His transistor radio informs him of the rubber price in São Paulo or Chicago. He makes between five and seven hundred dollars a month, as much as a metal worker in São Paulo, but he has no expenses. He derives most of his food from the forest and the river. He also has no transportation costs. Yet the colonization programs are displacing the *seringueiro* too. Another life-style compatible with the forest is being destroyed.

Brazil imports two thirds of its natural rubber consumption of approximately ninety thousand tons a year. By helping the *seringueiro* and by increasing the density of the rubber trees in the forest, which has already been proved possible by some small private enterprises, Brazil could easily have enough natural rubber for export. The monocultures of rubber trees that are now being promoted by the government will probably not last long. The experiment carried out in the 1930s by Ford was a failure. In monoculture the rubber tree is subject to all kinds of pest attacks.

The rubber tapper's income comes not only from rubber; he also collects Brazil nuts. He would be the ideal forest guard, requiring no pay from the government, and although in the past he contributed to the slaughter of the Indians, today, in many areas, rubber tappers and Indians have learned to live together in harmony. . . .

The federal government sees no difficulties in granting the rich title to tens of thousands or even hundreds of thousands of hectares, but it hardly ever gives useful tracts of land to the small operator. I visited one big project in Rondônia; it belonged to a firm that grew powerful in the south by devastating Araucaria forests. Some twenty thousand hectares were being put to pasture and an area much bigger was being logged. On this project, the company closed the road via which the *seringueiros* not affected by the project used to bring out their rubber and forced them to sell all the rubber to the company at prices far below market prices.

The life-style of Indians, *caboclos*, and *seringueiros* is compatible with the survival of the forest. Their life-style could easily be improved socially and ecologically by teaching them better cropping and collecting or fishing methods, storage methods, and hygiene. Almost nothing is being done in that direction, even though some very interesting research work already carried out at the Amazonian research agency (INPA) has shown how permaculture with palm trees, breadfruit, and others can produce up to ten times as much food per acre as the shifting agriculture now practiced by the *caboclo* and *seringueiro*. But official philosophy sees only backwardness in subsistence farming, even if it makes people happier. There is also no concern whatever for sustainability.

Poor Not to Blame

In Rondônia it is very easy to see how devastation, even when it is committed by small farmers, is always caused by the shortsightedness and greed of the powerful. The settlements now demolishing the forest in Rondônia are part of a classical colonialist structure of dependence and export. In the new towns of Rondônia, growing like mushrooms, it is almost impossible to find locally produced articles in the shops. Everything, even the broiler or the salad in the restaurant, comes from the industrial south. While enormous quantities of wood go up in smoke or rot in the fields people cook with bottled gas, brought in by truck over 2,500 kilometers. Local power stations also burn petroleum that comes by truck after crossing the ocean on its way from the Persian Gulf. Where the Madeira River passes the capital of Rondônia, Pôrto Velho, one can see thousands of tons of wood, logs, branches, whole trees, floating downriver. No attempt is made to use that wood. When a region has to import everything it consumes, it must pay with exports. Hence the agricultural policy of promoting only cash crops.

While unsustainable forms of agriculture are destroying the tropical rainforest in Rondônia, the regions in the south, from where many of the migrants come, are also being raped. Soybean monoculture to feed cows in the [European] Common Market, rather than people in Brazil, is causing erosion on a scale never seen before. All the rivers are dark brown or red with clay and silt. Monoculture is also destroying what is left of peasant culture. These soils could support a sustainable form of highly productive and diversified agriculture. Now food production in the former peasant regions is going down drastically. In the more mountainous areas of Santa Catarina, farmers plant corn on steep slopes, at enormous costs in terms of erosion, in order to rear chickens for export to Saudi Arabia. The farmers themselves often buy their food in the supermarket, the eggs and vegetables being imported from São Paulo.

If the methods of organic farming were promoted on the good, fertile soils in the south, the northeast, and in central Brazil, and only in those areas already cleared, without touching remaining wilderness, this would dramatically increase productivity with less pollution and erosion. Migration could cease, and could even be reversed. . . . A small step in the direction of organic soil management would immediately lead to dramatic increases in production with equally significant increases in employment. Brazil need not give up its present exports and could still produce more food. We already have a few examples of farms attesting to that.

Amazonia should be left to the Amazonians. The growth of capital and power at the expense of the ecology and the people of Amazonia is classical imperialism. It makes no difference whether the benefits accrue to powers from overseas or from other parts of Brazil.

Brazil's politics toward Amazonia must change. And they must change within this decade—or it will be too late!

12 Tadeu Valadares ◆ Deforestation:
A Brazilian Perspective

Tadeu Valadares, a Brazilian diplomat, expresses his government's perspective on the role of the Amazon rainforest in the nation's development. In this 1992 essay he does not question the desirability of developing the rainforest but instead focuses on how to develop rational policies for the use of the region's resources. Valadares admits that the government, especially during the military dictatorship, made mistakes in its management of the Amazon rainforest. He points out, however, that the Nossa Natureza (Our Nature) program announced by the Sarney government in 1988 offers a plan for incorporating the Amazon into the national economy without destroying the region's ecosystems. He claims that Brazil's new environmental program has benefited from past mistakes—especially those of today's industrialized developed countries (such as the United States), whose predatory actions during their own economic take-off seriously degraded the environment.

With the implementation of this and other environmental laws, the Brazilian government is attempting to bridge the gap between theory and practice. Coming in response to criticism by foreign as well as domestic environmentalists and development experts, Nossa Natureza represents a new recognition of the legitimate concerns and rights of various previously neglected groups of forest dwellers, as well as the need to maintain environmental health. It fails to address, however, some important factors in the destruction of the tropical rainforest, such as road building and large dam projects. The government's environmental policy also reveals how sensitive Brazil is (like most Latin American countries) about the issue of national sovereignty. Brazil's distrust and resentment of attempts by foreigners to dictate how to develop the Amazon is revealed clearly in Valadares's closing remark: "All other governments and international organizations must recognize that the Brazilian Amazon is first and foremost Brazilian."

In order to tackle the subject of deforestation in a rational and unemotional way, we must take into consideration a few preliminary facts. In a sense these facts are interconnected with the deplorable phenomenon of uncontrolled and illegal burning of forested areas in the Brazilian Amazon. First, in order to conduct a fair analysis of the problem, the sheer magnitude

From *Economic Development and Environmental Protection in Latin America*, 55–59, ed. Joseph S. Tulchin with Andrew I. Rudman. © 1991 by the Woodrow Wilson International Center for Scholars. Reprinted by permission of Lynne Rienner Publishers.

of the Legal Amazon must be acknowledged. This huge region comprises 60 percent of Brazil—approximately 5 million square kilometers. The area covered by the humid forest comprises only slightly more than half of this total, 2.8 million square kilometers. Recognition of the geographical extension of this continent within a continent helps one immediately understand the relevance of the Amazon for Brazil. The Amazon basin has an undeniable strategic significance for Brazil's national development. The integration of the Amazon basin into the national political economy is a goal shared by all informed citizens. Thus, how to mix the resources of the Amazon with other facets of the Brazilian economy is a topic of lively discussion. What is agreed upon by all, however, is that Brazil will be truly developed only if rational policies conducive to the optimum use of the resources offered by our tropical forest are devised and implemented immediately.

Approximately eighteen million people live within the boundaries of this gigantic area. This figure includes eight hundred thousand *garimpeiros* (mineral diggers) and less than two hundred thousand Indians. The inhabitants of the Legal Amazon are the manifestation of a larger historical process of population growth that gained momentum in the last two decades. In 1970 the Amazonian population was only 3.6 million, by 1980 the population had reached 7.6 million. The region is still experiencing rapid growth, as significant waves of migrants from other areas of Brazil are attracted there. From a demographic viewpoint, however, the region may be considered underpopulated.

The region's economy is characterized by all of the economic and social indicators usually associated with acute underdevelopment. Aside from a fragile urban economy based largely on trade, services, administrative activities, and fledgling industries, the mainstay of Amazonian economic growth continues to be agriculture, cattle raising, mining, and, to a much lesser degree, extractive industries. It is interesting to note that between 1970 and 1985 the number of rural properties increased by 91 percent and the number of cattle herds more than doubled.

The rural economy is characterized by a mix of large and small properties. Smallholders usually practice some kind of subsistence agriculture using a primitive technique, the *coivaras*, which consists of burning trees and secondary vegetation (*capoeiras*) in order to prepare the soil for agricultural use. Although this is a source of deforestation, the *coivaras* have only a minor impact on the deforestation problem. Inacio Rangel, one of Brazil's most respected economists, affirms: "Much of the most terrible devastation we have observed, especially in the Amazon, is not the smallholders' responsibility. It is the result of actions undertaken by large capitalist entrepreneurs." But Rangel emphasizes that the aggressive pattern of behavior displayed by some large agricultural enterprises may change over time as a result of technological progress and applied scientific expertise. On the other hand, the impoverished small producer lacks the financial resources that would enable him to use mechanical equipment and employ modern agronomic techniques and is therefore bound to continue using primitive techniques that invariably affect the environment in a negative way.

The uncontrolled and illegal burning of the forest is a most serious problem. The Brazilian government, civil society, and an absolute majority of public opinion are highly sensitive to the menace created by this vandalism. The indiscriminate burning of the forest irreversibly destroys one of our largest sources of future wealth and potentially endangers the ecological balance of the entire region. Government figures reveal that 200,000 square kilometers of the Legal Amazon were burned in 1987 and 120,000 square kilometers were burned in 1988. The government intends to reduce this to 60,000 square kilometers through new policies, recently enacted legislation, and innovative administrative measures.

How much of the forest has already been destroyed? Some say 12 percent; others say 7 percent. The Brazilian government indicates that the deforested area probably comprises 5 percent of the Legal Amazon. The underlying meaning of these figures is the bleak reality that an enormous area of tropical rainforest is already gone and an irreplaceable amount of wealth, life, and beauty has disappeared. Additionally, this unreasonable havoc produces nearly 4 percent of the carbon dioxide contributing to the greenhouse effect that threatens global ecology. In this context, however, it is important to remember that 85 percent of the greenhouse effect is directly produced by the unbridled consumption of fossil fuels in the advanced industrialized countries.

The Brazilian government's concern with the national environment predates the current situation in which so much of the national and international media is paying close attention to the Amazon. In fact, during the 1930s the first examples of what would today be called "environmental legislation" were adopted in Brazil. The adoption of a water code and mining code, the creation of the National Department of Public Works and Sanitation, and the establishment of the first national park all occurred under [Getulio] Vargas at that time.

During the long military cycle that began in 1964 and lasted until 1985, additional important legislative and administrative measures were undertaken. These included a forest code, established in 1965, a 1967 law on the protection of wildlife, the integration of environmental concerns in the theory and practice of public planning, the creation of a special secretariat on environment in 1973, and the establishment of a national policy on environment in 1981. The measures demonstrate the willingness of

Brazilians to address environmental issues irrespective of the character of the dominant political regime.

Nonetheless, it is also true that the environment has never received as extensive or systematic an analysis as the one undertaken by the Sarney administration. At the end of the military regime, the authoritarian model of centralized decision making resulted in an unsuccessful attempt to develop the Amazon, which in turn created an economic disruption compounded by aggressive ecological side effects. In the process of transition from authoritarianism to democracy, the Constituent Assembly drafted a new bill of rights. The final text was adopted in October 1988 and one of its most daring innovations is a new chapter that establishes the guidelines for state and society on environmental issues. Article 225 declares that the environment is a common heritage of the Brazilian people and entrusts government and society with the duty to defend and preserve it for present and future generations. Yet the unavoidable gap that exists between theory and practice, constitutional clauses and everyday life, is well known. In order to bridge this gap, President Sarney launched a new environmental offensive.

On October 12, 1988, the "Our Nature" program was presented to the Brazilian people as a new landmark on the long road in pursuit of the ancient dream of incorporating the Amazon into the national economy. This is to be accomplished without the destruction of the Amazonian ecosystem, with deep awareness of past mistakes, and with a critical evaluation of the predatory models followed by today's industrialized countries when they were in the take-off stage of economic development. The main goals of the program are (1) to halt predatory actions against the environment and renewable natural resources; (2) to create an environmental protection system for all of Brazil and specifically for the Amazon; (3) to promote environmental education and public consciousness regarding conservation of the Amazonian environment; (4) to regulate the settlement and exploitation of the Legal Amazon based on territorial planning; and (5) to protect Indian communities, the population living along the rivers, and those involved in sustained exploitation of natural resources.

This long-term effort has already produced a change in policy orientation. The government has created new forests. The Institute on the Environment was created to centralize government action concerning ecological issues, forestry exploitation, fishing, and the protection of ecological systems. A new concept of economic and social development for the Amazon is being designed, allowing for the fact that only 17 percent of the region is effectively suited for economic exploitation and that a new philosophy is needed to combine the ongoing flux of settlers with the economic and ecological potential of the area. We have recognized the need to accelerate agrarian reform in other parts of Brazil in order to diminish the waves of migrants who continue to enter the region. At the same time, Brasília adopted a new policy of giving priority to settlements in the central and western regions, ecologically less fragile than the Amazon.

The government has suspended all fiscal incentives and official credits for livestock and agricultural projects, and also prohibited exportation of timber "in natura." In the coming years the government will make a systematic effort to define areas of permanent preservation and to select microregions particularly appropriate for a range of economic activities. The government will also do whatever is necessary to enforce the law establishing 50 percent of each rural property as a protected site ("legal reserve") in forested areas. By 1995 reforestation is expected to provide 100 percent of wood consumption for all large steel projects like Grande Carajás as an additional means of protecting the rainforest. Protection of the rainforest also entails the establishment of fire prevention and extinction systems, which will be a priority of the "Our Nature" program.

The Brazilian government and civil society have clearly expressed their willingness to cooperate with other countries, international organizations, and interested institutions. In a world that is still, unfortunately, ruled by power politics and in an international arena where hegemonic behavior is an undeniable aspect of superpower strategy, the administration sets only one precondition: in order to be able to cooperate with the Brazilian government in the search for solutions to global environmental problems, all other governments and international organizations must recognize that the Brazilian Amazon is first and foremost Brazilian. When this basic fact is acknowledged by our eventual companions on the road toward an environmentally safer world, the Brazilian people are quite sure that Brazil and the international community will be able to advance the intertwined causes of economic development and sound environmental policies.

III

Why Save the Rainforest?

"Save the Rainforest" has become a rallying cry of environmentalists around the world, resulting in a high level of visibility for forest activists during the Earth Summit in Rio de Janeiro in 1992. Media coverage of the issue, however, rarely included discussion of the many interacting issues involved in rainforest conservation. Although the reasons given for forest preservation are ultimately interrelated, they tend to fall into several categories: ecological, economic, and cultural or ethical.

Tropical rainforests, in common with other wild ecosystems, involve a number of ecological functions that underpin our economies and make our lives possible. Referred to by some scholars as environmental services or subsidies, these functions include regulation of climate and water cycles, protection of the soil, and provision of materials that we need for housing, fuel, and various economic activities. The unique characteristics of the tropical rainforest, such as rapid infusion of water vapor into the atmosphere, a tendency toward infertile soils, and extremely high species diversity, make conservation of the tropical rainforest a critical environmental issue (Selection 13).

We have come to realize that destruction of neotropical forests has the potential to affect North American environments by precipitating climatic shifts or by decreasing migrant bird populations. Many birds that breed in North America overwinter in the tropical forests of Latin America (Selection 14). Declines in the population of these birds, therefore, might have substantial impacts on our ecosystems—in the control of insects, for example. Recent research in the tropical rainforest has revealed other interesting relationships between animal populations and their habitats. We now know that in the Amazon a number of fish species depend on the fruits of rainforest trees as a food source during the flood season and that the destruction of the rainforest could adversely affect the Amazon fishery—an important source of high-quality protein for the region's inhabitants. Conversely, a serious decline in certain fish populations could affect the ability of various tree species to disperse—particularly critical to the reestablishment of the forest in cleared areas. In fact, the biological diversity of tropical forests is so complex and poorly understood that we do not know how removing a particular species will affect the whole system. Modification of the forest, therefore, must be undertaken with great care so as not to destabilize the entire ecosystem.

The economic implications of ecological factors must also be considered (Selection 15). In addition to environmental services, tropical rainforests produce materials that can be turned into commodities in the world market. Studies have shown that the economic value of renewable products (such as oils, resins, nuts, and fruits) produced per hectare of wild rainforest can be greater than that produced by cattle ranches or monocultural plantations of equal size. Many tropical plants contain pharmacologically active substances of unknown potential, so that every plant that goes extinct represents a possible loss to pharmaceutical companies and to future generations (Selection 17). Preservation of the genetic diversity of the wild progenitors of our crop plants is essential to the breeding or genetic engineering of new crop varieties (Selection 16). And finally, nature tourism—ecotourism—based on the presence of wild tropical forests has the potential to provide more income in the long run for Latin American countries than the destruction of forests and the one-time exploitation of their resources. (Ecotourism is discussed in Part IV).

A number of arguments for saving the forest center on the human inhabitants of the tropical rainforest or on the actual or theoretical relationship between humans and nature. Some are practical considerations—such as preserving tribal peoples' knowledge and wisdom about the tropical rainforest accumulated during the hundreds or thousands of years they have coexisted with it (Selection 18). The knowledge of native healers, for instance, could increase the efficiency of the Westerner's search for new pharmaceuticals in the tropical rainforest. Unfortunately, the Native American's intimate knowledge of the forest and its useful properties is being lost rapidly as habitat destruction and acculturation lead to the demise of tribal cultures.

Deforestation raises ethical questions. Increasingly, destruction of the tropical rainforest is seen as a human-rights violation against the tribal peoples who require intact forest for their physical and cultural survival. The tropical rainforest is not simply the source of material benefits—it is the foundation on which the cultures of forest peoples are built, the resting place of their ancestors, the home of their deities. Their culture and environment are inextricably intertwined as parts of a single system. From this perspective, destruction of the tropical rainforest amounts to ethnocide. (A few people extend our ethical structure to nonhuman species, arguing that all living things have an intrinsic right to exist. In their view, human beings have no right to drive other species to extinction simply because they have the technological capability to do so.)

Other scientific and anthropocentric reasons are raised for preserving natural ecosystems. If large enough, wild ecosystems constitute natural laboratories for evolution and for future scientific research and training of scientists. In addition, most humans seem to have a psychological need for wild places, both for spiritual renewal and as a respite from the stresses of modern living. The rapidly growing visitorship to national parks, both in the United States and abroad, attests to our powerful need for nature.

Finally, a long history of failed attempts to settle and exploit tropical rainforest regions such as the Amazon should cause us to approach such development with caution. Selection 19 addresses some of the problems, particularly in terms of public health, that have plagued recent attempts to colonize the Amazon. Taken together, the selections in Part III provide a cautionary tale that should inform and influence planning for the future of the remaining rainforests of Latin America.

---

13 *The Ecologist* ◆ Tropical Forests: A Plan for Action

These excerpts from a 1987 editorial in The Ecologist *summarize the major ecological characteristics of the tropical rainforest, along with their significance. The editors point out the unprecedented scale of ecological change—particularly the loss of environmental services—now taking place and stress the threats to humans posed by tropical deforestation: loss of species (and the genetic resources they represent), disruption of the water cycle, accelerated soil erosion, and potential climate change. Preventing such environmental degradation is one of the major reasons for preserving the rainforest.*

Arguments in favor of preserving the tropical rainforest, such as those in this editorial, have been made for the past several decades. Despite their persuasiveness, however, and the growing evidence that supports them, most countries in Latin America continue to decimate their forests because various social forces encourage deforestation.

The Extinction of Species

Although tropical moist forests only cover some 6 percent of the total land surface of the globe, they contain at least 50 percent of the species on earth and, possibly, 90 percent.

From *The Ecologist* (July-November 1987): 129–31. Reprinted by permission of *The Ecologist*, Agriculture House, Bath Road, Sturminster Newton, Dorset DT10 1DU, England.

Indeed, the importance of tropical forests as a habitat for wildlife cannot be understated. Ninety percent of the world's nonhuman primates are found only in tropical rainforests, along with two thirds of all known plants, 40 percent of birds of prey, and 80 percent of the world's insects. The Amazon basin alone contains an estimated 1 million animal and plant species, including 2,500 species of trees, 1,800 species of birds, and 2,000 species of fish. A single hectare may contain 400 trees, every other one a different species. By contrast a typical temperate forest contains a mere 10 to 15 trees per hectare. One river in Brazil has been found to contain more species of fish than all the rivers in the United States.

As a result of tropical deforestation, at least one species is being condemned to extinction every day. In all likelihood, as Norman Myers points out, the true figure is even higher, amounting to "several species per day." Within another ten years, he predicts, the rate of extinction will have risen "to several species an hour." This view is endorsed by such eminent scientists as Paul Ehrlich, Edward O. Wilson, and Peter Raven.

Not only are species now being lost at an unprecedented rate—some four hundred times faster than at any other period during recent geological time—but the range of species affected is far wider than ever before. As Edward O. Wilson points out: "In at least one respect, this human-made hecatomb is worse than any time in the geological past. In earlier mass extinctions . . . most of the plant diversity survived: now, for the first time, it is being mostly destroyed."

Although nature undoubtedly has considerable resilience—ensured in part by the sheer number of species on earth—there is a limit to how far that resilience can be stretched. To illustrate the point, the biologists Paul and Anne Ehrlich have compared individual species, whether they be "bacteria, herbaceous plants, worms, mites, insects, frogs, lizards, or small mammals," to the rivets that hold together an airplane. Although we know that each species plays a crucial role in maintaining ecological systems, "in most cases, an ecologist can no more predict the consequences of the extinction of a given species than an airline passenger can assess the loss of a single rivet. But both can easily foresee the long-term results of continually forcing species to extinction or removing rivet after rivet."

Indeed, if the present mass extinctions are permitted to continue, "the end result will be as predictable as that of popping rivets from any flying machine—disaster." The Ehrlichs go on to warn: "Sooner or later, the vital functions of earth's ecosystems will be sufficiently impaired that the planet's carrying capacity for human beings will plummet, perhaps over a period of decades, perhaps within a single year. Then humanity will be faced with extinction."

Loss of Genetic Resources

In agriculture, as in medicine, preserving genetic diversity is of utmost importance. Modern farming practices have systematically reduced the number of crops used in farming; indeed, we now rely on just eight crops to provide 75 percent of our food. That lack of genetic diversity renders modern agriculture extremely vulnerable not only to pests and disease, but also to climatic change, current crop varieties being finely tuned to present climatic conditions. In future, therefore, wild species of plants may prove vital in order to fortify modern varieties against disease or a less propitious climate.

Droughts, Floods, Deserts, and Degradation

Undegraded forests perform numerous irreplaceable ecological services for free, and those services are now being widely disrupted by deforestation. As a result, droughts and floods are increasing and thousands of hectares are being transformed into degraded scrub or desert every year.

One of the most vital functions fulfilled by forests is the control of water runoff to rivers. Typically, in a well-forested watershed, 95 percent of the annual rainfall is trapped in the elaborate spongelike network of roots that underlies the forest floor. That water is then released slowly over the year, replenishing groundwater and keeping streams and rivers flowing during the dry season. When the forest is removed, however, there is no longer any "sponge" to absorb the water. As a result, the rains rush down the denuded slopes, straight into the local streams and rivers, only 5 percent of the rainwater being absorbed in what remains of the soil.

The consequence is massive flooding, which in the densely populated regions of the tropics can prove disastrous. According to the Independent Commission on International Humanitarian Issues, the number of people affected by flooding trebled between 1960 and 1980, with over fifteen million people suffering flood damage in the late 1970s. . . . Moreover, because the rainwater is no longer stored in the soil, the local streams and rivers are not replenished and thus quickly dry up once the rains are over. The result is the so-called drought-flood cycle, with massive floods during the monsoon periods alternating with devasting droughts during the dry season. . . .

Once stripped of their forest cover, the soils of the tropics are also increasingly vulnerable to erosion. Scientists working in the Ivory Coast have recorded massive differences between the rates of erosion in forested and deforested areas: they report that, even in mountainous areas, soil erosion in secondary forest is as low as 0.03 ton per hectare a year. Once deforested, the rate rises to 90 tons per hectare. . . . In Amazonia, the threat of erosion is such that Harald Sioli warns . . . : "There is a danger that the region may develop into a new dust bowl."

In that respect, the lushness of the world's rainforests is amazingly deceptive. For despite the profusion of plants and trees, the underlying soils are incredibly poor, almost all the nutrients being bound up in the vegetation. Once the forests have been cut down, those few nutrients that remain in the soil are quickly washed away, effectively transforming the land into a barren wasteland. Indeed, one of the greatest tragedies of tropical rainforest destruction is that it is all for nought: almost all the areas that are now being cleared for agriculture or ranching cannot support these activities for more than a few years at the most. In Brazil, for example, virtually all the cattle ranches established prior to 1978 had been abandoned by 1985. Similarly, as José Lutzenberger points out . . . attempts to open up Amazonia to agriculture have proved ecologically disastrous: almost all of the Brazilian colonists settled in Rondônia, for example, have been forced to abandon their new farms after the soils proved too infertile to make a living for more than a year or two. Some settlers have moved two or more times. . . .*

Climatic Change

Tropical forests play a critical role in regulating climate, both at the regional and the global levels. Their destruction not only threatens to disrupt world rainfall patterns but, more seriously perhaps, to destabilize the delicate chemistry of the earth's inner atmosphere.

At the regional level, deforestation is already disrupting the subtle hydrological cycles that control rainfall. At least half of the rainwater that falls on moist tropical forests is returned back into the atmosphere through evapotranspiration, hence the perpetual cloud that hangs over the world's great rainforests. That evaporated moisture is then carried by the wind to fall as rain in areas often thousands of miles away. Where the forests have been destroyed or degraded, however, there is no moisture for the winds to pick up; hence areas downwind of deforested areas no longer receive as much rain as previously, causing them to dry out. . . .

The climatic consequences of deforestation will undoubtedly extend beyond the regional level, however. As Peter Bunyard notes, much of the rain evaporated from the forests of Amazonia is carried by the trade winds

---

*See José A. Lutzenberger, excerpt from *Who Is Destroying the Amazon Rainforest?* in this volume.—Ed.

toward the higher latitudes. In the process, "Heat is transferred from the tropics to the higher latitudes, thus contributing significantly to a more equitable climate in temperate areas." Without the rainforests of the tropical countries, and in particular with the destruction of the forests of Amazonia, "the tropics would tend to be hotter and drier and the temperate regions both sides of the equator colder." Indeed, "the moist tropical forests of the world can be considered as a vital component in the process of pumping heat from the hot regions of the globe to the cooler regions."

In addition to disrupting regional and global hydrological cycles, deforestation is adding as much carbon dioxide into the atmosphere as that added by the burning of fossil fuels. The carbon dioxide results both from the burning of forest (and hence the oxidation of the carbon locked up in the vegetation) and through the rotting of cleared vegetation. It is now generally accepted that rising levels of atmospheric carbon dioxide will bring about a global warming via the so-called greenhouse effect, the carbon dioxide "trapping" the sun's solar energy, thus causing the temperature of the earth's atmosphere to rise.

Climatologists now predict that the combined effect of deforestation and the burning of fossil fuels will cause levels of carbon dioxide in the atmosphere to double, bringing about a two- to three-degree centigrade rise in global temperatures.

Scientists are agreed that rising global temperatures could completely alter the face of the earth. Many of the world's most fertile regions (notably the grain belts of North America and Russia) are likely to become drier and less productive, whilst regions such as India and the Middle East are expected to become wetter and more fertile. Tropical storms are predicted to become more violent and sea levels are predicted to rise as a result of thermal expansion of sea water. A rise in global temperatures of five degrees centigrade (by no means an impossibility) would melt the West Antarctica ice sheet, causing a five-meter rise in sea levels and drowning many coastal regions of the eastern United States and elsewhere. Even a modest rise in temperatures could have a dramatic effect on sea levels: a recent paper in *Nature* (12 November 1987) predicts that by 2025 the earth's temperature will have risen by 0.6–1.0 degrees centigrade, causing sea levels to rise by four to eight centimeters and directly threatening such cities as London, Bangkok, and Venice.

There are already worrying signs that the greenhouse effect is indeed becoming a reality. Scientists measuring the amount of solar radiation entering and leaving the earth's atmosphere, for example, have found that 0.1 percent more radiation is now retained than twelve years ago. Other worrying portents include the breaking off of a giant iceberg (measuring

100 miles by 25 miles) from the Ross Ice Shelf along the Bay of Whales in Antarctica.

Indeed it is clear that man's activities are destabilizing the world's climate, and that deforestation is one of the major causes of that destabilization.

---

14 John Terborgh ♦ A Glimpse at Some Tropical Habitats

By 1980 over one half the total area of Central America and the Greater Antilles had been cleared of forest. Because two thirds of the breeding pairs of North American woodland birds migrate to the Neotropics for the winter, the past decade witnessed a surge of interest in the consequences of tropical deforestation for the survival of these birds. It is clear that habitat destruction—both in North and Latin America—is a threat to the survival of species that inhabit forests. Some people believe that the extinction of birds due to habitat destruction is a warning of a similar fate, further down the road, for other species—including our own.

This reading, excerpted from Where Have All the Birds Gone? *(1989) by ornithologist John Terborgh, sets forth convincingly the current threat to birds posed by the widespread destruction of their habitats. Terborgh argues for preservation of all the habitats (including mature tropical forests) necessary to protect the full diversity of birdlife. He argues against accepting the fallacy of equivalency of species, which some scientists immersed in their bird counts tend to do. He reminds us of the great variety of forest types in the American tropics and that each is home to a different assemblage of bird species, both resident and migrant. Destruction of these forests will inevitably lead to extinction of some forest species, even if the overall number of birds remains the same (which is doubtful). Animal species that require forest for their survival cannot just move to another place; they must have an environment that meets their physical and behavioral requirements. In the tropics this is particularly important because many species have very narrow requirements and cannot easily adapt to other conditions. Some birds, although physically able to fly, will not cross a cleared area only one hundred meters wide—the open space creates an absolute barrier to them. Scientists are concerned that forest clearance will lead to massive extinction of not only bird species but of many other types of*

plants and animals as well. We do not know the full significance of this and
are therefore taking a large risk by destroying vast areas of forest.

To the uninitiated, the word *tropics* often carries the connotation of steamy jungles teeming with malevolent pests and awash with debilitating fevers. In reality, tropical landscapes are as varied, and often as beautiful, as anyone sees in the temperate regions. The vegetation may be lush and dense, but so may it be in some temperate environments. Perhaps it is the palms, vines, and epiphytes that create the exotic flavor of tropical vegetation. But once the novelty of these unfamiliar plant forms has worn off, tropical habitats can be seen to be as distinct and varied as those in the observer's homeland. The word *jungle* then ceases to have any meaning, just as it has no place in the botanical lexicon.

The environments in which North American migrants spend the winter are at least as varied as those in which they breed. Chilly mountaintops in Mexico, limestone scrub in the Antilles, the vast grasslands or llanos of Venezuela and Colombia, mangroves in Panama, cloud forests on the slopes of the Andes, the forbidding thorny fastness of the Paraguayan *chaco*, even Tierra del Fuego—all provide a retreat for one species or another.

A visitor viewing migrants for the first time in one of these environments would find both the expected and the unexpected. He or she would be reassured to note that most species choose winter homes that bear some obvious resemblance to their summer habitats. Louisiana waterthrushes course along clear pebbly streams, yellow-throated warblers creep around pine boughs, willow flycatchers sally from willowlike plants along rivers, and dickcissels throng to the grasslands and ricefields of the llanos. But a visitor would also find some disconcerting exceptions, such as indigo buntings in flocks of hundreds along Yucatán roadsides; eastern kingbirds, also in large flocks, feeding on avocadolike fruits in the canopy of the Amazonian rainforest; and chimney swifts darting over the Peruvian coastal desert.

There is another surprise when one finds species in seemingly incongruous combinations. A rainforest in the Dominican Republic, for example, might have Cape May warblers and gray-cheeked thrushes from the boreal forest; black-throated blue warblers, and redstarts from the Appalachians; and parula and worm-eating warblers from the eastern lowlands. There is nothing sacrosanct about the "communities" of species we find breeding together, for they recombine in many ways during the months they are beyond our purview.

It is also surprising to find so many species together. Rich eastern deciduous forests commonly harbor four to six warbler species, but perhaps due to the geographical congestion of the wintering grounds, one may find eight, ten, or even (in western Mexico) fifteen warbler species in a single homogeneous habitat (Hutto 1980). We now see that not only are the populations of individual species geographically concentrated in the winter, but the species may also be crowded into communities of extraordinarily high diversity. Once we realize this, we can appreciate that many tropical habitats, from a conservation standpoint, are even more precious than our own. . . .

We have seen that migrants pass the winter in a diverse array of environments—high and low, wet and dry, both north and south of the equator. As time goes on, many of these natural vegetation formations are being transformed by relentless economic pressures.

The magnificent pine and fir forests of the Mexican cordilleras are being felled to build houses in the crowded cities, and the once extensive evergreen forests of Mexico's Caribbean lowlands have been reduced to mere fragments to provide pasture for an ever-expanding market for beef. Lowland dry forests in Guatemala are being cleared for cotton growing and to raise winter crops, such as melons, for the North American market. Much of the natural vegetation of Cuba and the Dominican Republic has been replaced with sugarcane fields. In Jamaica, Guatemala, Panama, and other countries, coffee growing to supply export markets has drastically reduced the amount of mid-montane forest available to migrants. Lowland rainforests in Honduras, Panama, and Ecuador are being replaced with banana plantations, again for export to richer countries in the north. African oil palms are changing the landscape in Costa Rica, Ecuador, and elsewhere. Mid-elevation cloud forest has been discovered to offer a propitious climate for dairy farming in Costa Rica, Colombia, and Ecuador. And in the future there looms the truly grim prospect that many of these countries will have to devote major portions of their national territories to biomass plantations for alcohol production to reduce the cost of petroleum imports, as Brazil is already doing. When this happens, what will become of the migrants?

Not all of them will disappear, that is certain. Some species seem to benefit from disturbance; others, to varying degrees, adapt to it; and still others, we hope a minority, will decline in proportion to the disappearance of primary habitats. If we are not to blunder blindly into this future, we should make an effort to establish which species can adapt to disturbance and which cannot. Only then can we begin to define priorities.

Winter travelers in the New World tropics commonly remark on the conspicuous abundance of migrants in early successional habitats, such as gardens, hedgerows, brushy pastures, and young second growth (Karr 1976; Terborgh 1980). Observations of this type have led at least one author (Monroe 1970) to the sanguine conclusion that "opening up" the tropical forest could even lead to an increase in the capacity of the landscape to harbor overwintering migrants. If this were true, we could all rest comfortably and leave the tropical countries to cope with their own conservation problems.

But an impressionistic assessment, even if correct, should not be taken at face value without probing its implicit assumptions. Among the hidden assumptions, two are particularly crucial: first, that migrants in general would benefit; and second, that the new "habitats" generated by deforestation would be more conducive to migrants than the original forest. We shall see that neither of these projections is valid. To illustrate the point, let us proceed with . . . concrete examples.

In 1985 I surveyed migrants in the Quijos Valley of Ecuador. It is magnificent terrain on the eastern slopes of the Andes. Lush cloud forests sweep down from misty, unseen heights to roaring whitewater torrents in deep canyons below. It is the land of cock-of-the-rock and quetzal, breathtaking in its scale and beauty, but formidable of access.

The Ecuadorean government has recently completed a road down the valley to service a pipeline carrying oil from its eastern fields. When I was there in early 1985, the road was carrying a steady flow of settlers into the region, and scattered openings were beginning to punctuate the forested vistas. It is at this incipient stage in the modification of an erstwhile wilderness that one has the best opportunity to make "before" and "after" comparisons.

A representative area of natural forest contained a dazzling array of bird species, far too many to discover and enumerate in the span of a brief sojourn. Migrants were present in addition to the myriad residents, but in the verdant gloom of the cloud forest, birds of any kind were frustratingly difficult to find. It took me most of three days to accumulate an adequate sample of sightings, a hard-won goal in the brief bursts of sunlight between showers.

Yet my perseverance was rewarded. Migrants represented 16 percent of the tally. The species present were olive-sided flycatcher, Swainson's thrush, blackburnian, caerulean, golden-winged, and Canada warblers, redstart, and summer tanager—a set of birds with real class.

A few miles farther along the road, I found a narrow footpath that led sharply down a slope into one of the newly established clearings that are beginning to dot the landscape. Venturing forth, I was pleased to find that the peasant owner of this plot was cheerful and accommodating, and that his dogs were not prohibitively aggressive.

On a slope that was somewhat gentler than the rest, he was preparing pasture for a nascent herd of Brahman cattle. The forest had been cut and burned less than two years before, as one was reminded by the many charred snags that projected incongruously from the lush grass. Here, in the "after" setting, birds were conspicuous. They flew up from the edge of the path and sallied out from the many naked snags. Migrants seemed plentiful too, but *which* migrants? Not one of the species I had seen in the nearby cloud forest was in that pasture.

The total diversity of species was drastically diminished, to a mere 15 or 20 from the 150 or more that had inhabited the original forest. Gone were the colorful cocks-of-the-rock, tanagers, trogons, and hummingbirds. Flycatchers and seedeaters took their places in the pasture. As for migrants, the proportion remained about the same—18 percent—but there was only one species, the western wood pewee, instead of eight. Apparently the rough-hewn opening on the mountainside provided good conditions for hawking flying prey, for pewees were there by the dozen, sallying out from the sun-bleached branches of forest ghosts.

The lesson to be drawn from this example is a general one. When natural habitats are modified to serve human purposes, they lose the structural complexity and botanical richness that are required to maintain highly diverse bird communities. It may indeed be true that the *proportion* of migrants is unaffected by clearing the primary forest, but the total number of birds, and certainly their diversity, is bound to decline. That the birds are more conspicuous only creates a seductive illusion. . . .

"Opening up" the tropical forest does not automatically benefit migrants. The contrary impressions of earlier authors, although accurately reflecting their observations, were concerned more with quantity than quality. Disturbed habitats in some regions do support higher densities of migrants than undisturbed primary vegetation, but it is seldom true outside of lowland Amazonia that disturbed habitat supports more species (Fitzpatrick et al. in press). Furthermore, it has recently been pointed out that past comparisons of migrants in primary forest versus second growth, many of which were conducted with mist nets set on the ground, neglected the forest canopy. Now that special attention has been given to the canopy it has also been found to harbor considerable numbers of migrants (Greenberg 1981; Loiselle 1987).

The take-home message one derives from this is that disturbance nearly always leads to simplified communities. This was especially evident in the Ecuadorean cattle pasture, but was also apparent in the comparison of abandoned Yucatán milpas [crop fields] to regenerating forest. . . . True, one might retort, but in a slash-and-burn rotation system most of the land is fallow. If the cycle length is twenty years, then perhaps only 5 to 10 percent of the landscape is under cultivation at any time. The remaining 90 to 95 percent is undergoing succession and remains as suitable habitat for a wide range of migrants.

Although this argument might literally be true, it overlooks some important facts. First, as we have seen, the migrant species that use early successional vegetation are not the same as those that inhabit primary forest. The argument assumes the equivalency of all migrants, an assumption that many would be reluctant to accept. Second, slash-and-burn agriculture is on the way out and soon will be as obsolete as the shocks of corn that used to add an autumnal flavor to the landscape in my youth. In the ever more crowded world we live in, intensive, rather than extensive, agricultural practices are, of necessity, the current trend. Any realistic model of the future is therefore better represented by the Ecuadorean cattle pasture than by the abandoned milpas in Mexico. This future does not bode well for migrants, even if they are only catbirds and yellowthroats.

Literature Cited

Fitzpatrick, J. W., S. K. Robinson, and J. Terborgh. In press. "Distribution and Abundance of North Temperate Migrants in the Amazon Basin and Eastern Andes." *Biotropica.*

Greenberg, R. 1981. "The Abundance and Seasonality of Forest Canopy Birds on Barro Colorado Island, Panama." *Biotropica* 12:241–51.

Hutto, R. L. 1980. "Winter Habitat Distribution of Migrant Land Birds in Western Mexico, with Specific Reference to Small Foliage-gleaning Insectivores." In Keast and Morton 1980, pp. 181–204.

Karr, J. H. 1976. "On the Relative Abundance of Migrants from the North Temperate Zone in Tropical Habitats." *Wilson Bulletin* 88:433–58.

Keast, A. and E. S. Morton, eds. 1980. *Migrant Birds in the Neotropics: Ecology, Behavior, Distribution, and Conservation.* Washington, DC: Smithsonian Institution Press.

Loiselle, B. A. 1987. "Migrant Abundance in a Costa Rican Lowland Forest Canopy." *Journal of Tropical Ecology* 3:163–68.

Monroe, B. L., Jr. 1970. "Effects of Habitat Changes on Population Levels of the Avifauna in Honduras." In *The Avifauna of Latin America,* edited by H. K. Buechner and J. H. Buechner, *Smithsonian Contributions to Zoology* 26:38–41.

Terborgh, J. W. 1980. "The Conservation Status of Neotropical Migrants: Present and Future." In Keast and Morton 1980, pp. 21–30.

15 David R. Francis ◆ Natural-Resource Losses Reduce Costa Rican GNP Gains

Environmentalists have long been concerned about the way economists ignore the environmental consequences of economic activity such as defor-estation, dismissing them as "externalities." In recent years the field of environmental economics has developed, and its focus is on the environmental aspects of our economy, especially the costs of our current system of production and consumption. Our current accounting system measures only the economic growth that results from the exploitation of natural resources, while the costs of resource degradation, including pollution, are not considered as such. (Actually, to the extent that we must pay for pollution abatement or the restoration of degraded habitats, environmental degrada-tion actually increases the gross national product [GNP]—because we count the jobs and production created but do not subtract the costs involved, especially the ones levied on future generations.)

In this article, originally published in 1991 in The Christian Science Monitor, *David R. Francis summarizes the results of a study of the Costa Rican economy by Robert Repetto, an environmental economist. Repetto found that forest clearance and subsequent agricultural practices have caused a depreciation in the value of Costa Rica's forest resources and soils on the order of 5 percent of GNP per year for the past twenty years. This translates into a 25 to 30 percent reduction in potential economic growth in that country. Studies such as Repetto's are causing some economists to call for a revision in the way GNP is calculated, to factor in the costs of environmental degradation. If this were done, under some circumstances it would make more economic sense to preserve rainforest than to convert it to other uses.*

B etween 1970 and 1989, national output in the Central American republic of Costa Rica grew at an average annual rate of 4.6 percent.

To economists, that's handsome progress. It beats the high 2.5 percent annual growth in Costa Rica's population and thus raised living standards.

But to economist Robert Repetto there's a serious flaw in those numbers. They don't take account of the destruction of natural resources in this tropical democracy.

In a report of the World Resources Institute (WRI) in Washington and the Tropical Science Center in San José, Costa Rica, Mr. Repetto and several other authors note that Costa Rica's conventional national accounts record timber output, fish harvest, and crop production as income but ignore the costs of deforestation, overfishing, and soil erosion. Natural resource assets worth more than one year's gross national product (about $4.1 billion in 1984 United States dollars) vanished without a trace in those two decades, the study calculates.

"A nation's depletion of its natural resources—consumption of national capital—can . . . masquerade as growth for decades, even though it will clearly reduce income prospects from resource sectors in the future," notes James Gustave Speth, president of WRI. "Just as ignoring the deterioration of man-made assets skews economic assessments, so does overlooking the degradation of natural assets."

Idea Gains Favor

This idea of taking account of resource depletion in the measurements of a nation's economy is "catching on," Dr. Repetto says

Developing countries such as Mexico, El Salvador, Chile, Brazil, the Philippines, Indonesia, Malaysia, and India have been studying the issue. China, switching from the old communist measure of "net material product" to the broader Western system of national accounting, has also examined measures of resource depletion.

Among industrial nations, Norway, Germany, the Netherlands, Canada, and Australia are looking into the issue. France has a "patrimony" account that attempts to include natural resource factors. In the United States, Congress appropriated funds two years ago for a study by the Bureau of Economic Analysis in the Commerce Department.

Repetto would like the United Nations' Statistical Commission, which is in the process of revising the UN system of national accounts (SNA), the standard-bearer for measuring economic developments in countries around the world, to include measures of changes in natural resource assets.

"The current UN system of national accounts is a cover-up for the environmental degradation that's occurring," he states. "There is a dangerous asymmetry in the way economic performance is analyzed that validates the notion that rapid economic growth can be achieved and sustained by exploiting the environment. The UN's national income accounting framework is a relic of the 1930s when raw materials were cheap and few economists could foresee environmental threats."

The study suggests that the UN should announce at the June 1992 meeting in Brazil of the UN Conference on Environment and Development that "this distortion in the treatment of natural resources will be removed in the ongoing revisions to the SNA."

The Brazil conference follows the 1987 report of the World Commission on Environment and Development, which called for "sustainable development" that meets the current generation's needs without depriving future generations by drawing down productive assets.

Potential Growth Cut 30 Percent

In Costa Rica, the study used remote sensing and satellite imaging, detailed field studies, scientific samplings, and Geographic Information Systems methodologies and mapping to measure natural resource losses.

They found that the depreciation in the value of Costa Rica's forests, soils, and fisheries averaged 5 percent of GNP per year over the 20 years of the study or one third of gross capital formation. This means a 25 to 30 percent reduction in potential economic growth. Net capital formation was in effect overestimated by at least 40 percent.

---

16 Norman Myers ◆ A Cornucopia of Foods

In this chapter from The Primary Source *(1984), Norman Myers discusses the importance of the tropical rainforest as a powerhouse of evolution and a source of genetic material (germplasm) for the improvement of existing crop plants or the breeding of new ones. Because of the extremely high biodiversity of the tropical rainforest and the tendency of its species toward patchy distributions, its widespread clearance will inevitably result in the extinction of certain gene pools. As the population of a plant or animal species shrinks, it loses some of its genes, even if the species itself continues to exist. This ultimately reduces the flexibility of the species to adapt to changing conditions and reduces the opportunity of future generations of humans to benefit from presently unknown but potentially useful properties of wild plants and animals. Many scientists believe that this subtle erosion of the genetic diversity of life on earth is one of the greatest threats posed by the destruction of the tropical rainforest.*

Our daily wake-up cup of coffee owes its far-past origin, and its currently acceptable price, to tropical forests. Perhaps we shall shortly sweeten that cup of coffee with a natural sweetener that contains next to no calories;

From Norman Myers, *The Primary Source: Tropical Forests and Our Future* (New York, 1984), 189–205, by permission of W. W. Norton & Company, Inc. © 1984 by Synergisms Ltd.

if so, the plant from which the sweetener is prepared will almost certainly come from tropical forests. At breakfast, we may well enjoy a slice of papaya, a banana, a mango, an avocado, or any of at least two dozen fruits that derive from tropical forests. As a measure of our daily delight in these tasty offerings of tropical forests, a typical citizen of North America and Western Europe consumes about 10 kilograms per year of bananas; worldwide, people eat their way through 40 million tons of bananas each year, plus 13 million tons of mangoes, and about 1.5 million tons each of papaya and avocado. We can assert much the same about many other items that turn up in our daily diets, right through to the late-evening cup of hot chocolate.

Of course these items do not come to us directly from tropical forests. They come from plantations. But as is the case with many established crops around the world, tropical fruits, plus beverages such as coffee and drinking chocolate, cannot keep on flourishing without season-by-season infusions of new genetic material from their wild relatives, among other sources of "support germplasm."[1] However much we may suppose that a banana plantation remains superbly productive because the farmer throws masses of fertilizer and pesticides at it, the key lies rather with its genetic underpinnings. Indeed, all modern crops, being the refined products of selective breeding, constantly require new genetic material in order to maintain and even expand their productivity, to enhance their nutritive content, to improve their taste (or to restore it), and to resist emergent types of diseases and pests, as well as environmental stresses such as cold and drought.

During the past several decades, genetic resources from tropical forests have saved a number of important crops, including cocoa, banana, and coffee. Wild germplasm for cocoa is found in the species' native habitats in western Amazonia and in relict patches of forest in the Pacific coast zone of Ecuador—where one particular variety of the cocoa plant has now been reduced to just a few surviving individuals in the 1.8 square-kilometer biological reserve at Rio Palenque. It is a type of cocoa with better taste and other virtues than almost all other gene pools of wild cocoa.[2] Another example is the sugarcane crop. During the mid-1920s, sugarcane growers in the Deep South of the United States ran into trouble from a mosaic virus transmitted by aphids, which brought the crop crashing from over 180,000 tons per year to only 43,000 tons. Fortunately, mosaic-tolerant varieties of sugarcane were found in a wild species that grows in secondary forests of Java, saving the U.S. sugarcane industry from bankruptcy.[3] Since that time, further wild types of sugarcane have supplied resistance to red rot, gummosis, and other pathogens that plague sugarcane growers.

More recently, coffee growers faced a major setback in 1970 when a rust disease appeared in southern Brazil. This was no ordinary type of disease. It revealed at least thirty different races and types. The rust soon spread to Central America, threatening the economies of several countries where coffee exports are the premier source of foreign exchange, earning a total of $3 billion a year. Coffee growers tried conventional methods of fighting the rust, principally by spraying of fungicides. But the cost ran to $200 per hectare, more than many farmers could afford. Again, it was crop geneticists who saved the day. A rust-resistant strain became available from germplasm collected in forests of Ethopia—the original source of genetic variability for coffee. Even though at least four fifths of Ethiopia's original forests have been eliminated, and the rest are facing imminent threat, germplasm collectors reached the wild gene reservoirs in time—whereupon coffee growers in Latin America were saved from catastrophe, and coffee drinkers around the world were saved from the one-dollar cup of coffee.[4] Even health addicts benefit from wild sources of coffee germplasm. A new variety of wild coffee, containing not a trace of caffeine, has been discovered in such tiny patches of forest as still survive in the Comoro Islands off eastern Africa.

Significant as these instances have been, the most remarkable contributions from wild germplasm almost certainly lie ahead of us, provided we safeguard the wild gene reservoirs in time. An illustration of the wild gene support yet to come involves the recent discovery, in a small patch of montane forest in south-central Mexico, of a weedy-looking form of wild teosinte, the closest relative of corn.[5] Curiously enough, this proved to be the first perennial type of teosinte with the same chromosome makeup as corn, allowing it to be crossbred with conventional, that is, annual, varieties of corn. A hybrid strain might eventually eliminate the heavy year-by-year costs of ploughing and sowing, since the crop would spring up by itself with every new season, just like daffodils. The wild corn also offers resistance to several diseases, including at least four out of eight major viruses and mycoplasmas that are more than troublesome to corn growers and to corn consumers worldwide.[6] Corn appears not only in cornflakes and popcorn, but in preserves, salad dressing, catsup, soft drinks, beer, and bourbon. Moreover, since the wild species has been discovered at elevations between 2,500 and 3,250 meters, where its cool mountainous habitats are often damp, it may well thrive in wet soils that have hitherto been beyond the survival capacities of conventional corn. The wild species could thus expand the cultivation range of corn by as much as one tenth, or many millions of hectares. Overall benefits for the global corn industry could eventually be measured in billions of dollars per year.[7]

Entirely New Foods

Tropical forests not only support modern agriculture through their genetic contributions to established crops, they offer hosts of opportunities for entirely new crops, in the form of foods that we may scarcely have thought about thus far. Unaware as we may be, forest plants of the humid tropics have supplied us with many staple foods, including cereals such as rice and millet; pulses such as peanut and mung bean; roots and tubers such as yam and taro; and other well-known items such as cassava and pineapple, to name but the leading foods.[8] But the fact that these crops are so widely grown does not necessarily mean that they are the best crops. We can argue that today's crops are accidents of history. While we may well believe that rice and other staple products of the tropical forest zone—together with wheat, potatoes, and two dozen other basic foods from other parts of the world—are eaten by the great majority of humankind each day on the grounds that they constitute the world's best food plants, we actually grow these plants because it turned out they were suited to cultivation by Neolithic man. The plants that were selected as most appropriate 10,000 years ago still supply virtually all items on our meal tables today. Many new crops could be awaiting our attention, capable of becoming front-rank crops in many lands if they were given a chance.

As an example of a plant with unusual promise, let us look at the winged bean, a plant from the forests of New Guinea.[9] Because of the shape of its pods, it is also known as the four-angled bean and the asparagus pea; and it has long been known to forest tribes of its native New Guinea as a crop with outstanding nutritional content. The vinelike plant contains far more protein than occurs in potatoes, cassava, and several other crops that serve as principal sources of food to many millions of people each day in the tropics. The winged bean offers nutritional value equivalent to soybean, with 40 percent protein and 17 percent edible oil, plus vitamins and other nutrients. It is not to be decried as a poor man's crop, a vegetable to be dismissed as a second-rate product for third-rate communities. Its capacity to match the soybean's nutritional value might remind us that the United States used to produce only scattered patches of soybean, for at least one century before the plant was finally upgraded to a widespread crop. Today the soybean is the principal protein crop in the world, flourishing in dozens of temperate-zone countries. Could not a similar prospect be in store for the winged bean, scheduled to become the long-sought "soybean of the tropics"? The bean has received a crash program of development and improvement during the last few years, until it now helps enhance human diets in more than fifty countries of the developing tropics.

Probably fruits offer the greatest promise for new foods. Temperate-zone forests have yielded only about 20 major fruits, whereas tropical forests feature at least 250 fruits that please human palates in their millions, and many more are enjoyed locally. In New Guinea alone, 251 tree species bear edible fruits, most of them consumed, at one time or another, by local communities—yet a mere 43 have become established as cultivated crops, and only about one dozen reach the marketplace, indicating the scope for future development.[10] There could well be 2,500 fruit species in tropical forests for human consumption—and of these, perhaps 250 are widespread, 50 are well known, and 15 rank as major commercial species.[11]

To get an idea of what these fruits might consist of, let us look at a couple that deserve to become as widely established as bananas and mangoes. First, the pummelo, a citrus fruit that appears splendidly suited to the warm, moist areas of the lowland tropics. Virtually all other citrus fruits require subtropical environments, with cool, damp winters followed by warm, drier summers. But the pummelo thrives in year-round warmth and moisture. Native to Southeast Asia, it prefers lowland areas, and it can even prosper in shoreline soils, revealing a high tolerance for saline conditions—a trait that would allow it to be grown in brackish, marshy areas. The pummelo is the largest of the citrus fruits, larger even than a grapefruit. As a measure of our global appetite for citrus fruits, we eat 55 million tons per year, and a U.S. citizen consumes an average of ten kilograms per year, probably enjoying the sharp flavor of oranges and so forth virtually every day. Second, a fruit from tropical America, the soursop. A large fleshy fruit that can weigh four kilograms or more, with a white juicy interior, the soursop's smell is akin to that of a pineapple, but its taste is a striking mixture of musky and acidic flavors. The fruit can be eaten raw, or it can be pulped for use in ice cream and soft drinks.

Similar accounts could be presented, without further field research, for many dozens of other tropical fruits; for instance, the mangosteen of Malaysia, described as "perhaps the world's best tasting fruit."[12] So when we visit the fruit section of our local supermarket and marvel, as we rightly may during certain seasons of the year, at the bountiful variety of fruits shipped in from the tropics, let us reflect that these represent but a tiny fraction of the array that we could enjoy if botanists and agriculturists were to exploit the far greater variety of fruit trees available in tropical forests—and that steadily decline toward extinction before the axe and the chainsaw.

As for vegetables, we find that nutritious leaves and other greenery of tropical forests are equally diverse. At least 1,650 plants of tropical forests offer vegetablelike materials of various sorts.[13] Having looked at tropical forest fruits in some detail, we shall not linger with an instance-by-instance account of vegetables—except to note a distinctive way of deriving high-quality food from forest greenery, in the form of leaf protein.[14] This type of food is not yet something that we can purchase in cans in our local supermarket, yet it could become, in just a few more years, a significant factor in our diets—and even more importantly, a common item among protein-deficient areas of the world. Through a process that is sometimes known as green-crop fractionation, plant leaves and stems can be ruptured to release juices and saps that contain several proteins, also sugars, salts, lipids, and vitamins. The process is relatively simple. Leaves are passed through a pulper, the juice is drained and then heated to 70–80 degrees Fahrenheit, causing the protein to coagulate, whereupon it can be separated by means of a filter press. The protein material, dark green and cheeselike in appearance, is mixed with established foods as a protein reinforcer.

A key question is, Which plants best lend themselves to supply of protein through this technique, that is, which offer the greatest quantity of best-quality protein in their tissues, which grow fastest, which best tolerate less-than-ideal conditions, and so forth? Thus far, scientists have been inclined to focus on a series of legumes, with a protein content between 12 and 36 percent. Given present technology for green-crop fractionation, we can generate leaf protein from legumes at a cost of only one fifth as much as soybean protein, and one seventeenth as much as protein in the form of milk or meat. Via experimental projects, protein of this sort has been extracted from alfalfa, clover, oats, spinach, Chinese cabbage, water hyacinth, and numerous grasses. Now that we know that green-crop fractionation can be applied to a wide variety of leafy plants, the challenge is to find the most suitable candidates. Plainly, the best bet for investigators lies with the zone that features almost as many plant forms as in all the rest of the earth.

Natural Sweeteners

In the wake of the cyclamate and saccharin controversies, there is urgent need for an alternative non-nutritive sweetening agent, that is, one that does not add calories to our diet and centimeters to our waistlines. Although sweetness is only one of four basic tastes of humans, it commands far more attention than all the others combined—to the detriment of our health and our appearance, since a single cola drink contains as many calories, in the form of sugar, as half a kilogram of potatoes. We must break ourselves of our sugar habit, since we already consume far too much—100 million tons worldwide each year, or almost twenty kilograms for each global citizen. The average American consumes at least forty-five kilograms of sugar per year, making it a key factor in overweight problems and associated diseases such as heart disorders and tooth decay.

Many plant pigments, such as carotenoids in sweet-tasting fruits, attract birds, insects, and other herbivores. Almost certainly, then, they are not toxic to mammals, including humans. The problem with the natural sweeteners of fruits that we consume is that they are nutritive sugars—glucose, fructose, and sucrose—and we already consume far more of them than is good for us. Fortunately we are finding that a few natural sweeteners in fruits are made up of protein compounds; and these materials, identified only during the last ten years, make up an entirely new class of natural sweeteners.[15] They are all 1,000 times sweeter than sucrose, and at least 300 times sweeter than saccharin.

A leading example of a source of protein sweeteners is the so-called miracle fruit *Synsepalum dulcificum*, a berry from West African forests. It causes sour foods to taste splendidly sweet, as anyone can tell by merely chewing on a berry at the same time he or she is eating lemons, limes, rhubarb, or grapefruit. Another fruit from West Africa's forests, known as the serendipity berry, *Dioscoreophyllum cumminsii*, has a sweetness 3,000 times greater than that of sucrose. The red, grapelike berry derives its curious name from an occasion in 1965 when an American scientist, Dr. George Inglett, was exploring West African forests for sweet fruits. Coming across the plant by chance, he was surprised to find that its berries tasted so sweet; he had gotten no indication from scientific reports.

Still more important than these two is a third fruit from the forests of West Africa. The katemfe, *Thaumatococcus danielli*, contains two sweet-tasting proteins, thaumatin I and II, both of which are 1,600 times sweeter than sucrose. Thaumatin is now widely marketed by the noted sugar corporation in Great Britain, Tate and Lyle Limited, under the trade name Talin. It is becoming strongly established in Japan, where it is used as a sweetener in such diverse products as candies, chewing gum, salad dressing, coffee drinks, soups, jellies, pickles, frozen desserts, fish and meat products, and table-top sachets. It should soon become available in the United States after surviving tests by the Food and Drug Administration.

Control of Agricultural Pests

Tropical forests can further support agriculture by supplying materials to help keep down the many insect pests that account for the loss of 40 percent of all food grown around the world each year. A sound way to control insect pests is to exploit chemicals from plants that have developed mechanisms to resist insects. The finest source of such plants lies with tropical forests and their exceptional variety of plant forms that have co-evolved in equilibrium with associated insects.[16] Tropical forest plants constitute a vast storehouse of chemical substances for defense against insects—not only biocompounds that serve as insect repellents and toxicants, but feeding deterrents of various sorts, inhibitors of insect growth and development, and the like. Since multitudes of plants and insects have evolved symbiotic relationships within their tropical forest ecosystems, we can surmise that there must be many other insect-resisting substances available in the forests, not only of the types listed, but of novel and unrecognized forms as well.

Moreover, all these compounds are biodegradable. This means that they do not accumulate in organisms and thus do not contribute to the environmental problems associated with synthetic chemical insecticides. Perhaps most important of all, they generally cause little, if any, harm to higher animals, such as birds and mammals, including humans.

By way of illustration, let us note two main categories of toxic compounds—the pyrethrins, from chrysanthemum-type plants, and the rotenoids, from roots of tropical forest legumes. Rotenoids are the more widely distributed, known to occur in the roots and seeds of at least sixty-seven plant species found across Amazonia and Southeast Asia. Especially important as a source of rotenoids is the *Derris* group of woody climbing plants in Southeast Asia; their roots contain powerful toxins that have long been used by forest tribes as fish poisons. So powerful are these root compounds, that one part of plant to three hundred thousand parts of water is sufficient to kill fish. It was the use of these rotenoids as fish poisons that enabled their toxic characteristics to be identified by Western scientists, and today a series of *Derris*-based insecticides are used in the form of plant sprays for field crops, and as dips and dusting powders for livestock.

In the American tropics, a major agricultural pest consists of leaf-cutting ants. These ants make their living by stripping leaves from plants, including crop plants. Fortunately, at least one species of tropical forest tree produces a chemical compound that actively repels the ant—thus opening up the prospect that the compound could be used to produce an insect repellant. Better still, of course, would be to identify the genes that enable the tree to produce its own internal insect repellant, and then to splice the chemical-generating genes into certain of our food crops. The same approach could apply to many other plant-produced materials, for example the anti-feedant compound found in bark extracts of forest trees in Papua New Guinea.[17]

But while a gene-splicing strategy will represent by far the most efficient way to use anti-insect compounds produced by plants, the strategy will depend on the greatest possible stocks of genetic variability among wild plants. As the burgeoning industry of genetic engineering reaches a stage where inter-species crosses become not only possible but relatively straightforward, the industry will seek a maximum array of plants with insect-repelling and insect-killing capacity (as they will seek other prized traits, such as resistance to diseases, saline soils, drought, etc).

At the same time, we should bear in mind that insect pests include variations that can multiply in numbers to overcome plant defenses in as little as ten years, sometimes a mere three years. Hence there is all the greater need to derive further genetic combinations of plants to enable farmers to "stay ahead of the game"—otherwise, they will start to encounter increasing numbers of immune insect strains.

Not all anti-insect defenses in plants are chemicals that make the insect feel sick to its stomach, or worse. A number of chemicals cause insects to moult at the wrong phase of their life cycle; or they inhibit the growth of an infant insect into an adult, leaving it as a perpetual juvenile of harmless scope; or they suppress the reproductive mechanisms of insects; or they make life more than difficult for insects in dozens of other ways.

Pest Control through Natural Enemies

Yet another weapon for the farmer to mobilize against insect pests lies with natural enemies. Certain insect species in the wild operate as predators or parasites to hold down the numbers of their host species—and it is precisely these hosts that frequently proliferate to become pests in agriculture. Predators and parasites attack the eggs, larvae, pupae, and adults of their target species.[18] Since many predators and parasites are highly specific in their choice of prey, they are inclined to target only certain species without doing damage to others. By contrast, the broad-scale use of persistent toxic chemicals tends to kill off far more insects than is necessary.

In any case, many insect pests are growing resistant to chemical insecticides. Among certain species, as few as fifteen generations are needed to build up resistance. According to the Food and Agriculture Organization of the United Nations, more than three hundred species of insects, mites, and ticks throughout the world are known to have become resistant to one or more pesticides, and dozens more are suspected of becoming resistant. In the United States, entomologists in the Department of Agriculture estimate that approximately seven hundred insect species do significant damage to crops within the continental limits (not counting Hawaii, where the problem is still more acute); the loss is calculated at $5 billion per year. Of these seven hundred insect species, around half have developed resistance to at least one pesticide, some to two or more. American farmers apply four hundred thousand tons of chemical insecticides to their crops each year, ten times as much as in 1950, yet they lose twice as much food to insects. Hence the rationale for the natural enemies strategy. The track record of this approach is encouraging. Entomologists have recorded at least 250 cases of pest control accomplished through introduction of predators and parasites that attack troublesome species. For example, citrus growers in Florida have been able to save their industry $40 million each year through a onetime outlay of $35,000 in 1973 for the introduction from the tropics of parasitic insects that attack citrus-tree pests.[19]

Furthermore, natural enemies can be used against another form of pest, weed plants. In the United States, alligator weed has proved a notorious and costly problem for rivers and lakes, irrigation canals, waterways for boats, etc. No herbicide proved equal to the task. Fortunately a solution has been found in the form of a flea beetle from South American forests, which regards the alligator weed as its preferred host.[20] Another prominent weed in the United States, as elsewhere in the world, is the water hyacinth; a mere ten plants can multiply to six hundred thousand in just eight months, forming a carpet a quarter of a hectare in size, and a carpet thick enough for a person to walk across. A promising response to the water hyacinth problem lies with herbivorous insects from tropical forests of South America.[21]

The economics of the natural enemies strategy are often highly positive. Across-the-board performance indicates that there is an average of a thirty-dollar return for each dollar expended on importation of beneficial organisms (in contrast to the 4:1 benefit-to-cost ratio for chemical pesticides). In California alone, during the period 1928–1979, a series of natural-enemy projects has reduced crop losses to insects, and has reduced the need for pesticidal chemicals, for savings worth just short of $1 billion (at 1979 prices).[22]

At least 250 insect pests in the United States, accounting for around one half of all crop losses to insects, are species of foreign origin. It is precisely against these imported pests that alien introductions of natural enemies offer the greatest promise.[23] According to preliminary estimates by the U.S. Department of Agriculture, a full 1,000 species of foreign organisms—not only insects, but also mites and pathogens—could be profitably introduced into the United States, at a cost of less than $40 million over a period of twenty years. Much potential is available in the form of, for example, wasps that act as parasites or predators, notably the chalcid wasps, among others that are numerous in tropical forests. At least as much potential appears to lie with the ichneumonid or braconid wasps, and with certain groups of beetles. To date, American pest experts have called on the services of natural enemies from abroad to overcome many dozens of foreign insect pests: the best times still lie ahead.

Forest Animals for Food

Thus far, this chapter has emphasized tropical forest plants that are new sources of food. Let us now take a look at animals.[24]

Within the forests of the Thailand-Kampuchea border lives a secretive, cowlike creature with resplendent horns: the kouprey. A bull kouprey sports horns that are longer and wider than those of any other living wild cattle except the buffalo; a female's are lyre-shaped, corkscrewing upward in a manner akin to those of the lesser kudu in Africa. The kouprey is believed to have been one of the wild ancestors of the humped zebu cattle of southern Asia, which means that further crossbreeding between the two bovids could boost cattle raising throughout the entire region. In particular, the kouprey appears immune to rinderpest, a widespread disease that is fatal to cattle. Regrettably, the kouprey's very survival is doubtful, due to military activity in its habitats during the past several decades. Perhaps only a few individuals remain.

Other wild bovids of Southeast Asia's forests could likewise help cattle husbandry, notably the so-called dwarf water buffaloes, more correctly termed the seladang, the tamarau, and the anoa. But as with the kouprey, the numbers of all these wild cattle have been severely reduced through human disruption of the forest ecosystems. In addition, the forests of Southeast Asia support the babirusa, a distant relative of the pig that seems to be a rudimentary ruminant and, through its distinctive approach to the challenge of converting rough forage into good meat, could upgrade some of the half-billion pigs around the world.

When speculating on the potential contributions of these wild creatures to modern livestock, let us bear in mind that the ancestral stock of the domesticated water buffalo includes the wild *Bubalis arnee* of southern Asia; that among the progenitors of Indian cattle is the gaur, *Bos gaurus*; and that livestock people in Indonesia already use a hybrid animal, known as the madura—a cross between conventional cattle and the banteng, *Bos banteng*.

As for birds, we might reflect, the next time we enjoy a chicken supper, that this most numerous bird on earth, numbering at least five billion, originated from a pheasantlike creature of India's forests, known as the red jungle fowl, together with some genetic support from the guinea fowl of West Africa.

Wild Meat

In a number of tropical forest countries, wild meat counts as an important item in people's diets.[25] In Nigeria, for example, where the forest cover has been reduced by at least 90 percent, local people still derive a renewable harvest of almost 100,000 tons of good, solid meat per year from animals including grass-cutters (giant rats), small antelopes including bushbuck and duiker, and sundry monkeys. Four people out of five enjoy game meat as a regular item in the cooking pot. On average, it constitutes one fifth of all animal protein of whatever sort for people in Nigeria's forest zone. In Zaire it rises to almost 27 percent, and in Cameroon, Ivory Coast, and Liberia, to a massive 70 percent.

Wild meat comes not only from mammals. In Amazonia, seven species of river turtles could, if properly managed, become sustainable sources of high-grade meat.[26] Turtles feed readily on aquatic plants of all sorts and conditions; they survive temporary food shortages at the end of the dry season without adverse effect; they have low metabolic rates, so they do not become nearly so hungry as warm-blooded creatures; and they appear to need far less living space than higher vertebrates. According to some theoretical calculations, a one-hectare lake of turtles could produce well over two tons of meat each year, in contrast to the fifty kilograms of beef that could come from one hectare of average cattle pasture in the humid tropics. Other creatures of South American forests provide abundant meat, notably the tapir, agouti and paca (rodents of Amazonia), plus peccaries (wild pigs), monkeys, and other mammals, and also snakes and lizards. In two separate areas of Peru's sector of Amazonia, people living outside townships depend on wild meat for 80 to 85 percent of their animal protein.

To date, the offtake of wildlife in Amazonia has tended to range from next to no harvest at all, to severe over-exploitation. If, however, a controlled-cropping system were to be mounted, the result could be encouraging, according to some preliminary figures worked out by Dr. Angel Paucar, of the Wildlife Division in Ecuador, and Dr. Alfred L. Gardner, of the U.S. Fish and Wildlife Service.[27] Their calculations represent no more than a tentative and speculative attempt to illuminate a situation that remains almost entirely unexplored. So the numbers represent best-judgment guesstimates—no more and no less.

In Ecuador's sector of Amazonia, local people have long taken a self-renewing harvest of wildlife products, partly in the form of meat for consumption and partly in the form of skins and hides for export. In some localities the offtake has been excessive in the case of certain species. But by and large, wildlife has proved itself to be a strongly renewable resource, given the low levels of exploitation to which it has generally been subjected. So few people live in this part of Amazonia, that only a moderate harvest can make a sizable contribution. As much as 85 percent of animal protein consumed by local people comes from wild animals, notably peccaries, deer, tapirs, pacas, and agoutis, among some forty species of mammals in all. A sustainable harvest of wild meat can, according to Paucar and Gardner, amount to 240 kilograms per square kilometer, with a market value of about $1.8 per kilogram, or a total of almost $440 overall. (Were the harvest to be systematized, and expanded to include birds, turtles, and fish, the minimum potential value could be increased as much as ten times.) Furthermore, since almost one third of Amazonian Ecuador consists of swamps and rivers, there is plenty of scope for harvest of caimans, at least two per hectare per year. A caiman measuring 1.5 meters in length is worth $145. Thus one square kilometer of such habitats could yield $14,550 per year for hides alone, rising to $16,370 when we include meat from the caimans. In addition, each square kilometer of forest can renewably produce twenty primates each year for biomedical research, an individual being worth between $200 and $300. So a sustainable harvest of wild primates could generate a minimum of $4,000 per year. Many readers may object to the prospect of using wild primates to foster human health. In the past, the wild primate stocks have almost invariably been overexploited, sometimes critically so. But if this crucial factor can be taken care of, need any objection remain, particularly when a sustainable harvest of primates helps to promote the survival of their forest habitats?

This all means that a forest tract of five hundred square kilometers could, under scientific management, produce a self-renewing crop of wildlife with a potential value of at least $10 million per year, or slightly more than $200 per hectare. These revenues are to be contrasted with a return from commercial logging of only a little over $150 per hectare—and hardwood timber . . . tends to be harvested as a once-and-for-all product, leaving little prospect that a further harvest can be taken within several decades at least.

In conclusion, then, we can accept that tropical forests, while making significant contributions to modern agriculture already, play only a trifling part in the life of the farmer compared with what they could supply. Were we to undertake a systematic exploration and selective extraction of whatever "agricultural" materials are available from tropical forests, we could surely look for a steady stream of new products. Were this chapter to be rewritten in the year 2000, who can guess at the host of exotic articles that it might enumerate? The problem surely does not lie with tropical forests themselves, with their extreme abundance of resources waiting to be brought into the mainstream of our lives. Rather, the deficiency lies with our imaginations: we constantly fail to grasp the scale of potential products from tropical forests that could enrich our lives.

Notes

1. P. Carlson, editor, 1980, *Biology of Crop Productivity*, Academic Press, New York; J. R. Harlan, 1975, *Crops and Man*, American Society of Agronomy, Madison, Wisconsin; N. Myers, 1983, *A Wealth of Wild Species*, Westview Press, Boulder, Colorado; M. L. Oldfield, 1981, Tropical Deforestation and Genetic Resources Conservation, *Studies in Third World Societies*, 14:277–346.

2. A. H. Gentry, 1982, Patterns of Neotropical Plant Species Diversity, in M. K. Hecht, B. Wallace, and G. T. Prance, editors, *Evolutionary Biology*, 15:1–84.

3. J. R. Harlan, 1975, *Crops and Man*.

4. F. P. Ferwerda, 1976, Coffees, in N. W. Simmons, editor, *Evolution of Crop Plants*, 252–60, Longman, New York.

5. H. H. Iltis, J. F. Doebley, R. M. Guzman, and B. Pazy, 1979, Zea diploperennis (Gramineae), a New Teosinte from Mexico, *Science*, 203:186–88.

6. L. R. Nault and W. R. Findley, 1981, Primitive Relative Offers New Traits for Corn Improvement, *Ohio Report* 66(6):90–92.

7. A. C. Fisher, 1982, *Economic Analysis and the Extinction of Species*, Department of Agriculture and Resource Economics, University of California at Berkeley; N. Myers, 1983, *A Wealth*.

8. M. Chai, E. Soepadmo, and H. S. Yong, editors, 1979, Proceedings of Workshop on Genetic Resources of Plants, Animals and Microorganisms in Malaysia, *Malaysian Applied Biology, Special Issue* 8(1); M. A. Rifai, editor, 1979, *ASEAN Grain Legumes*, Central Research Institute of Agriculture, Bogor, Indonesia; J. T. Williams, C. H. Lamoureux, and N. Wulijarni-Soctjipto, editors, 1975, *Southeast Asian Plant Genetic Resources*, BIOTROP, Bogor, Indonesia.

9. National Academy of Sciences, 1975, *The Winged Bean: A High Protein Crop for the Tropics*, National Academy of Sciences, Washington, DC.

10. K. Jong, editor, 1979, *Biological Aspects of Plant Genetic Resource Conservation in Southeast Asia*, Institute of Southeast Asian Biology, University of Aberdeen, Scotland, UK.

11. S. Nagy and P. E. Shaw, editors, 1980, *Tropical and Subtropical Fruits*, AVI Publishing Company, Westport, Connecticut; J. A. Samson, 1980, *Tropical Fruits*, Longman, New York; and for several illustrative examples, see National Academy of Sciences, 1975, *Underexploited Tropical Plants with Promising Economic Value*, National Academy of Sciences, Washington, DC.

12. National Academy of Sciences, 1979, *Tropical Legumes: Resources for the Future*, National Academy of Sciences, Washington, DC.

13. G. A. C. Herklots, 1972, *Vegetables in Southeast Asia*, George Allen and Unwin, London, UK; F. W. Martin and R. M. Ruberte, 1979, *Edible Leaves of the Tropics*, Institute of Tropical Agriculture, Mayaguez, Puerto Rico; J. J. Ochse, 1977, *Vegetables of the Dutch East Indies*, A. Asher and Company Publishers Ltd., Amsterdam, Netherlands; J. C. Okafor, 1980, Edible Indigenous Woody Plants in the Rural Economy of the Nigerian Zone, *Forest Ecology and Management* 1:235–47; H. A. P. C. Oomen and G. J. H. Grubben, 1977, Tropical Leaf Vegetables in Human Nutrition, in *Communication* 69:24–41, 51–55, Department of Agricultural Research, Koninklijk Instituut voor de Tropen, Amsterdam, Netherlands; and R. L. Villareal and R. T. Opena, 1976, The Wild Vegetables of Southeast Asia, *American Horticulturalist* 55(3):1–4.

14. J. A. Duke, 1981, *The Gene Revolution*, Office of Technology Assessment, U.S. Congress, Washington, DC; N. Mohan and G. P. Srivastava, 1980, Studies on

the Extractability and Chemical Composition of Leaf Proteins from Certain Trees, *Journal of Food Science and Technology* 18:48–50; N. W. Pirie, editor, 1975, *Food Protein Sources*, Cambridge University Press, London, UK.

15. J. A. Duke, 1983, *Ecological Amplitudes of Crops Used as Sweeteners*, Plant Genetics and Germplasm Institute, Agricultural Research Service, Beltsville, Maryland; J. D. Higginbotham, 1979, Protein Sweeteners, in C. A. M. Hough, K. J. Parker, and A. J. Vletof, editors, *Developments in Sweeteners*, Applied Science Publishers, London, UK; G. E. Inglett, 1981, Sweeteners—A Review, *Food Technology*, March 1981, 37–41.

16. L. E. Gilbert and P. H. Raven, editors, 1975, *Coevolution of Animals and Plants*, revised edition, University of Texas Press, Austin, Texas; D. H. Janzen, 1975, *Ecology of Plants in the Tropics*, Arnold, London, UK.; R. L. Metcalfe, 1977, Plant Derivatives for Insect Control, in R. S. Seigler, editor, *Crop Resources*: 165–78, Academic Press, New York.

17. W. Kraus et al., 1980, New Insect Antifeedants from *Toona* Species (*Meliaceae*), in *Proceedings of Fourth Asian Symposium on Medicinal Plants and Species*: 127–35, Government of Thailand in Conjunction with UNESCO and Faculty of Science, Mahidol University, Bangkok, Thailand.

18. S. W. T. Batra, 1982, Biological Control in Agroecosystems, *Science* 215:135–39; C. P. Clausen, editor, 1978, *Introduced Parasites and Predators of Arthropod Pests and Weeds: A World Review*, Agricultural Research Service of U.S. Department of Agriculture, Washington, DC; C. B. Huffaker, 1980, Use of Predators and Parasitoids in Biological Control, in R. C. Staples and R. J. Kuhr, editors, *Linking Research to Crop Production*: 173–98, Plenum Publishing, New York; J. S. Marsden, G. E. Martin, D. J. Parham, T. J. Ridsdill-Smith, and B. G. Johnston, 1980, *Returns on Australian Agricultural Research*, Division of Entomology, Commonwealth Scientific and Industrial Research Organization, Canberra, Australia; R. I. Sailer, 1981, Progress Report on Importation of Natural Enemies of Insect Pests in the U.S.A., in J. R. Coulson, editor, *Use of Beneficial Organisms in the Control of Crop Pests*: 20–26, Entomological Society of America, College Park, Maryland; R. Van den Bosch, P. S. Messenger, and A. P. Gutierrez, 1982, *An Introduction to Biological Control*, Plenum Publishing, New York.

19. V. L. Delucchi, editor, 1976, *Studies in Biological Control*, Cambridge University Press, Cambridge, UK.

20. D. M. Maddox, L. A. Andres, R. D. Hennessey, R. D. Blackburn, and N. R. Spencer, 1971, Insects to Control Alligatorweed, *BioScience* 21:985–91.

21. National Academy of Sciences, 1976, *Making Aquatic Weeds Useful*, National Academy of Sciences, Washington, DC.

22. C. B. Huffaker, 1980, Use of Predators; R. Van den Bosch et al., 1982, *Introduction to Biological Control*.

23. R. I. Sailer, 1981, Progress Report.

24. M. L. Oldfield, 1981, *The Value of the Conservation of Genetic Resources*, Department of Agriculture, University of Texas, Austin, Texas; N. D. Vietmeyer, 1983, *Little-Known Asian Animals with a Promising Economic Future*, National Academy Press, Washington, DC.

25. S. S. Ajayi, 1979, *Utilization of Forest Wildlife in West Africa*, Food and Agriculture Organization, Rome, Italy; A. DeVos, 1977, Game as Food, *Unasylva* 29:2–12; W. Krostitz, 1979, The New International Market for Game Meat, *Unasylva* 31(123):32–36; J. B. Sale, 1983, *The Importance and Values of Wild Plants and*

Animals in Africa, International Union for Conservation of Nature and Natural Resources, Gland, Switzerland.

26. R. A. Mittermeier, 1978, South America's River Turtles: Saving Them by Use, *Oryx* 14(3):222–30.

27. A. Paucar and A. L. Gardner, 1981, *Establishment of a Scientific Research Station in the Yasuni National Park of the Republic of Ecuador*, National Zoo, Washington, DC.

17 Mark Plotkin ◆ The Healing Forest

Shamans (native healers) hold the keys to unlocking the pharmacological potential of rainforest floras in their knowledge of the curative properties of tropical forest plants. Unfortunately both forests and shamans are disappearing at an accelerating rate, and with them dies a wealth of potential cures for a variety of ills. In this 1990 article ethnobotanist Mark Plotkin makes a strong argument for the preservation of the tropical rainforest and for the protection of the tribal peoples who live there. Shamans need to be encouraged to maintain and pass on their traditional knowledge—and their wisdom about how to live in and make use of the tropical rainforest without destroying it. Plotkin and a number of other researchers have begun to challenge the dominant Western perception of tribal peoples as ignorant, backward, and in need of our help. These scholars suggest that perhaps we have more to learn from indigenous people than vice versa. The question is whether Plotkin's perspective will become widely accepted before the rainforests—and their native inhabitants—disappear forever.

The rate of species extinction is increasing at an alarming pace. The majority of the world's threatened species—both animal and plant—inhabit the tropical forests. These forests cover less than 10 percent of the earth's surface, but they are believed to contain more than half the world's species. Among the devastating impacts of the current destruction of tropical forests will be the loss of raw materials for future medicines and the loss of the knowledge needed to utilize them. Rainforest plants are complex chemical storehouses that contain many undiscovered biodynamic compounds with unrealized potential for use in modern medicine. We can gain access to these materials *only* if we study and conserve the species that contain them.

The amount of species diversity concentrated in tropical regions is staggering. For example, the Rio Negro in central Brazil contains more

Reprinted from *The Futurist* (January-February 1990): 9–14, by permission of the World Future Society.

species of fish than are found in all of the rivers in the United States combined. Manu National Park in southeastern Peru is home to more species of birds than are found in the entire United States. A hectare of forest in the U.S. northeast typically contains about twenty species of trees, whereas a similar plot in western Amazonia may contain more than three hundred.

One problem faced by biologists working to prevent diminution of biological diversity is the lack of basic knowledge about most of the world's species. Carolus Linnaeus inaugurated the Latin binomial system in 1753, and approximately 1.7 million species of plants and animals have been described since then. The total number of species in the world is still uncertain. In 1979, Norman Myers, author of *The Sinking Ark*, estimated the total number of species on earth as ten million. But increasingly sophisticated sampling techniques have caused scientists recently to rethink the magnitude of the diversity of life on earth. For instance, Terry Erwin of the Smithsonian Institution now estimates that, worldwide, there are over thirty million species of insects alone.

Compared with the insects, the angiosperms (flowering plants) are much better known. It is estimated that some 250,000 species exist worldwide, 90 percent of which are already known to science. Nevertheless, major expeditions to the tropics, particularly the Amazon region, continue to bring back new species.

The flora of the tropics, like the fauna, face serious threats to their very survival. For example, as much as 95 percent of the Atlantic coastal forest of eastern Brazil has already been destroyed, according to Russell A. Mittermeier of the World Wildlife Fund. On the island of Madagascar, where it is believed that 80 percent of the flowering plants exist nowhere else on earth, well over half of the original forest cover has been removed or seriously disturbed, says Mittermeier. In the Hawaiian archipelago, where more than 90 percent of the plant species exist nowhere else, as much as 14 percent are already believed to be extinct.

Natural and Unnatural Extinction

Extinction is a natural process. Since the origin of life ten million years ago, many species have disappeared. Yet, to view these recent extinctions as natural is to misinterpret the geological record. E. O. Wilson of Harvard University postulates that the present rate of global species extinctions is four hundred times faster than in the recent geological past and that this rate is rapidly accelerating. The only similar examples in the history of this planet were the massive species die-outs at the end of the Paleozoic and Mesozoic eras.

A striking feature of these historic natural disasters, however, is that the extinctions were of primarily animal rather than plant species. Indeed, there is little evidence in the fossil record of mass extinctions of vascular plants. In the past, plants were presumably more resistant to extinction than the dominant animal life forms such as dinosaurs. Consequently, plant diversity has increased through time.

The unpleasant conclusion is that man is causing the first major reduction of global plant diversity since the origin of life.

Plants and Medicine

Plants have traditionally served as man's most important weapon against the bacteria that cause disease—in fact, it seems that even the Neanderthals knew and made use of medicinal plants. As early as 2000 B.C., the Chinese were using molds to treat festering ulcers, and the ancient Egyptians are known to have applied moldy bread to open wounds.

It is only relatively recently, however, with the advent of modern technology and synthetic chemistry, that we have been able to reduce our almost total dependence on the plant kingdom as a source of medicines. Nonetheless, we continue to rely on plants to a much greater degree than is commonly realized. Almost half of all prescriptions dispensed in the United States contain substances of natural origin—and more than 50 percent of these medications contain a plant-derived active ingredient. In 1974 alone, the United States imported $24.4 million worth of medicinal plants.

There are four basic ways in which plants that are used by tribal peoples are valuable for modern medicine. First, plants from the tropics are sometimes used as sources of direct therapeutic agents. The alkaloid D-tubocurarine is extracted from the South American jungle liana *Chondrodendron tomentosum* and is widely used as a muscle relaxant in surgery. Chemists have so far been unable to produce this drug synthetically in a form that has all the attributes of the natural product, and we therefore continue to rely on collection of this plant from the wild.

Surprisingly, harvesting medicinal plants is often less costly than synthesizing drugs artificially. In 1973, less than 10 percent of the seventy-six drug compounds from higher plants used in U.S. prescription drugs were produced commercially by total chemical synthesis. Reserpine, an important hypotensive agent extracted from *Rauwolfia*, is a good example. The synthesis of the drug in the mid-1970s cost approximately $1.25 per gram, whereas commercial extraction from the plant cost only about $.75 per gram.

The second way in which modern medicine can use tropical plants is as a starting point for the development of more complex semisynthetic compounds. An example of this would be saponin extracts that are chemically altered to produce sapogenins necessary for manufacturing steroidal drugs. Until relatively recently, 95 percent of all steroids were obtained from extracts of neotropical yams of the genus *Dioscorea*.

Third, tropical plants are also sources of substances that can be used as models for new synthetic compounds. Cocaine from the coca plant, *Erythroxylum coca*, has served as a model for the synthesis of a number of local anesthetics, such as procaine. New and unusual chemical substances found in plants will continue to serve as "blueprints" for novel synthetic substances and will prove to be increasingly important in the future.

Fourth, plants can also be used as taxonomic markers for the discovery of new compounds. From a plant-chemistry standpoint, the plant kingdom has been investigated in a very haphazard manner; some families have been relatively well studied, while others have been almost completely overlooked. For example, many uses have been documented for Liliaceae, and the family is known to be rich in alkaloids. Although little was known of the chemistry of the Orchidaceae, plants of this family were investigated because of its close relationship to the Liliaceae. The research demonstrated that, not only were Orchidaceae rich in alkaloids, but many of these alkaloids were unique and thought to be of extreme interest for the future.

Of the hundreds of thousands of species of living plants, only a fraction have been investigated in the laboratory. This poor understanding of plants is particularly acute in the tropics. The noted Brazilian plant chemist Otto Gottlieb wrote in 1981: "Nothing at all is known about the chemical composition of 99.6 percent of our flora." It is worth noting that Brazil probably has more species of flowering plants—approximately fifty-five thousand—than any other country on earth.

Ethnobotany

In a region like the Amazon, home to tens of thousands of plant species, how do we begin to decide which plants are of potential use? Randomly screening plant materials for new biodynamic compounds has proven to be very expensive. A more cost-effective method to find new and useful plant compounds is the science of ethnobotany.

Ethnobotany is the study of tribal peoples and their utilization of tropical plants. The importance of ethnobotanical inquiry as a cost-effective means of locating new and useful tropical-plant compounds cannot be overemphasized. Most of the secondary plant compounds employed in modern medicine were first "discovered" through ethnobotanical investigation. There are some 119 pure chemical substances extracted from higher plants that are used in medicine throughout the world, and 74 percent of these compounds have the same or related use as the plants from which they were derived.

The rosy periwinkle (*Catharanthus roseus*) represents a classic example of the importance of plants used by local peoples. This herbaceous plant, native to southeastern Madagascar, is the source of over seventy-five alkaloids, two of which are used to treat childhood leukemia and Hodgkin's disease with a very high success rate. Annual sales of these alkaloids worldwide in 1980 were estimated to reach $50 million wholesale prior to 100 percent markup for the retail market, according to International Marketing Statistics. This species was first investigated in the laboratory because of its use by local people as an oral hypoglycemic agent. Thus, we can see that investigation of plants used for medicinal purposes by "unsophisticated" peoples can provide us with new biodynamic compounds that may have very important applications in our own society.

Some of the earliest evidence of plant use by Native Americans are fossil remains of peyote (*Lophophora williamsi*), a hallucinogen, excavated from caves in Texas and dated about 7000 B.C. In lowland South America, artifacts from coastal Ecuador indicate that coca (*Erythroxylum* sp.) was in use in 2100 B.C. The Sinú culture (A.D. 1200–1600) of northwestern Colombia produced numerous gold pectorals with mushroomlike representations, possibly of hallucinogenic mushrooms of the genus *Psilocybe*. That no South American tribe is known to consume hallucinogenic mushrooms today makes one wonder about the quantity of ethnobotanical information that has already been lost.

A major barrier to knowing where to focus our research efforts in the search for new plant medicines is the haphazard way in which most of the early ethnobotanical data were collected. A turning point in the history of South American ethnobotany was the arrival of Richard Evans Schultes, now director of the Botanical Museum at Harvard, in Amazonian Colombia in 1941. After completing his doctoral dissertation on the ethnobotany of the Indians in Oaxaca, Mexico, he decided to initiate a study of plants employed in the manufacture of arrow poisons.

Schultes remained in the northwest Amazon until 1954, living with the Indians, participating in their native rituals, and conducting ethnobotanical research. Although he eventually went to work on the U.S. Department of Agriculture project to harvest natural rubber from the Amazon during World War II, he continued collecting, eventually sending home more than twenty-four thousand plant specimens.

Nearly two thousand of these species had been employed medicinally by the natives, while others had been used for everything from clothing to contraceptives. Most of the ethnobotanists working in South America today are following in Schultes's footsteps.

Native Knowledge

Tropical-forest peoples represent the key to understanding, utilizing, and protecting tropical-plant diversity. The degree to which they understand and are able to sustainably use this diversity is astounding. The Barasana Indians of Amazonian Colombia can identify all of the tree species in their territory without having to refer to the fruit or flowers—a feat that no university-trained botanist is able to accomplish.

Nevertheless, to this day, very few tribes have been subjected to a complete ethnobotanical analysis. In 1981, Robert Goodland of the World Bank wrote: "Indigenous knowledge is essential for the use, identification, and cataloguing of the [tropical] biota. As tribal groups disappear, their knowledge vanishes with them. . . . The preservation of these groups is a significant economic opportunity for the [developing] nation, not a luxury."

Since Amazonian Indians are often the only ones who know both the properties of these plants and how they can best be utilized, their knowledge must be considered an essential component of all efforts to conserve and develop the Amazon. Failure to document this ethnobotanical lore would represent a tremendous economic and scientific loss to mankind.

What can modern medicine learn from the witch doctor? Certainly, much more than one might think. To most of us in industrialized countries, the witch doctor or medicine man or shaman is an object of some derision. In countless films, he has been portrayed in a grass skirt with a bone through his nose, waving rubber snakes and shouting gibberish. Those of us, however, who have been fortunate enough to live in the tropical forest and work with these people have a very different impression.

These medicine men usually have a profound knowledge of tropical plants and the healing properties for which they may be employed. A single shaman of the Wayana tribe in the northeast Amazon, for example, may use more than a hundred different species for medicinal purposes alone. Furthermore, a great many of the remedies *are* effective. Fungal infections of the skin are a common affliction in the humid tropics, and modern medicine can only suppress—not cure—serious cases. On more than one occasion, I have had serious infections successfully treated by shamans using jungle plants.

Unfortunately, however, the oral tradition of these medicine men is not being passed on to the next generation. With the advent of Western medicine in many of these remote areas, the young members of the tribe demonstrate little interest in learning the traditional ethnomedical lore. Of all the shamans with whom I have lived and worked in the northeast Amazon, not a single one had an apprentice. We are, in my opinion, facing a critical situation—

unless we act now, thousands and thousands of years of accumulated knowledge about how to use rainforest plants is going to disappear before the turn of the century.

The Search for New Jungle Medicines

What can the medical community do to aid both the struggle to conserve tropical forests and the search for new jungle medicines? Certainly, a much more prominent role needs to be played if both of the aforementioned efforts are to prove successful. Many reasons for species conservation have been presented to the general public—aesthetic, ethical, etc.—but the most relevant for the medical profession is the utilitarian: that species are of direct benefit to us. The few examples I have mentioned are indicative of the kinds of undiscovered compounds that are undoubtedly out there.

We now know that synthetics are not the only answers to our medical needs. European pharmaceutical firms are showing renewed interest in the potential of the tropical flora, and there is heightened awareness in the United States, as well. The National Cancer Institute recently awarded more than $2.5 million in contracts to the New York Botanical Garden, the Missouri Botanical Garden, and the University of Illinois to collect and test tropical-plant species for antitumor activity.

With the moral and financial support of the U.S. medical community, the conservation movement can help protect and utilize tropical species for human welfare.

We must also consider the importance of medicinal plants in the developing countries themselves. The World Health Organization has estimated that 80 percent of the people in the world rely on traditional medicine for primary healthcare needs. In many cases, developing countries simply cannot afford to spend millions of dollars on imported medicines that they could produce or extract from tropical-forest plants.

Several African and Asian nations have begun to encourage traditional medicine as an integral component of their public healthcare programs. Indigenous medicines are relatively inexpensive, locally available, and usually readily accepted by the local populace.

The ideal scenario for the future would be the establishment of local pharmaceutical firms in developing countries of the tropics. These firms would create jobs, reduce unemployment, reduce import expenditures, and generate foreign exchange. Beyond the economic advantages, however, such enterprises would encourage documentation of traditional ethnomedical lore and would promote the conservation and sustainable use of the tropical forest.

18 Darrell A. Posey ◆ Alternatives to Forest
Destruction: Lessons from the Mêbêngôkre Indians

*Recent research has shown that indigenous peoples manage forest resources
in a complex and sustainable way based on extensive knowledge of their
local flora and fauna. Modern land-use practices in Amazonia are inherently
unsustainable, and in destroying Indian societies they are destroying a vital
source of information as to how people can live in and enrich, rather than
destroy, the forest. Darrell Posey claims here, in a 1989 essay, that indigenous
knowledge of the environment and how to manage it successfully deserves
to be seen as a major intellectual contribution to humanity. Research by
Posey, Mark Plotkin (Selection 17), Katherine Milton (Selection 5), and
other ethnoscientists is beginning to change the way Westerners perceive
the remaining tribal peoples of Latin America and elsewhere.*

Indians in Brazil have historically been considered, at best, as "relatively
incapable" human beings that must be "protected" as wards of the federal
government. The Brazilian Indian Foundation (Fundaçao Nacional do Indio—
FUNAI) serves as the official organ responsible for Indian affairs. Under
past national constitutions, FUNAI was considered the only legal institution
that could represent or defend native peoples. Land demarcation, sales of
mineral and timber rights, judicial proceedings, even labor contracts and
agricultural sales could only legally be conducted by FUNAI officials.

Claims of corruption within FUNAI have now swollen to a level equal
to accusations against its predecessor, Sociedade para Proteçao do Indio
(SPI), which was disbanded due to its scandalous activities, in 1967. A
former president of FUNAI, Romero Jucá Filho, has been charged with
involvement in the illegal sale of gold and timber rights on Indian lands.
This did not stop him, however, from being named acting governor of the
Federal Territory of Roraima, where some of Brazil's richest mineral and
natural reserves are located—mostly in indigenous reserves.[1]

As Carneiro da Cunha points out, "The Indian question today is centered
around disputes over mineral and natural resources on Indian soils and sub-
soils." Native peoples, by virtue of their low numbers (approximately
1 percent of the Brazilian population) and cultural, social, and political
differences, are markedly disadvantaged in the battle against the powerful

From *The Ecologist* (November-December 1989): 241–44. Reprinted by permission of the author and *The Ecologist*, Agriculture House, Bath Road, Sturminster
Newton, Dorset DT10 1DU, England.

forces of international capitalism behind those who seek to exploit these resources.

Maintaining Stereotypes

Much of the general strategy of the exploiters of Indian lands depends upon the maintenance of traditional stereotypes of "primitive" Indians. In a country where paternalism is as much a part of the national fabric as *carnaval*, it has been all too easy to mask attempts to thwart native independence movements with rhetoric about "helping" Indians to make decisions about "what is best for them." Rarely have Indian leaders been heard, because, it is said, they could not possibly know enough about white man's society to make good judgments.

It is equally important for those who wish to exploit Indian lands—especially in Amazonia which is the refuge of over half of Brazil's remaining aborigines—to say that such lands are unproductive and/or unoccupied. The whole of the Amazon basin is considered empty—one great frontier where only a few "primitive" Indians and "cultureless" *caboclos* (peasants) struggle to survive. As Carneiro da Cunha notes: "Indian lands are . . . treated as 'no-man's-land': always considered as the first option for mining, hydroelectric projects, land reform, and development projects in general." This strategy has been relatively easy to maintain over the years because of the inability of native peoples and *caboclos* to organize in a dominant society where minority rights have never been considered an issue.

The Human Tragedy

The destruction of Amazonia is a human as much as an ecological tragedy. *Caboclos*, with few exceptions, are ignored in Amazonian studies as though they were devoid of any culture whatsoever. Expelled from their lands as squatters (*posseiros*), they are forced into poverty and dependency in sprawling slums (*favelas*) where they pay the price of "development."

Indians reflect clearly the tragic human costs of Amazonian development.[2] Brazilian Indian populations have declined from approximately eight million, at the time of the first European contact, to less than two hundred thousand today. Eighty-seven Indian groups have become extinct during this century in Brazil alone.[3] With the decimation of each indigenous group, the world loses thousands of years of accumulated knowledge of adaptation to tropical ecosystems. Such precious information is overlooked without the least consideration: the rapid pace of economic development cannot be halted even long enough to take note of what it is about to destroy.

Indian cultures offer a rich and untapped source of information on the natural resources of the Amazonian basin.[4] Recognition of the value of indigenous knowledge by our civilization would permit Indians to be seen as major intellectual contributors to humanity, rather than mere exotic footnotes to the pages of history books. This recognition could provide an "ideological bridge" through which Indians can prosper with the dignity they need and the respect they deserve.

The Mêbêngôkre and the Kayapó Project

The Kayapó Indians once inhabited a territory the size of France between the Araguaia and Tocantins rivers in eastern Amazonia. Today they live on a five million-acre proposed reserve that includes a variety of tropical ecosystems, ranging from high forests to vast grasslands. All groups within the Kayapó nation call themselves the Mêbêngôkre ("people of the water's source") and speak a language of the Je family of languages.

The knowledge of the Mêbêngôkre Indians is an integrated system of beliefs and practices. Much generally shared information is to be found in a Mêbêngôkre village, in addition to the specialized knowledge held by a few. There are specialists in soils, plants, animals, crops, medicines, and rituals. Each and every Mêbêngôkre believes that he or she has the ability to survive alone in the forest for an indefinite time. Such a belief engenders a strong sense of personal security and is interwoven into daily life.

Forest Islands

The creation of forest "islands" (*apete*) in tropical savannas, demonstrates to what extent the Mêbêngôkre can alter and manage ecosystems to increase biological diversity. Such ecological engineering requires detailed knowledge of soil fertility, microclimatic variations and species' niches, as well as the interrelationships among species which are introduced into these human-made communities. The succcessful *apete* results not only from knowledge of immediate soil and biological properties, but also from the long-term relationships that develop as these forest "islands" become established and increase in density and height. Because numerous plants are cultivated to attract game animals the *apete* can be viewed as both agroforestry plots and hunting reserves.[5]

The Mêbêngôkre frequently speak of *ômbiqwa-ô-toro* plants, or those plants which are "good friends" or "good neighbors" to one another. The Indians are aware of some species combinations that develop more vigorously when planted together. Such synergistic groups often include dozens of plant species, require complex cultivation patterns, and are characterized in terms of "plant energy." Thus, a Mêbêngôkre garden is created by careful combinations of different "plant energies," just as an artist blends colors to produce a work of art. Planting practices based on plant energies can be compared with ecological principles which allow us to understand, from the viewpoint of Western science, the underlying logic of Mêbêngôkre management.

Mêbêngôkre techniques of long-term management of forest savannas, with regard to both floral and faunal resources, represent an alternative to the destructive development models offered by timber extraction, agroforestry, agriculture, and cattle ranching. Native animal and plant species can be utilized, while being conserved, if indigenous integrated management principles are adopted.[6] Mêbêngôkre understanding of forest growth also holds useful lessons for those studying the restoration of degraded forest ecosystems.

Ethnopedology: Indian Understanding of Soils

The Mêbêngôkre have a sophisticated understanding of soils, which are classified according to horizontal and vertical distinctions based on texture, color, drainage qualities, friability, and stratification. Soil qualities are frequently related to indicator plant species that allow Indians to predict the flora and fauna associated with specific soil types, each of which is managed differently according to its individual characteristics.

The Indians modify local soils by using different types of ground cover such as vegetation, logs, leaves, straw, and bark to influence soil moisture, shading, and temperature. Holes are sometimes filled with organic matter, refuse, and ash to produce highly concentrated pockets of rich soil. Old banana leaves, stalks, rice straw, and other organic matter are piled (and sometimes burned) in selected parts of fields to create additional local variations.

The Mêbêngôkre have dozens of types of plant ash, each of which is said to have certain qualities preferred by specific cultivars. Plant ash is an important component in all aspects of indigenous agriculture.

The well-known *terra preta dos indios*, the soils formed through Indian occupation, are extremely rich and are distributed throughout Amazonia, but little is known of their formation as they have been considered to be the results of historical practices that are no longer followed. There are, however, numerous Indian groups like the Mêbêngôkre that continue to manage soils to improve fertility and productivity.[7]

The study of indigenous uses of ground cover, mulch, organic matter, and ash could lead to the development of modern agricultural systems in Amazonia that succeed in improving, rather than degrading, soils.[8]

Ethnozoology

Indians are astute observers of many aspects of animal behavior: mating, nesting, feeding, hunting, predator-prey relationships, diurnal and nocturnal habits, etc. They teach these lessons to their children partly through the rearing of pets in the village, and also by encouraging children to learn the behavior patterns and feeding habits of different animal species that are considered to have their own "personalities." Like other tribes, the Mêbêngôkre conscientiously study animal anatomy, giving special attention to the stomach contents of game animals.

A precise knowledge of insect behavior is utilized by the Mêbêngôkre in the control of agricultural pests. For example, nests of ants of the genus *Azteca* are deliberately placed by the Indians in gardens and on fruit trees which are infested with leaf-cutter ants (*Atta* sp.). According to the Mêbêngôkre, the Azteca ants have an odor which repels the leaf-cutter ants. In the same manner, the Indians cultivate several plants which have extra-floral nectar glands, often on the leaves or stems, which attract predatory ants to serve as "bodyguards," for the plant. Several species of predacious wasps nest preferentially under the leaves of banana trees which Indians plant to form a living wall around their fields. Thus, knowledge of insect behavior is an important aspect in the manipulation of the natural biological control of agricultural pests.[9]

Ethnomedicine and Ethnopharmacology

One of the most productive areas of ethnobiological research is ethnopharmacology. Plants used medicinally by native peoples are a prime source of useful drugs for the pharmacological industry. Intensive study of indigenous plant and animal preparations and their administration, can enrich conventional medical knowledge. Data on the parts of the plants which are used in medicines, the ecological preferences of these plants, the seasonal cycle of their flowering and fruiting, and the soils in which they grow are important since these factors influence the amounts of pharmacologically-active ingredients in the harvested plants.[10]

Not only can ethnopharmacological studies contribute to the discovery of unknown drugs, but [they] also reveal new sources of known pharmaceuticals. This is especially important for countries like Brazil where imported medicines are exorbitant in cost.

Ethnopharmacology should be coupled with ethnomedicine to be truly effective. For example, Elisabetsky and Posey have suggested how research into two Mêbêngôkre folk disease categories can advance knowledge of symptoms that complicate diarrhoea and dysentery—the major killers in the humid tropics.[11] The Mêbêngôkre classify over 150 types of diarrhoea/dysentery, each of which is treated with specific medicines. Ethnopharmacologists and physicians frequently forget that disease categories are, like all phenomena, socially classified and not universal: folk categories, as in the Mêbêngôkre case, are often more elaborate and detailed than their Western counterparts.

Ethnoagriculture and Agroforestry

Research into indigenous agriculture has resulted in valuable information on pest control without costly chemical sprays and additives. The use of natural predators, insecticides, and fertilizers make indigenous agriculture both inexpensive and energy efficient. Intercropping of cultivars appears to be another key factor in natural control, as does the extensive use of "trap crops" within and at the margins of plots. "Natural corridors" maintained between Mêbêngôkre fields serve as biological reserves that maintain species diversity, while facilitating the re-establishment of plants and animals during forest regeneration.

When applying the restrictive term "agriculture" to Mêbêngôkre management of domesticated and semidomesticated plants, one must consider that indigenous agriculture begins with a forest opening into which useful species are introduced and ends with a mature forest of concentrated resources, including game animals. The cycle is repeated when the old-field forests become too high and dense for efficient production and are cleared again.

The Mêbêngôkre also practice long-term management strategies to maximize firewood production using a number of techniques, including seasonal cutting schedules, pruning, vertical extraction preferences, limb and trunk size choices, maturation decisions, and drying capabilities.

There is an urgent need in Amazonia for the implementation of integrated agricultural and forest management, which would include both plant and animal resources and not be destructive to the local environment. Indigenous systems, like those of the Mêbêngôkre, have functioned successfully for millennia and offer many ideas for the successful implementation of diversified and sustainable agricultural and forestry practices.

Myths and Ecological Concepts

A knowledge of complex ecological interrelationships is sometimes expressed in the highly codified and symbolic forms of myth and ritual. These can only be understood when one lives and participates in an Indian society for some length of time.

The Mêbêngôkre recognize two mythological entities that illustrate how beliefs can function as ecological concepts. One is *Bepkororoti*, which is the spirit of an ancient shaman unjustly killed by fellow tribesmen while seeking his hereditary share of tapir meat after a hunt. His spirit now manifests itself in the form of rain, lightning, and dangerous storms, which can kill people or destroy crops. He becomes angry when people do not share, and fear of his vengeance compels the Mêbêngôkre to be generous. To placate *Bepkororoti*, Indians cater to his fondness for honey by leaving behind a portion of honey, pollen, and brood in raided hives. As a result, some species of stingless bees return to disturbed hives and re-establish colonies. The belief in *Bepkororoti* thus serves to preserve bee colonies and ensure continued honey production.

The *mry-kàák* is an entity that takes the form of an electric eel-like animal, twenty or more meters in length, that lives in deep pools of water. It is the most feared of all creatures, since it can kill with its powerful electric shock from a distance of five hundred meters or more. It is thought to subsist on minnows and, whenever the Mêbêngôkre see schools of spawning fish or minnows, they stay clear of the area for fear of the *mry-kàák*. This practice serves to protect the minnows, which are the basic element of the aquatic foodweb of the river.

An Ideological Bridge Between Peoples

Mêbêngôkre ecological adaptations and agricultural methods offer new models for resource management of the Amazon without incurring the wholescale destruction which characterizes present development policies. If indigenous experience were taken seriously and incorporated into research and development programs, then the Indians would be recognized for what they truly are: a diligent, intelligent, and practical people who have adapted successfully to their Amazon environment over thousands of years. It is imperative that Indians and their respective systems of ecological management be protected so that they can develop according to their own social and cultural rules which we, in our ignorance, have only just begun to appreciate and understand.

Notes

1. *Survival International News* 22, 1988, 6.
2. Davis, S., *Victims of the Miracle: Development and the Indians of Brazil*, Cambridge University Press, 1977.
3. Ribeiro, D., *Os indios e a civilizaçao*, Ed. Civilizaçao Brasileira, 1970.
4. Posey, D. A., "Indigenous Knowledge and Development: An Ideological Bridge to the Future," *Ciência e Cultura* 35, 7, 1983, 877–94.

5. Anderson, A. and Posey, D., "Reflorestamento indígena," *Ciência Hoje*, 6, 31, 1987, 44–51.

6. Posey, D. A., "Indigenous Management of Tropical Forest Ecosystems: The Case of the Kayapó Indians of the Brazilian Amazon," *Agroforestry Systems* 3, 1985, 139–58.

7. Hecht, S. B. and Posey, D. A., "Management and Classification of Soils by the Kayapó Indians of Gorotire," in Posey, D. and Balée, W., eds., *Resource Management by Caboclos and Indians in Amazonia*, New York Botanical Gardens, New York, 1987.

8. Kerr, W. E. and Posey, D. A., "Nova informaçao sobre a agricultura dos Kayapó," *Interciência* 9, 6, 1984, 392–400.

9. Overall, W. L. and Posey, D. A., "Uso de formigas *Azteca* para controle biológico de pragas agricolas entre os indios Kayapó," *Rev. Brazil. Zool.*, 1987.

10. Elisabetsky, E. and Posey, D. A., "Pesquisa etnofarmacológica e recursos naturais no trópico úmido: o caso dos indios Kayapó e suas implicaçoes para a ciencia médica," *Primeiro Simpósio sobre os Trópicos Umidos*, Belém, Embrapa, 1987.

11. Elisabetsky, E. and Posey, D. A., "Etnofarmacologia dos indios Kayapó do Gorotire," *Rev. Brazil. Zool.*, 1987.

---

19 Nigel J. H. Smith ◆ Colonization Lessons from a Tropical Forest

These excerpts from geographer Nigel Smith's classic study of the Transamazon Highway clearly demonstrate the failure of development programs based on the building of roads into rainforest frontier zones. Focused upon the problems associated with colonization of the Amazon basin by family farmers, this article discusses a number of aspects of rainforest colonization, including the causes of forest clearance. It provides a wide-ranging discussion of the many problems associated with agricultural colonization, thereby showing why the current approach to land use may not be the most appropriate one for the Amazon.

Smith shows how the Amazon has repeatedly defeated human attempts to tame it. Despite the claims of the proponents of developing the Amazon, the region has not proved to be a "motor of development." The Transamazon project certainly failed to meet its goals—at least by 1981, when this article was written—and these failures are due both to the characteristics of the Amazon's environment and to inappropriate development planning. Using colonization of the tropical rainforest as a substitute for real reform of the highly inequitable agrarian systems in long-settled regions does not work because it does not encourage sustainable development in either source

Reprinted from *Science* (November 13, 1981): 755–61, by permission of the author and the American Association for the Advancement of Science. © 1981 by the AAAs.

area or destination. Instead, it leads to massive forest destruction and associated environmental and social or economic impacts, such as degradation of soils, public health problems, and the loss of genetic stocks for future crop varieties and for commercially useful products, such as pharmaceuticals and industrial lubricants. Smith points out that the only lasting solution is to deal with the forces that cause the poor to migrate to the frontier. Inappropriate development policies only worsen matters, as the results of industrialization and large-scale agricultural modernization in northeast Brazil have shown.

In 1970, the Brazilian government announced plans to integrate the Amazon region with the rest of the country. The forest-clad region was to be crisscrossed by a web of pioneer roads with the east-west Transamazon Highway serving as the backbone for the system. The 3,300-kilometer Transamazon slices across the forest blanketing the southern interfluves of Amazonia, starting in Estreito on the Tocantins River and finishing in Cruzeiro do Sul near the Peruvian border. The entire road was opened with bulldozers by 1975. Plans called for settling one million families on one hundred-hectare farms along the highway by 1980.

The Transamazon Highway was designed to accomplish three main goals. First, this two-lane dirt road would provide a safety valve for the poverty-stricken northeast, a region with thirty million inhabitants increasing by one million a year. The 1970 drought that seared the backlands of the region and uprooted some three million people triggered the government's decision to build the Transamazon. Second, the highway would help fill a demographic void in a region occupying half of Brazil's territory but containing only 4 percent of the nation's population. The Brazilian government was reluctant to leave such an immense space vulnerable to the covetous eyes of foreign concerns, and saw the Transamazon Highway as placing an indelible stamp of sovereignty on a land surrounded by an ever-increasing population and experiencing a growing scarcity of natural resources. Finally, the highway would create access to mineral and timber reserves that would fuel the country's spectacular 10 percent annual economic growth.

The Transamazon scheme has largely failed on all three counts. With the colonization phase of the highway now completed, only eight thousand families have been settled by the Instituto Nacional de Colonizaçao e Reforma Agraria (INCRA), the federal agency responsible for administering the project. Even allowing for the estimated sixteen hundred families that have settled spontaneously at the end of side roads and in forest reserves, the highway scheme has clearly not even come close to achieving the colonization target.

Although three quarters of the colonists were supposed to be northeasterners, only 40 percent of the settlers have come from that parched region. The humid valleys of the Transamazon have accommodated twenty-three thousand *nordestinos*, but since the highway was built, the population of the northeast has grown by six million. The Transamazon has thus absorbed less than 1 percent of the region's population growth. The failure of the highway to relieve the demographic pressures and social strife in the northeast was highlighted in 1980 when drought once again struck the region. This time, the lives of nine million people were disrupted, resulting in food riots in several towns in the state of Paraíba.[1] The drought has continued into 1981 and the incidence of ransacking stores for food has spread to other states.

A major objective of the highway scheme, that of unlocking resources, has only been partly realized. Neither lumber nor mineral operations provide significant income for the Transamazon settlers. Only eight sawmills operate along the highway, and all are small. The most commercially important woods, such as mahogany (*Swietenia macrophylla*) and cedar (*Cedrela odorata*), have been mostly cleared within a fifteen-kilometer zone on either side of the highway. The high cost of transport fuel, and the enormous distances between sawmills, preclude the large-scale exploitation of other, less valuable tree species.

The highway has not led to the discovery of any sizable mineral deposits. Only one company, Mineração Taboca, extracts minerals along the Transamazon. The company has built a side road leading south from the Humaitá-Prainha stretch of the Transamazon to take out tin ore. The 1978 production from the mines totaled nineteen hundred metric tons, representing a quarter of Amazonia's reported tin ore production for that year. The ore is trucked to São Paulo in the industrial heartland of Brazil. Mining activity thus occurs only along a short stretch of the Transamazon.

The sluggish colonization rate and disappointing economic performance of the scheme triggered a major policy shift in the Brazilian government.[2] With the demise of a large number of the one hundred-hectare homesteads, planners rethought their strategy for developing the Amazon with family-sized units. In 1973, the highway was opened for large-scale entrepreneurs, principally cattle ranchers. Plot sizes ranging from five hundred to sixty-six thousand hectares were made available for wealthy individuals and for companies. These vast parcels of land, set further back from the highway than the one hundred-hectare lots, are now being cleared. They total 2.7 million hectares, three-and-a-half times the area zoned for small farms. In order to better assess the viability of the smallholder in the agricultural development of Amazonia, the major ecological, cultural, and institutional factors that have retarded the progress of settlement along the Transamazon need to be highlighted.

The Ecological Setting

It is no accident that, historically, people have settled mostly along the margins of rivers in Amazonia.[3] Silt-laden rivers, such as the Amazon, create generous floodplains with fertile soils, abundant fish, and the convenience of cheap water transportation. In contrast, the interfluvial forests of the basin generally mask poor soils, leached by millions of years of torrential rainfall. The Transamazon Highway was clearly not designed to provide access to the better soils of the region.

The highway transect vividly reveals this unfavorable base for agricultural colonization. . . . Only 3 percent of the soils in the vicinity of the highway can be classified as naturally fertile. . . . Fertilizer prices are exceptionally high in Amazonia because the product must be imported from other regions. Consequently, farmers rely largely on nutrients that are captured in plants and released when the vegetation is burned in field preparation.

The thin layer of ash left on the ground after the annual burning is vulnerable to erosion and rapid leaching. Storms can be intense. In the Marabá area of the Transamazon, for example, sixteen centimeters of rain fell within a few hours in February 1974. The onset of heavy rains coincides with the planting season when garden plots are bare and the soil surface is exposed. Up to one hundred tons of topsoil per hectare can be lost within a year on fifteen-degree slopes planted to annual crops.[4] The severe loss of topsoil recorded from some fields along the Transamazon is not unusual in the humid tropics. . . .

The idea has been advanced that soil erosion in the tropics is not always detrimental to agricultural productivity. By stripping the highly leached mantle, it is argued, plant roots can penetrate closer to the weathering zone in the subsoil where nutrients are being liberated.[5] But in other parts of the Amazon basin, soil erosion clearly drains the nutrient reserves of the soils since most of the fertility is concentrated in the top five centimeters of soil.[6]

Erosion of roads is at least as serious as topsoil losses in Transamazon fields. From jet-cruising altitude, the Amazon forest appears to be growing on a monotonously flat plain. But the canopy conceals a generally crumpled topography. The relief of the Precambrian Brazilian shield, where close to half of the Transamazon colonists have settled, varies from sharply to moderately undulating. . . . Most of the highway transect is a seemingly endless sea of hills. During the rainy season, some sections of the highway are cut by lateral erosion which must be repaired during the dry season.

Many of the side roads are cut off entirely for several months. Harvested rice, the principal cash crop along the highway, frequently rots in fields because the grain cannot be removed and sent to driers.

The broken terrain slows traffic and boosts transportation costs. Trucks and buses cannot climb certain rain-soaked hills, and tractors have to pull the vehicles over the crests. Accidents due to the slippery road surface are frequent. . . .

Agricultural Yields

A major factor in the slowdown of the colonization rate has been the disappointing agricultural yields. Poor soils and erosion have already been mentioned as two important constraints to agricultural productivity. But a host of other ecological and sociological factors have led to low crop yields.

A poor selection of crops by planners is partly responsible for the generally depressed crop performance along the Transamazon. INCRA envisaged upland rice as the main cash and subsistence crop for Transamazon colonists. Favored by fiscal incentives, rice accounted for 30 percent of the 1978 income of 155 settlers sampled by the author. But heavy dependence on one crop for food and cash income is a risky policy, particularly in the tropics where weeds and pests proliferate all year. Most Transamazon farmers cannot afford to buy insecticides, fungicides, or herbicides. . . .

One of the reasons that rice yields are so low is that inappropriate varieties have been promoted by INCRA and Empresa de Assistência Técnica e Extensao Rural (EMATER), the agricultural extension service. The most commonly planted variety, IAC 101, was developed in Campinas in southern Brazil, barely within the tropics. The IAC 101 strain is unsuited to the climatic conditions of the Amazon basin. . . . In an effort to introduce more advanced agricultural techniques, planners overlooked local varieties of rice traditionally used by peasants.

Manioc, a basic staple of the Amazon region, was relegated to a minor role in the agricultural strategy of the colonization project. The root crop was perceived as a primitive cultivar with little economic potential. Nevertheless, manioc has several crucial advantages over rice as a catalyst for agricultural development, especially during the start-up phase of a settlement scheme in Amazonia.

The myth that manioc is an economically unattractive crop has been dispelled by the Transamazon experience. On first-year plots, yields of the root crop easily attain twenty tons per hectare, in part because of the light pest damage.[7] Most of the crop is converted to flour for domestic consumption and sale. . . . A family of six can comfortably harvest three hectares of the tubers within a year and earn three thousand dollars from the sale of flour.

Although the relative financial advantage of manioc cultivation will vary according to such factors as market conditions and variety planted, in most cases cropping the tuber is more profitable than rice cultivation.

Manioc enjoys several other advantages over rice as a cash and subsistence crop in the uplands (*terra firme*) of Amazonia. Since the roots can be harvested from six months to three years after planting, farmers do not compete with each other for labor or machinery at harvest time, as in the case of rice. Rather, manioc cultivation fosters mutual assistance, because neighboring families often help each other to process the crop. The roots can stay in the ground until roads are passable, and the flour can be stored for months with little deterioration. Finally, the tubers are a far more productive and reliable source of carbohydrates, providing three times more calories per hectare than rice.

What crops are planted is determined largely by bank policy. Farmers can obtain bank loans, arranged through EMATER, to plant rice, but not for manioc or other root crops. Most of the colonists are poor, so they depend heavily on loan installments to purchase equipment and to hire workers.

The credit system operating along the highway has worked against the interest of settlers in other ways. The processing of loans takes considerable time and farmers must make several financially onerous trips to town to expedite paperwork and to pick up installments.[8] Sometimes a loan payment is released after the dry season has begun and when newly planted crops will wither. Furthermore, the state-owned Bank of Brazil provides more generous loans for farmers willing to grow crops in fields cleared from mature forest since yields are usually higher than in garden plots opened in second growth. Consequently, the bank policy encourages a wasteful destruction of forest; settlers often clear far more space than they can use.

As a long-term solution to the cash crop problem, EMATER and INCRA have encouraged the planting of perennial crops. A perennial vegetative cover is far preferable to annual cropping for most of the *terra firme* of Amazonia.[9] Pepper, bananas, cacao, and cattle pasture have been especially promoted along the Transamazon. Although these crops provide better soil cover than annuals, in most situations they still require fertilization to maintain productivity over the long term. Costs of maintaining yields of the perennial crops are likely to increase because of a buildup of pests and plant diseases.

The Transamazon was envisaged as a fresh beginning for tropical crops. For the most part, the highway slices through wilderness containing few species-specific crop pests and diseases. But it did not take long for fungi and agricultural insect pests to disperse along the corridor of disturbance created by the highway. By 1975, for example, a disease caused by the fungus *Fusarium solanum piperi*, resistant to chemical control, was severely damaging pepper plantations along the Transamazon.[10] The fungus probably penetrated the colonization zone with infected cuttings or stakes. The useful life of a pepper plantation has been reduced from an expected fifteen years to an average of seven years, and now the crop is marginally profitable.

Banana growers have also felt the destructive impact of introduced plant diseases. Initially, bananas were produced in abundance along the highway, and much of the crop during the first few years of settlement rotted on the ground because the local markets were too small to absorb the output. After 1974, the prospects for banana growers along the Transamazon improved markedly when the Belém-Brasília highway was paved. Truckers were able to buy bananas from Transamazon colonists and transport the fruits to markets in Belo Horizonte, Rio de Janeiro, and São Paulo before they spoiled. As marketing opportunities improved for banana growers along the highway, disease struck. Several fungi, especially species of *Fusarium*, now severely attack banana groves, often before a lucrative harvest can be cut.

Although most of the agricultural pests and diseases have seemingly spread along the Transamazon Highway in the wake of settlement, some crop damage undoubtedly occurs from insects that were already present in the forest before the highway was built and from insects and other potentially damaging organisms that flourish in light gaps created by tree falls. Some crops are at risk because their wild relatives in the forest act as reservoirs of disease. . . .

Public Health Problems

Diseases in humans have also played an important role in depressing agricultural yields. As in the case of crop diseases, the forest serves as a pool for some pathogens potentially transmissible to settlers. The forest shelters parasites and vectors, and human modification of the landscape favors disease transmission. However, the most important public health problems have been introduced by colonists.

The popular image of the rainforest teeming with tropical diseases that enervate settlers has not proved to be the case along the Transamazon. Few of the zoonoses in the forest have actually infected settlers. . . .

The most serious public health problems along the Transamazon are caused by the importation of pathogens by people. For example, in any given year, from 5 to 25 percent of the highway population contracts malaria, which can debilitate a person for a month or more. In a 100 percent sample of patients from the Transamazon region admitted to the Marabá and Altamira hospitals in 1973, malaria accounted for 53 percent of the admissions, exclusive of maternity patients. In 1978, the disease still accounted for 44 percent of admissions from the Transamazon region.[11]

Although much remains to be learned about the epidemiology of malaria in the Amazon basin, it is clear that incoming settlers and migrant workers, especially from the northeastern state of Maranhão, are responsible for bringing the etiological agents *Plasmodium falciparum*, *P. vivax*, and *P. malariae* to the Transamazon region. No nonhuman reservoirs have been found in the wild for these parasites; however, alterations of drainage conditions have favored the buildup of potential vector populations that already existed in the forest prior to settlement.

The identity of the vector, or vectors, of malaria along the Transamazon has not been established with certainty, but *Anopheles darlingi* is the most common vector for the disease in most of the Brazilian Amazon and is implicated as a major vector along the Transamazon. The mosquito prefers partially shaded, neutral, unpolluted, and relatively still water for breeding, conditions rarely found in the rainforest where streams are generally strongly acid and heavily shaded.[12] However, water culverts under the Transamazon were often installed above the gradients of streams crossed by the road; consequently, hundreds of watercourses have backed up forming small lakes which vary in surface area from 0.5 to 10 hectares. The artificially created ponds allow sunlight to penetrate the water, while soil erosion from cleared banks introduces nutrients and reduces the acidity of the water, thereby creating more favorable breeding conditions for anopheline mosquitoes. Since settlers often build their homes close to the ponds they are easily exposed to malaria vectors. . . .

Other major public health problems along the highway, such as gastroenteritis and helminthiasis, are related to poor standards of hygiene. Contaminated drinking water is a primary source of gastrointestinal disease among all age groups along the Transamazon. Less than 10 percent of the highway population has access to piped water; most people obtain their drinking water from streams, ponds, and poorly covered wells. Less than 5 percent of the Transamazon settlers use latrines on a regular basis; most of the colonists take care of physiological necessities in a nearby patch of vegetation. Although less than 1 percent of the highway settlers required hospital treatment for intestinal problems in any given year, the entire population probably suffers from some form of gastroenteritis during a twelve-month period. Diarrheal diseases, as in other regions where hygiene standards are low, are a leading cause of infant mortality.[13] Gastroenteritis was responsible for 48 and 51 percent of the hospital deaths of children under five years old in 1973 and 1978, respectively.

Lessons

It is not enough to open up frontier areas with highways, divide the land into parcels, provide credit, and expect largely illiterate farmers with few capital resources to flourish. This approach has led to disappointing results in other tropical regions, such as Indonesia's outer islands.[14] Along the Transamazon, many settlers soon fell victim to a biased and inefficient credit system, a poor selection of crops, infertile soils, and isolation from large markets.[15] Planners need to pay closer attention to ecological factors, such as the suitability of soils and proposed cultivars. State colonization projects in Malaysia have generally been more successful than those in Amazonia, partly because the soils of settlement zones are more fertile and because there has been an emphasis on tree crops that protect the soil surface and discourage weeds.[16]

The failure of the Transamazon scheme is also due to an inadequate screening procedure. Some colonists arrived with land speculation in mind and little or no prior experience with agriculture. The colonization scheme not only failed to absorb a significant portion of the landless in the northeast, it did not provide a secure environment for the few thousand families it did accept. Close to half of the Transamazon lots have been sold at least once.

It is an unwise policy to regard Amazonia as a convenient depository for the landless from other regions. In most instances the incoming settlers contribute little to the development of the Amazon basin.[17] On the contrary, massive forest destruction, degradation of soils, and the loss of genetic stocks for future agricultural experimentation and drug plants ensue.[18] The forces responsible for driving the itinerant folk need to be dealt with in order to slow the flow of migrants to manageable proportions. In the northeast, for example, the government-subsidized strategy of industrialization and irrigation has created few jobs while displacing more farmers than have been settled.[19] More effective attempts at land reform, easier access to birth control methods, and increased attention to rural development engaging small-scale farmers would alleviate some of the demographic pressure in the region. In southern Brazil, diminishing plot sizes, steeply rising land prices, and severe frosts in recent years are forcing many families to migrate north, particularly into Rondônia.[20]

Political expediency and the buffer of an immense, sparsely settled region will inevitably result in a continued stream of settlers into Amazonia. In order to better accommodate the influx of land seekers, future colonization schemes could be located along the floodplains of silty rivers such as the Amazon, Madeira, and Purus. In this manner, colonists could take advantage of fertile alluvial soils which are annually rejuvenated, abundant fish supplies, and cheap water transportation. Most major towns and cities in

Amazonia are located along rivers, so large markets would be more accessible to floodplain farmers. While the alluvial soils are flooded during the four- to seven-month high-water seasons, colonists could attend to perennial crops, such as cacao and rubber, on nearby uplands. Unrestricted settlement of floodplains could nevertheless trigger serious ecological effects. Many of the fishes important in subsistence and commerce depend heavily on floodplain forests for shelter and food; large-scale disruption of their habitat would considerably reduce their numbers, thus restricting supplies of a major source of dietary protein in the basin.[21]

The Brazilian government has spent close to $500 million on the Transamazon project. Few Third World countries, Brazil now included, can afford to invest such sums in schemes that produce limited social and economic benefits. The Transamazon Highway was conceived when the cost of petroleum was only two dollars a barrel on the world market; Brazil currently pays close to thirty-six dollars a barrel for the product. In 1980, Brazil spent $11 billion, half of her export earnings, to import petroleum. Considering Brazil's mounting external debt, now approaching $60 billion, it would be wise to concentrate scarce public funds on consolidating the gains of earlier colonization efforts in the Amazon region, and to focus any new settlement projects on floodplains where settlers can benefit from the world's largest network of rivers.

The Transamazon project fits a pattern of the repeated failure of government-directed settlement schemes in South America.[22] Blueprints are usually drawn up with little or no understanding of the ecological and cultural conditions of settlement areas. Bureaucratic controls often hamper the development of colonization zones. Spontaneous migrants, already highly motivated, should be given land titles relatively quickly and access to an efficient credit system. It is unrealistic, though, to expect pioneer zones to foster the blossoming of egalitarian communities. The great diversity of soil types and the different cultural values of settlers will usually lead to social stratification.

Notes

1. N. J. Smith, *Rainforest Corridors: The Transamazon Colonization Scheme* (Univ. of California Press, Berkeley, 1982); R. J. Goodland and H. S. Irwin, *Amazon Jungle: Green Hell to Red Desert?* (Elsevier, Amsterdam, 1975).

2. E. F. Moran, *Developing the Amazon* (Indiana Univ. Press, Bloomington, 1981).

3. B. J. Meggers, *Amazonia: Man and Culture in a Counterfeit Paradise* (Aldine/ Atherton, Chicago, 1971); H. O'R. Sternberg, *The Amazon River of Brazil* (Erdkundliches Wissen, Wiesbaden, 1975), vol. 40; N. J. Smith, *Ann. Assoc. Am. Geogr.* 70, 553 (1980).

4. N. J. Smith, thesis, University of California, Berkeley (1976), p. 111.

5. J. E. Spencer, *Shifting Cultivation in Southeast Asia* (Univ. of California Press, Berkeley, 1966).

6. I. Falesi, *Bol. Tec. Inst. Pesqui. Exp. Agropecu. Norte* 55, 1 (1972); and see N. J. Smith, thesis.

7. Reported yields for manioc in other tropical areas generally range between five and fourteen tons per hectare [E. S. Normanha and A. S . Pereira, *Bragantia* 10, 179 (1950)]; W. C. Jones, *Manioc in Africa* (Stanford Univ. Press, Stanford, Calif., 1959); C. H. Hendershott et al., *Feasibility of Manioc Production in Northeast Brazil* (Univ. of Georgia, AID/LA 681, Athens, 1971). In most tropical regions, manioc is often planted last in the cropping sequence, when soil nutrient reserves would normally be low. In Amazonia, yields are usually higher because pest and disease attack is lighter [M. Albuquerque, *A Mandioca na Amazonia* (Superintendencia de Desenvolvimento da Amazonia, Belem, 1969)].

8. E. F. Moran, *Agricultural Development in the Transamazon Highway* (Latin American Studies Working Papers, Indiana University, Bloomington, 1976).

9. R. Goodland, H. S. Irwin, and G. Tillman, *Ciencia e Cultura* 30, 275 (1978); R. Goodland, *Environ. Conserv.* 7, 9 (1980).

10. P. M. Fearnside, *Turrialba* 30, 35 (1980).

11. See N. J. Smith, thesis; the decrease in the number of patients entering the public hospitals from the Transamazon is not due to improved health conditions among highway settlers. Whereas the Transamazon population grew modestly during the 1973–1978 period, that of the towns of Marabá and Altamira spurted. In 1973, approximately 20,000 people lived in Marabá; by 1978, that number had reached 40,000. The population of Altamira also doubled during the same period, from 15,000 inhabitants in 1973 to an estimated 30,000 by 1978. The public hospitals of Altamira and Marabá, operated by Serviço Especial de Saúde Pública (SESP), contained 95 beds in 1973. Five years later, only 125 beds were available in the two hospitals in spite of the increased demand for patient care.

12. G. Giglioli, *Agric. J. Br. Guiana* 9, 197 (1938); L. M. Deane, O. R. Causey, M. P. Deane, *J. Hyg. Monogr. Ser.* 18, 1 (1946); L. M. Deane, O. R. Causey, M. P. Deane, *Rev. Serviço Espec. Saúde Públ.* 1, 827 (1948); L. M. Deane, J. F. Ledo, E. S. Freire, V. A. Sutter, J. Cotrim, G. C. Andrade, *Anais do Setimo Congresso Brasileiro de Higiene Sao Paulo* 1, 455 (1949); A. Vargas and A. C. Sá, ibid., p. 385; M. Pinotti, *Trans. R. Soc. Trop. Med. Hyg.* 44, 663 (1951); F. M. Bustamante, *Rev. Bras. Malariol. Doenças Trop.* 9, 181 (1957).

13. W. Ascoli, M. A. Guzman, N. S. Scrimshaw, J. E. Gordon, *Arch. Environ. Health* 15, 439 (1967).

14. J. M. Hardjono, *Transmigration in Indonesia* (Oxford Univ. Press, Kuala Lumpur, 1977); W. L. Collier, *Prisma* 18, 32 (1980).

15. C. H. Wood and M. Schmink, in *Changing Agricultural Systems in Latin America*, E. F. Moran, ed. [special issue of the *Journal of Third World Studies* (1978)], pp. 77–93.

16. R. Wikkramatileke, *Ann. Assoc. Am. Geogr.* 55, 377 (1965); *Geogr. Rev.* 62, 479 (1972).

17. R. F. Skillings and N. O. Tcheyan, *Economic Development Prospects of the Amazon Region of Brazil* (Center of Brazilian Studies, Johns Hopkins Univ., Washington, DC, 1979).

18. A discussion of the importance of preserving large areas of tropical rainforests as a genetic resource can be found in N. Myers, *The Sinking Ark* (Pergamon, Oxford, 1979).

19. A. L. Hall, *Drought and Irrigation in North-East Brazil* (Cambridge Univ. Press, Cambridge, 1978).

20. R. Wesche, *Rev. Bras. Geogr.* 40, 233 (1978).

21. M. Goulding, *The Fishes and the Forest* (Univ. of California Press, Berkeley, 1980); N. J. Smith, *Man, Fishes, and the Amazon* (Columbia Univ. Press, New York, 1981).

22. M. Nelson, *The Development of Tropical Lands* (Johns Hopkins Press, Baltimore, 1973).

IV

Prospects for Development: Alternative Futures for Latin America's Tropical Rainforests

At present a great debate rages over what to do with the remaining forested regions of Latin America. The failures of past attempts to exploit the resources of regions such as Amazonia, as well as the growing political power and sophistication of groups seeking to preserve the tropical rainforest, have encouraged nontraditional approaches to developing these regions. Selections in previous sections of this book examine the problems associated with large-scale projects, such as Carajás and colonization programs along frontier roads. The selections in Part IV explore some of the alternative approaches to developing the tropical rainforest. Most represent attempts to find a path to "sustainable development."

Sustainable development is itself a contested subject, with different meanings to different groups of people. As used in this book, however, it refers to economic development based on sustained-yield use of renewable resources and an equitable social system in which everyone receives some of the wealth created by economic development. In other words, it has both environmental and social components. The success of sustainable development is measured not by economic growth alone, but by actual improvements in the quality of people's lives—which includes environmental health as well as improved family incomes or access to the resources necessary to meet basic needs.

In tropical rainforest regions, sustainable development entails preservation of some mature forest while encouraging ecologically sound exploitation and management of other forested areas. Inevitably, some areas will be converted to other uses entirely. The challenge is to identify the appropriate mix of land uses for the remaining tropical rainforest regions. Experts from the various natural and social sciences can provide information about the probable environmental and human consequences of alternative land uses in specific zones. The actual land use that materializes, however, will undoubtedly result from political struggles over rights to rainforest resources. Chico Mendes (Selection 20) provides some insight into the political aspects of development policy.

One approach to preserving the rainforest is to provide it with legal protection from commercial exploitation. The most traditional way to do this is through the establishment of national parks. In recent decades a number of Latin American countries have established national parks in an attempt to prevent the complete destruction of their forests. The troubled existences of most such parks reveal the difficulties associated with the uncritical adoption of models of conservation from the developed countries. In the underdeveloped economies of Latin America, conservation needs a different approach if it is to succeed. As long as the economic and social pressures that fuel deforestation persist in Latin America, and public support for parks is weak or absent, the boundaries of national parks will not be respected. Furthermore, when the inhabitants of designated parks are ignored during park planning, as they usually are, they will continue to use the resources of the park in order to meet their basic survival needs, as they have for generations. Tiny, underfunded national park agencies cannot protect the integrity of parks under these circumstances. The result has been the creation of "paper parks"—national parks drawn on maps but receiving little real development or protection. James Nations discusses in Selection 25 some aspects of the relationship between parks and Latin American society that should be considered in conservation planning.

The problems encountered by national parks are partly due to policymakers' lack of awareness of the human inhabitants of the forest. In a few countries, however, forests are protected as Indian homelands. By protecting the human rights of indigenous people, this kind of forest reserve also tends to ensure the ecological integrity of the forest. Peter Bunyard (Selection 21) shows how the Colombian government has recognized that the best guardians of the forest are, in fact, its indigenous inhabitants, who have preserved the forest over the thousands of years that they have lived in it.

Finally, preservation of some national parks and other reserves has been engineered by means of debt-for-nature swaps in a few Latin American countries. The debt-swap concept is widely seen as a model for funding conservation projects in the Third World. This new method for simultaneously reducing a country's crushing foreign debt and preserving some of its natural heritage is critiqued in Selection 24.

The tropical rainforest can provide the foundation for ecotourism. Tourism is a dynamic sector of the world economy, and nature-based tourism is one of its fastest growing segments. By 1990 in Costa Rica, for example, tourism had surpassed coffee exports as the number one foreign exchange earner. There is considerable controversy over ecotourism, however. Proponents argue that tourism attracted by intact tropical rainforest can provide good economic returns year after year, not just the one-time windfall produced by current methods of timber and cattle production. But critics point out that tourism revenues are notoriously volatile. Michael Lipske, in Selection 30, describes the positive effects of ecotourism in Belize. The exponential growth of unregulated ecotourism in Amazonia, however, has had its negative impacts, as discussed by Ty Harrington in Selection 29.

Another approach is to preserve forests as extractive reserves for the exploitation of renewable commodities on a sustained-yield basis. Such renewable forest products include latex (rubber), Brazil nuts, and babaçu (palms) in Amazonia (Selection 20) and resin in Honduras (Selection 22). Extractive reserves, as proposed by Mendes and others, represent a way for traditional forest people to continue living in—and making a living from—the tropical rainforest. Along these lines using the forest as a source of genetic material or pharmacologically active chemicals represents another alternative for simultaneously preserving mature forest and producing income (Selection 28). On the other hand, Selection 23 raises questions about this aspect of conservation by exploring some of the ethical issues involved in appropriating the accumulated knowledge of tribal peoples without crediting or paying royalties to them. Critics, however, point out that these approaches have limited possibilities for preserving large expanses of Amazonian forest. They support only a relatively sparse population, and not all areas of forest have adequate densities of exploitable resources. Proponents respond that densities of economically valuable species can be increased, and that there are probably as yet undiscovered resources in the forest that could be the foundation of future extractive economies. Furthermore, a system of extractive reserves could form just one part of a multi-approach model of forest conservation that also includes national parks, autonomous Indian lands, and national forests used for sustained-yield forestry.

Although timber has not been extracted in a sustainable way in the past, it could be in the future, given the economic and political will to encourage sustained-yield methods. Ecologists and foresters are in the process of exploring new forestry systems for the tropics. The Tropical Science Center in Costa Rica, for example, has developed a system of rainforest management based on the dynamics of natural forests that is described in Selection 27. John Browder (Selection 26) provides an overview of various options for managing production in tropical forests that were previously considered unmanageable because of their complexity.

At present a number of innovative and promising alternatives for developing tropical rainforest regions are emerging from both research and practical experience. The political struggles of traditionally powerless groups, such as Indians and rubber tappers, have focused the world's attention on the social aspects of what has generally been considered an environmental issue. The empowerment of the poor and dispossessed that has resulted from their struggle over rights to the tropical rainforest has led to powerful critiques of the traditional approach to development—and has generated many of the innovative alternatives presented in Part IV.

---

20 Chico Mendes ◆ Fight for the Forest: Building Bridges

Chico Mendes was an internationally renowned leader in the struggle of forest people against powerful Brazilian landowners over access to tropical forest resources. He was born in 1944 into a rubber tapper's family in Xapuri, in the state of Acre, near Brazil's border with Bolivia, and went to work tapping rubber at age nine. He never had the opportunity to attend school and did not learn to read until adulthood, when a Brazilian activist settled in Xapuri after fleeing Bolivian authorities who sought to stop his organizing of the peasants in their country. The activist taught Mendes not only literacy but also raised his consciousness about social justice and political action. Rubber tappers traditionally lived under virtual slavery, bound by debt to a seringalista *(owner of a tract of rubber-producing forest). Mendes joined the growing rural trade union movement, which, in the 1970s, had some success in breaking the hold that* seringalistas *had over the rubber tappers.*

During this period, however, a new threat to the rubber tappers arose: the expansion of cattle ranches. As seringalistas *sold off their holdings, the land frequently was purchased by cattle ranchers. They proceeded to clear the forest and replace it with pasture for their herds. Obviously the rubber tappers would lose their livelihoods if cattle ranching continued to expand. As the resistance movement by rubber tappers gained strength, so did the violence of the tactics employed by the cattle ranchers. A number of rural union leaders and other activists have been killed in this struggle. Chico Mendes joined their ranks in December 1988—number ninety in that year's catalog of murdered rural workers and their supporters.*

These excerpts from his own writings, published in 1989, describe the link between the economic interests of forest people and the preservation of the Amazon rainforest. Mendes proposes the establishment of extractive

From Chico Mendes (with Tony Gross), *Fight for the Forest: Chico Mendes in His Own Words* (London, 1989), chap. 3, by permission of the Latin American Bureau.

reserves as the mechanism for preserving both the forest and the livelihoods of the people who live there. He indicates the economic potential of an Amazon economy based on the extraction of renewable resources on a sustainable basis. Finally, he points out that the alliance forged between rubber tappers and Indians in the rural unions and trade associations has greatly strengthened the grass-roots movement to save the Amazon rainforest. Now the traditional animosity between these groups has given way to the need to join forces in the battle for their livelihoods and, in many cases, their lives.

We realized that in order to guarantee the future of the Amazon we had to find a way to preserve the forest while at the same time developing the region's economy.

So what were our thoughts originally? We accepted that the Amazon could not be turned into some kind of sanctuary that nobody could touch. On the other hand, we knew it was important to stop the deforestation that is threatening the Amazon and all human life on the planet. We felt our alternative should involve preserving the forest, but it should also include a plan to develop the economy. So we came up with the idea of extractive reserves.

What do we mean by an extractive reserve? We mean the land is under public ownership but the rubber tappers and other workers that live on that land should have the right to live and work there. I say "other workers" because there are not only rubber tappers in the forest. In our area, rubber tappers also harvest brazil nuts, but in other parts of the Amazon there are people who earn a living solely from harvesting, while there are others who harvest babaçu and jute.*

So what are we really after? Despite the threats, we're fighting for better marketing and price guarantees for rubber. We want better marketing policies and better working conditions for those harvesting nuts. But there are an infinite number of natural resources in the forest, so we also want the government to encourage the industrialization and marketing of other forest products that it has always ignored in the past.

There are other questions to be considered. A sustainable fishing industry could be developed, exploiting the resource in a rational way. The enormous variety of plants with medicinal properties in this forest could prove very important to the country, if only some research was done. The universities, not only in Acre, but throughout Brazil, should spend time researching the Amazon region. I believe if this happened, and if the government took it all

---

*Babaçu refers to either of two palm species, *Orbignya martiana* and *O. oleifera*, whose fruit and leaves have a number of uses, both commercially and for subsistence. Jute is a fiber crop.—Ed.

seriously, then in ten years the Amazon region could be very rich and have an important role in the national economy. . . .

Where did we get the idea of setting up the CNS [National Council of Rubber Tappers]? We discovered there is something called the National Rubber Council which represents the interests of landowners and business-men but not the interests of the rubber tappers, so we thought, why not create an organization as a counterweight to all that bureaucracy and try to stop the government messing the rubber tappers about? The First National Congress set up the CNS and elected a provisional executive committee.

The CNS is not meant to be a kind of parallel trade union, replacing the Xapuri Rural Workers' Union, for example. It is just an organization for rubber tappers. The growth of the trade unions was very important for us, but other agricultural workers including day laborers and so on are also members of the same union. Other kinds of agricultural workers have been seen as having particular needs and interests, but not rubber tappers; it's as though we were something that existed only in the past. So one of the reasons for creating the CNS was to recognize the rubber tappers as a particular group of workers fighting for a very important objective—the defense of the Amazon forest. The idea went down very well.

We also wanted to seek out the leaders of the Indian peoples in Acre and discuss how to unite our resistance movements, especially since Indians and rubber tappers have been at odds with each other for centuries. In Acre the leaders of the rubber tappers and Indian peoples met and concluded that neither of us was to blame for this. The real culprits were the rubber estate owners, the bankers, and all the other powerful interest groups that had exploited us both.

People understood this very quickly, and from the beginning of 1986 the alliance of the peoples of the forest got stronger and stronger. Our links with the Indians have grown even further this year. For example, a meeting of the Tarauacá rubber tappers was attended by two hundred Indians and six of them were elected to the Tarauacá Rubber Tappers' Commission. Indians are now beginning to participate in the CNS organizing commissions. In Cruzeiro do Sul about two hundred Indians are active in the movement and this year they have even joined in our *empates* [mass occupations of forest slated for clearing in order to stop the loggers from cutting the trees].

Our proposals are now not just ours alone, they are put forward together by Indians and rubber tappers. Our fight is the fight of all the peoples of the forest.

When the minister of agriculture met a joint commission of Indians and rubber tappers in his office, he was really taken aback. "What's going on?" he said. "Indians and rubber tappers have been fighting each other since the last century! Why is it that today you come here together?"

We told him things had changed and this meant the fight to defend the Amazon was stronger. People really took notice of that.

21 Peter Bunyard ◆ Guardians of the Forest: Indigenous Policies in the Colombian Amazon

Colombia has about 450,000 Indians, living mainly in the Amazon basin where they comprise about 95 percent of the population. The area they occupy, too, is substantial, representing about one quarter of the country's territory. The Colombian government recognizes that these indigenous tribal groups possess superior knowledge of how to live in the rainforest without destroying it, and it has set a remarkable precedent by granting them inalienable rights to millions of hectares of land. But the right to ancestral land is only half of the equation, as Peter Bunyard points out in this 1989 article in The Ecologist, *and will not alone guarantee conservation of the rainforest. Indians must be allowed, even encouraged, to maintain their traditional values and ways of life so that they can coexist with the market economy of the outside world.*

The Colombian Amazon encompasses some forty-seven million hectares—approximately one quarter of the entire territory of Colombia and nearly double the size of Great Britain. Over the last thirty years, annual deforestation throughout Colombia has varied between 660,000 and 880,000 hectares. Such a rate, if continued, would see most of the country's forests vanish within fifty years. However, much of Colombia's Amazonian forest is still intact, a consequence in part of its isolation from the remainder of the country.

At present, twenty-five million hectares of the Colombian Amazon are utilized by Indians, but at a very low population density. The population of the entire region is some 550,000, the majority of whom are recent settlers who live at the margins of the rainforest, having cleared it. Some thirty-eight million hectares were once covered in tropical moist forest, of which as much as six million hectares have been lost as the result of colonization, particularly following the "Era of Violence" which began in the 1950s and led to an exodus of thousands of peasants from their traditional homes in the Andean cordillera.

For the most part the colonization took place either in the Andean piedmont itself or just east of it in the llanos (savannah plains lying between

From *The Ecologist* (November-December 1989): 255–58. Reprinted by permission of the author and *The Ecologist*, Agriculture House, Bath Road, Sturminster Newton, Dorset DT10 1DU, England.

Colombia and Venezuela to the north of the Amazon rainforest). Such colonization and the resulting deforestation has had major environmental consequences, with massive erosion, landslides, and the drying up of small rivers. As in other parts of Latin America, much of the forest is converted into pasture for extensive cattle raising. Particularly during the 1970s, both the Colombian government and the World Bank gave support to the conversion of forest into pasture for cattle, despite the exceedingly poor returns and the ecological devastation. Such intervention has only aggravated the trend toward large holdings at the expense of the poorer peasant who was yet again displaced to wreak more damage on the forest ecosystem. Support for cattle raising appears to have become institutionalized within government agencies such as the Colombian Institute for Agrarian Reform—INCORA—and the Caja Agraria—the Agrarian Bank.

The situation in the lower Amazon region of Colombia appears to be stable at present, with little pressure on the forests. Nonetheless, schemes exist for the exploitation of the Colombian Amazon, for its timber and its supposed agronomic resources. Undoubtedly, pressures for deforestation are currently worse in other parts of Colombia, in particular in the forests along the Pacific coast which are now being exploited by Japanese timber companies. With their extremely high rainfall—10,000 mm per annum—these forests are some of the richest in ecological terms in the world. Their need for protection is a priority.

The eastern part of the Colombian Amazon, aside from the gold mining areas close to the border areas between Colombia and Brazil, and towns such as Leticia, La Pedrera, and Mitú, has virtually no colonists. In fact, the population consists almost entirely of some seventy thousand Indians organized into fifty different ethnic groups belonging to some ten different linguistic families. Where the forest is still intact the indigenous peoples make up 95 percent of the population.

Restoring the Forests to the Indians

The Colombian government is now deeply concerned over the future of the Amazon basin, not just those parts within its own territory, but also in the wider context of the effect of changes to the basin taking place in neighboring countries, and especially in Brazil, which has far surpassed all the other countries of the Amazonian Treaty (Ecuador, Peru, Bolivia, Guyana, Surinam, and Venezuela) in terms of the rate and extent of destruction. The Colombian government has therefore been actively seeking ways in which it can implement policies that will protect the forest and safeguard it into the distant future. Its hope is that other countries of the treaty will follow suit, as it is appreciated that destruction of the forest in one region may have repercussions on the well-being of the forest in others, especially as a result of climatic and hydrological changes.

Over the past fifteen years the Colombian government, under its various presidents, has been taking into consideration the rights of the indigenous population of its Amazonian territories. Negotiations between the various government agencies, including the Caja Agraria, the land reform agency (INCORA), the Institute for Natural Resources, Environment and National Parks (INDERENA), and the Division of Indigenous Affairs, came to fruition in April 1988, with the returning of the Predio Putumayo region into the hands of the Indians. Indeed, President [Virgilio] Barco's government has now begun a massive program of conferring land rights to all the many indigenous communities living in the country's Amazonian territories.

Over the past few years, more than twelve million hectares have been granted to the respective indigenous peoples, nearly half of which was handed over in April 1988. The Colombian word for these indigenous lands is *resguardo* and indicates the conferring of special rights that go beyond the notion of "reserve" or "reservation" insofar as the latter suggests a kind of bountiful "set aside" rather than an acceptance of prior rights. These rights, as enshrined in the laws concerning *resguardos*, signify that the land is the collective property of the Indian communities and is inalienable. The land cannot therefore be sold or transferred to non-Indian hands. The legal character of the *resguardos* is guaranteed by the government.

Discussion is now in progress over the granting of another six million hectares as *resguardos* in the northern part of the Colombian Amazon, in the State of Guainía, on the border between Colombia and Brazil. Should this land be granted as *resguardos*, some 200,000 indigenous people will have land rights over an area the size of Great Britain. Colombia has an estimated 450,000 indigenous peoples, approximately double the numbers officially recognized as being indigenous in neighboring Brazil.

Indigenous Peoples: Guardians of the Forest

As a result of the indigenist policies being pursued by Colombia, numerous indigenous communities now have the right to an exclusive territory that will serve them as a base for the development and fulfillment of their productive activities. They have the right to their own forms of organization, to establish their own rules, and to choose their own authorities. Moreover, they will be enabled to pursue a degree of autonomy in the management of their internal affairs and to enjoy the right to pursue development models that harmonize with their own needs. The hope is that, given the respect and recognition of the integrity of their territory, of their organization, customs, and traditions, they will be able to enjoy a peaceful and prosperous existence.

Acceptance of the prior rights of the Indians to the land is a major factor in the restoring of ownership, but equally significant is the government's recognition that the Indians alone to date have achieved a mode of existence in the rainforest that enables sustainability without causing long-term damage. They can therefore be considered its protectors: a role that the white colonizers have patently failed to fulfill.

Traditional indigenous peoples manage the forest in a fundamentally different way from that of the colonists. Nowhere is this more apparent than in their different approaches to farming the forest. For instance, the Indians avoid using the *vegas*—the fertile wetlands along the river—but create their *chagras* (or gardens) on firmer ground, one reason being their use of perennial rather than annual crops.

They also assiduously leave as much forest intact as possible since they see it as the fount of regeneration and of game and useful wild plants. Their forest economy is thus based on leaving a buffer zone a hundred or even a thousand times larger in area than that used around their communal houses for subsistence produce. Meanwhile, cattle have no meaning for them and, for the most part, they see little point in having them. To keep one cow necessitates the destruction of at least one hectare of forest.

In making their *chagras*, the Indians purposely do not burn the boundaries of the clearings nor cultivate them. In many of the *chagras*, they also plant various species of fruit trees and these form microhabitats which attract birds and bats and therefore accumulate their droppings, which invariably contain the seeds of a number of species which in germinating also contribute to the swift process of regeneration. Usually, the Indians plant some twenty-five to fifty fruit trees per hectare.

A *chagra* is chosen for the nature of its soil and vegetation. Primary forest is chosen in which there is little understory and not too great a concentration of surface roots, especially root mats. When understory is present that implies that the canopy is open and light is getting through, or that the soil is too wet, while root mats are difficult to burn and may need several burnings at intervals of one to two months. The soil must be between sand and clay, the former being good for yuca (cassava) and tuberous plants, while clay favors plantains, coca, and other fruit bushes. The Indians avoid flooded areas, finding the right places as a result of their hunting operations through the forest.

The settlement in any one area is maintained until the resources, especially the *chagras* and orchard, begin to dwindle. In general, the community may stay in one place for some twenty-five years, during which time they may have moved their gardens some dozen times.

Surviving the Market

The Colombian government has made it clear that the granting of indigenous rights over such extensive areas does not correspond exclusively to the needs of the Indian population but seeks the conservation of tropical rainforest ecosystems known to possess some of the greatest variety of fauna and flora of the entire Amazon region.

However, the fact that Indians are still living in the Colombian Amazon does not ipso facto guarantee the conservation of the forest. The introduction of a consumer-oriented western model of development into those areas could destroy within a generation the adherence of Indians to their own models, especially by undermining the authority of the traditional leaders— the community "captains" and shamans—whose role it is to oversee the activities of the entire community. The indiscriminate killing of game during the time of the skin trade in the 1950s and 1960s, carried out primarily by Indians in the pay of white dealers, can certainly be attributed to the breakdown of traditions within the communities and the loss of respect for the traditional leaders.

At present the Indians have little to market. They produce some rubber but by the time they have got it to market using Japanese outboard motors and extravagant quantities of fuel, the profits are practically zero. The Indians are at the mercy of the dealers, who come from Brazil and can keep the Indians waiting in town until they have no choice but to accept the low prices being offered. It would undoubtedly make all the difference to the communities if they could get a reasonable return on the rubber. Some leaders have suggested that if some of the profits on selling rubber were set aside, the accumulated funds could be used for such ventures as community schools.

Whatever activity is undertaken to get cash, the Indians are increasingly insistent that it should not interfere with the rituals and the underlying traditions of their society. Indeed, if all members of a community had conventional jobs, then the tribal structure would almost certainly break down. It is only through reinforcing ritual and tribal beliefs that authority is vested in the captains and shamans and a coherent community structure is maintained.

If the Indian communities are to survive, then it is vital that they retain their models of looking at the world and are not forced or persuaded to accept ours. Their most urgent challenge is to achieve a balance between the desire for certain manufactured goods and the desire to retain their cultures and the environment around them. The challenge is to achieve a useful and continuing dialogue between the Indians and both government and nongovernment agencies concerned with their welfare.

The task is formidable. Throughout the history of contact with whites—a history of slavery, torture, massacre, and disease—the most common method of getting the Indians wholly dependent has been to sell them goods, such as machetes and guns, and then keep them working until they have paid off their debts, which they never do, since the prices of the goods and the cost of labor are totally controlled by the white overlords, whether they be missionaries or dealers.

In an attempt to undermine this system of debt-peonage, and counteract its destructive cultural influence, the Division of Indigenous Affairs in the government tried to establish shops within the communities themselves which would be controlled and operated by the Indians. Such ventures were not wholly successful, a prime reason for their failure being the contradiction in the captain's role as giver and provider in a complex of reciprocal relationships with members of the community and the need to bring in hard cash to pay for the goods. Thus some captains who took on the responsibility of running the community shops, finished up giving away the goods that they had had to procure through paying hard cash because the giving away fitted in with the traditional role of captain.

Resilience in the Face of Change

Yet, despite the pressures, the Indians express an extraordinary resilience in their ability to recreate their traditions and ways of life. In all probability, such resilience is a consequence of a way of life that necessitates shifting the entire community every few years to a new base in the forest. Reconstruction and recuperation are very much part of the Indians' vocabulary, and they have seen enough of the misery and destruction following in the wake of white colonization and exploitation to be wary of the so-called benefits of development and progress. In effect, the regeneration of the forest itself following slash-and-burn gardening provides the Indians themselves with a model of the cycle of life and the natural forces of recuperation.

At this stage the indigenous communities require assistance in establishing a sound economic base which provides sufficient returns on their work so as to enable the acquisition of essential goods but does not undermine traditional and cultural activities. Help is also needed to overcome the health problems brought about largely through contact with colonizers and dealers. Again any assistance must be integrated with traditional methods of coping with disease. Finally, there is a need to provide education that is adapted to the cultural needs of the communities concerned. Here again, there must be subtle integration between the two cultures so as not to undermine the extant traditions.

Meanwhile the communities have a vital role to play in the conservation and protection of the Amazon basin. The creation of national parks within the territories of the Indians should provide a unique opportunity for showing that indigenous cultures and environmental management are wholly interlocked.

A Model to Follow

The Colombian government's open recognition of the close coupling between the traditions of the various communities and their management of the environment has clearly brought about a uniquely enlightened policy.

On April 23, 1988, Virgilio Barco, the president of Colombia, flew to La Chorrera in the Putumayo, and in the presence of the captains, leaders, and governors of the various Indian communities, signed the handing over of the Predio Putumayo. He told the Indians: "I bring you my greetings. I have come to give you some good news, a word of truth. At last your land is yours."

The Colombian government has now given the world a model of how to deal with the vexed problems of environmental degradation and of indigenous peoples with intrinsic rights to land and their cultures. It is to be hoped that the other countries of the Amazon Treaty of Co-operation will look closely at the initiatives emerging from Colombia and will do their part in protecting this most diverse of terrestrial ecosystems.

At least in the Colombian Amazon, there is a good chance, given continuing support from outside including both government and nongovernment sources, that the indigenous communities and the important elements of their traditions will survive. That being so, the forest too will have a far better chance of surviving intact. As Barco pointed out at that historic meeting in La Chorrera, "Land and indigenous peoples belong to each other."

22 Denise Stanley ◆ Demystifying the Tragedy of the Commons: The Resin Tappers of Honduras

Ever since 1968, when Garrett Hardin published his landmark paper "The Tragedy of the Commons" in Science, *it has been widely accepted that public lands are subject to overuse and degradation because there is no owner to take responsibility for their care. But a growing body of literature is challenging this "conventional wisdom" and is represented here by*

From *Grassroots Development* 15, no. 3 (1991): 27–35.

Denise Stanley's 1991 study of Honduran resin tappers. Stanley demonstrates that peasants are rational, goal-oriented, economic actors who respond to the economic, political, and institutional systems in which they live. She shows how government policies can have unintended negative impacts on rural people, who are largely invisible at the scale of the national economy. In particular, their stewardship of local natural resources goes virtually unrecognized by the urban elite classes and by government institutions such as departments of forestry or agricultural extension.

Stanley contends that within traditional economies, common land generally is not open access or unmanaged land; it is managed for the community's long-term benefit. Furthermore, private ownership does not guarantee stewardship, as the results of Latin America's beef boom have clearly shown (Selection 7). She concludes that the key to successful community forestry is controlling access to the resource base and developing rules for managing its use. Her study of resin tappers in Honduras provides a model of community forestry that could help preserve forests throughout Latin America.

"This forest belongs to the people of San José de Protección, Comayagua," says don Víctor Manuel Sánchez, founder of the community's agroforestry cooperative and a member of the national federation of resin tappers. He speaks slowly and firmly, giving voice to sentiments commonly heard in the rural highlands of Honduras. Yet his circumstances convey the precariousness of his convictions. Sánchez is speaking from the jail where he and other co-op leaders are being detained after being arrested the night before for trespassing.

For years members of the cooperative have tapped resin from pine trees growing on lands under the jurisdiction of the ejido, or the local municipality. Recently, a large tract of ejidal land was sold to an outsider from the capital city of Tegucigalpa who wished to enclose it for other purposes. When local resin tappers persisted, the new landowner had their leaders arrested.

Although the facts seem straightforward, the roots of the conflict are tangled. The landowner has title to the soil, but the state owns the trees. In the past, a state agency had given the cooperative's resin tappers usufructure rights and assigned them a production quota. Now it claimed neutrality.

Here, in microcosm, is the renewal of a long-standing debate over who owns the nation's forests and how they should be used. These questions were supposed to have been answered in 1974, when Honduras established the Sistema Social Forestal, or Social Forestry System, within the Corporación Hondureña de Desarrollo Forestal (COHDEFOR) to halt clearcutting by European and North American lumber companies, regulate the extraction and marketing of forest products, and finance government development programs. In effect, Law 103 nationalized the forests and created

COHDEFOR to administer their use. COHDEFOR would implement its mandate by encouraging farmers to join cooperatives or other work groups that would harvest forest resources, combat fires, and prevent overgrazing, illegal cutting, and slash-and-burn agriculture.

By the early 1990s, the system was in disarray. While producing only 15 percent of the nation's exports, woodlands continued to shrink at such an alarming rate they would vanish by the turn of the century. More than one third of the rural population still lived in forested areas, yet they remained among the nation's poorest people. Critics charged that drastic reforms were needed to prevent Honduras from falling victim to what an influential body of research has called "the tragedy of the commons."

This term was coined by Garrett Hardin in 1968 to describe how communal lands are inevitably degraded as population pressure rises and people rush to use available resources before others can do so. At about the same time, Harold Demsetz (1967) assigned blame for this depletion to communal forms of ownership that "fail to concentrate the cost associated with any person's exercise of his communal rights on that person." The remedy was to establish clear private property rights since an individual owner would "attempt to maximize [the land's] present value." Later writers of "the property-rights school," including Theodore Panayotou (1989), argued that public ownership also led to resource exhaustion and should be privatized along with other forms of communal property.

Arguments concerning the relative superiority of public or private ownership misinterpret the value and legitimacy of common property and communal management. Other authors have stressed the logic and sustainability of common property regimes. As [Daniel] Bromley (1989) writes, a confusion of terms exists. A common property regime is not a situation of open access; common property has a well-defined group of authorized users, a well-defined resource that the group will manage and use, and a set of institutional arrangements with rules of use for the resource. Like private property, common property can contribute to sustained forest management. S. V. Ciriacy-Wantrup and Richard Bishop (1975) also argue that common property, and communal management of resources, is not a disaster: "Common property is not 'everybody's property.' The concept implies that potential resource users who are not members of the group of co-equal owners are excluded."

Although the failures of the Honduran Social Forestry System are increasingly obvious, the diagnosis and cure are not. In reality, neither state, private, nor common property regimes have spotless records in environmental protection. The experience of cattle ranching in much of Latin America shows how private ownership can contribute to deforestation (Nations and Komer 1983), while the experience of Swiss and some African livestock herders shows that communal grazing systems can be ecologically sound (Netting 1976; Swallow 1990), suggesting that factors other than property ownership are at work.

Identifying those factors is crucial not only for Honduras, where the government is considering the privatization of its woodlands, but for rubber tappers in Brazil, nut gatherers in Peru, and other promising community efforts elsewhere in Latin America to increase incomes among the poor while protecting dwindling forests. The experience of the resin tappers in the Federación Hondureña de Cooperativas Agro-Forestal (FEHCAFOR) suggests how the tragedy of the commons can be avoided. A look at two affiliates—the Cooperativa Villa Santa-Los Trozos and the Cooperativa San Juan de Ojojona—reveals three determining factors: secure tenure, economic incentives, and institutional capacity.

Secure Tenure

"If a tree is productive, it can last twenty to twenty-five years," says Rosalio Espinal, president of FEHCAFOR and member of the Cooperativa Villa Santa-Los Trozos. "These trees are our livelihood, so we must protect them."

Juan Francisco Martínez, secretary of the Cooperativa San Juan de Ojojona, adds that "the government says the forests belong to COHDEFOR, but we are the ones who put out the fires, clear the underbrush, and look after the trees."

Long years of stewardship have convinced resin tappers that the forest is theirs, but despite their passionate conviction, national policymakers remain unconvinced that the rural poor can manage this resource. As the country undergoes a program of economic restructuring, reforms are being proposed for the state forestry system that threaten to reduce access by resin tappers and other community groups. These reforms are unlikely to work if they misread the cause of the past failures, confusing public ownership with common property and common property with open access. That is, one must understand the relationship between the prescribed Social Forestry System and actual tenure, that "bundle of rights" to extract value from an area that includes how people perceive, partition, own, and defend resources, formally and informally (Fortmann and Ridell in Raintree et al. 1987).

Currently, Honduran resin tappers operate under a combination of common, state, and individual property regimes. As previously mentioned, the state owns the trees, while the topsoil is privately, nationally, or municipally owned. Although Article 29 of Law 103 establishing the Social Forestry System apparently assigns to cooperatives and community groups exclusive access rights to tap resin and extract timber from national forests, legal tenure, in practice, is highly conditional.

To begin with, each cooperative must renegotiate its lease annually through a sales contract with COHDEFOR that spells out how many barrels of resin can be taken and how many board feet of lumber can be cut. The cooperative can only sell its timber to the authorized local sawmill, which has exclusive rights for marketing products from its "tributary" area. The contract also binds the cooperative to "submit unconditionally" to COHDEFOR's forest management plans in the area, forbids the cooperative from trying to block any contracts COHDEFOR signs with third parties, and specifies that "access to the area of resination is unrestricted."

The cooperatives that have prospered under the Social Forestry System have been able to informally organize and defend their tenure rights and the forest itself. The Cooperativa Villa Santa-Los Trozos is a prime example.

Villa Santa is a rural town of twenty-five hundred people in the municipality of Danli in the department of El Paraíso. Covered by a thick pine forest canopy and receiving abundant rainfall in excess of 1.5 meters annually, the surrounding mountainous zone is being populated by settlers from the parched southern areas of Honduras, including Sabana Grande and Nueva Armenia.

On May 16, 1973, the town's residents blockaded the main road for twenty-four days to keep tractors from an Italian sawmill from clearcutting the forest. "We felt obliged to defend the forest, even though we did not know what it could give us," says Policarpo Alvaringa. Assisted by university students and lawyers from Tegucigalpa, twelve strike leaders, who became known as *los primitivos*, or the wise old men, decided to form the cooperative Alvaringa would one day lead. A concession to use twenty-two thousand hectares of national forests was obtained from the newly organized COHDEFOR, and the co-op obtained 216 sets of modern tapping equipment on consignment from the Maya resin-processing company. After dividing the land among individual members for care and harvesting, the community was in business.

Members paid a quota into a savings fund for each barrel of resin they tapped, allowing the cooperative to purchase a truck for transporting resin from centrally located pickup stations to the processing plant in Tegucigalpa. A consumer store was opened to buy staples and agricultural supplies in bulk for discount sale. In 1980, the co-op began to market logs from trees past the resin cycle; they then diversified their income sources by marketing tree sprigs as binding material to tobacco companies in a nearby valley. By 1989, the cooperative had nearly two hundred members and a reserve fund of nearly thiry thousand dollars.

The key to this success has been the cooperative's ability to limit access to the forest. Today, most members have fenced in their tracts and live near enough to monitor entry. Forest claims can be bequeathed to family members after death, or transferred following resettlement, by making provisions with the cooperative secretary. A sharecropping arrangement, or *medias*, has been worked out that allows members to rent out their trees to a worker, who receives half the resin collected. And on two occasions, the co-op leadership has met with the national director of COHDEFOR to stop sawmill logging and other outside incursions.

The Cooperativa San Juan de Ojojona, located in the department of Francisco Morazán, has not been so fortunate. The area, which has been a resin-tapping center since the practice was introduced to Honduras in 1913, is marked by extreme poverty, growing aridity, rapidly dwindling forest cover, and high out-migration to nearby Tegucigalpa. In 1966, sixty peasants from several villages in the municipality of Ojojona joined together to form the nation's first cooperative for marketing resin. The Cooperativa San Juan blossomed under the Social Forestry System initiated in the early 1970s, growing to more than three hundred members, acquiring a truck, and starting a consumer store. Co-op leaders rose to prominent positions in the new national federation, FEHCAFOR.

The bubble burst in 1979 when the president, who was a former mayor of the municipality, absconded with nearly fifty thousand dollars. The organization was left in shambles. By 1989, resin production had plummeted to only 180 barrels, or 45 metric tons, less than 7 percent of the production in Villa Santa. Today, the Cooperativa San Juan has only thirty-five members, and has reserve capital of only about one thousand dollars.

The San Juan resin tappers live far from each other and far from their assigned plots, making it difficult to tend trees properly or defend them from outsiders. Cooperative President Bienvenido Martínez sadly noted that "anyone can come in to steal our resin cups, cut wood, and start fires . . . because the forests are ejidal, and there are no fences."

In this arid zone above valleys deforested by the cattle expansion of the 1950s, trees are increasingly sparse, and the rate of natural regeneration is low. Even if the cooperative had the knowledge and resources to reforest, the prevailing system of "open access" makes it futile. Both resin tapping and the forest verge on extinction.

The experience of these two cooperatives shows that the key to viable community forestry is the ability to control access to the resource base and develop rules for managing its use. The package of new legislative proposals to reform the Social Forestry System threatens to undermine strong cooperatives that have managed, despite COHDEFOR's policies, to achieve informal tenure rights, and push the weaker ones quickly over the edge.

Some of these proposals are intended to give economic incentives for forest protection, while potentially increasing government revenues. COHDEFOR's monopoly on wood exports has ended, and the stumpage fee for logging trees has nearly doubled. Also being discussed is a plan in which farmers would be paid to plant trees, tree ownership would be ceded to private property owners, and tax breaks would encourage conservation and rational use.

The transfer of usufructure rights to private owners would have an immediate impact on resin tappers such as those in San José de Protección, where outsiders are rapidly buying up the land. The main threat, however, comes from legislation to privatize public lands. One scenario would expand the fifty-eight tributary areas over which sixty-three functioning sawmills currently have jurisdiction, and give them exclusive rights to manage all production activities, including resin tapping, and the responsibility for reforestation. An alternative approach would pass forest jurisdiction from COHDEFOR to municipal governments, but resin tappers suspect the result would be the same. Lumber companies have the capital to promise greater short-term profits, and FEHCAFOR manager Salvador Meza wonders if the resin tappers' case will be misunderstood by "mayors who are very open to political pressure, and know little or nothing about forest care."

If lumber companies are able to enclose the forests and lock out community enterprises, it will affect both the rural poor and the environment. Sap can be harvested from a tree for as long as forty years, after which it can be cut for firewood or milling. Stands are kept intact for long periods, providing habitat for flora and fauna, maintaining watersheds, and preventing soil erosion. By offering small farmers a long-term, environmentally sound "cash crop," resin tapping discourages slash-and-burn agriculture by co-op members, and can sow the seeds for increased farmer receptivity to more sustainable methods of subsistence farming as well. Farmers living "with" the forest prove to be effective firefighters against both natural and manmade blazes, and cooperatives have mobilized their members on numerous occasions to keep their livelihoods from going up in smoke.

Meanwhile, FEHCAFOR officials and forestry technicians point to numerous examples of overexploitation by Honduran sawmills under the existing tributary system, and wonder, since many are foreign owned, if the mills will be committed to preserving the nation's forests over the long term once restraints are removed. Even if lumber companies are required to reforest, clearcutting disrupts habitat and magnifies many of the other ecological threats resin tapping avoids.

In late 1988, FEHCAFOR placed an advertisement in *La Tribuna*, Honduras's most prominent daily newspaper, warning the public that expansion of the tributary areas will "deliver [the forest] to the service of a few sawmills, hurting the majority of the Honduran people, who would be converted into poorly paid day laborers." Falling income will presumably increase the rate of migration to already burdened urban areas, and those who remain behind will have little incentive to protect someone else's property.

Whether resin tappers earning long-term income from pine trees or whether sawmills turning those trees into plywood for quick export will better safeguard forest cover is yet to be determined. What is certain is that cooperatives, like the one in Villa Santa, can operate as private corporate bodies to efficiently use forest resources and spark rural development among campesino farmers.

Economic Incentives

Secure tenure is a prerequisite for successful forestry cooperatives, but it is not sufficient. Evaluating tree-planting programs in Haiti, anthropologist Gerald Murray has said: "Ecological protection and reforestation occur only as secondary effects to activities that generate income. . . . Peasants are not villains or the blind [who need] to be educated, but rational, goal-oriented, economic actors."

Rosalio Espinal of the Villa Santa cooperative explains it more directly, saying, "We do not want to cut pine trees before they finish the resin cycle because that would be like butchering a milk cow."

Most resin tappers are small farmers who have taken up the trade to earn cash income to buy needed consumer goods and tide them over during the lean months while subsistence crops are being planted and before they are harvested. Working alone, a farmer can spend two or three days a week installing tubes and plastic drain cups into pine trees of the species *Pinus oocarpa, tecun amania, caribaiea, pinabeta,* and *costanero*, thinly scoring the bark with a blade to avoid damaging the wood, and pouring sulfuric acid into the scars to increase the flow. During the height of the resin-tapping cycle from January to May and during midsummer, a farmer can collect as much as a quarter metric ton of resin sap monthly per stand of five hundred trees, earning approximately three hundred dollars for the annual season. In Villa Santa, some tappers have access to as many as two thousand trees, with the average being around one thousand.

Unfortunately, the terms of trade have been highly volatile during the past decade, and future profitability is in question. Drastic price swings in the international market have created a boom-and-bust cycle, rising to forty-one dollars per quarter metric ton in the early 1980s, before plummeting to sixteen dollars in 1984, and inching back up to twenty-eight dollars four years later. From this fluctuating gross price, resin tappers paid nearly ten dollars per quarter metric ton in steady taxes to COHDEFOR and municipal governments and in co-op dues.

Part of the problem has been the resin tappers' inability to obtain market leverage domestically. They sell their resin to three companies that process it for export to the United States, Japan, and Europe as turpentine, or as rosin for soaps, dyes, and adhesives. The three firms have formed a legal oligopsonistic accord known as the Resin Fund, which sets the fixed price they will pay tappers and divides the processing pie into equal wedges. The fund does offer price stability for the six-month tapping season, but it has also been pegged to quality standards that tend to exclude resin collected from the poorest tappers and from marginal woodlands.

These economic trends affect farmers' decisions about whether to continue resin tapping. With the Resin Fund refusing to buy much "dirty" resin and having been burned by the wild price swings of the past decade, a number of cooperatives, many of them affiliated with the Central Nacional de Trabajadores del Campo, a national farm federation, have abandoned resin tapping for cutting firewood. Moreover, economic changes in 1990 make the situation precarious.

In March of that year, newly elected Honduran President Rafael Leonardo Callejas announced a liberalization of the foreign exchange system, a de facto devaluation that inadvertently threatened to drive resin tappers out of business. The action was designed to encourage exports for Honduran agro-industries while cutting imports and the trade deficit. The resin-processing companies were able to improve their domestic balance sheets by converting at a higher rate dollars earned abroad, while using their control of the resin market to avoid passing any of the profit through to tappers by paying them higher prices. Meanwhile, tappers were being squeezed at the other end as their input costs soared after import duty waivers and sales tax exemptions were abolished. The price of inputs such as sulfuric acid doubled, while the costs of plastic cups and steel blades increased by 30 percent.

After the companies refused to raise product prices, in May 1990 the FEHCAFOR cooperatives decided to withhold their resin from the market. By July, the cooperatives had negotiated a price increase of 20 percent, and sales resumed. Following another six months of tortuous negotiations, the Resin Fund announced that a further increase to fifty-two dollars per quarter metric ton would take effect in February 1991.

The common element in the dangers posed by plans to change the forest tenure system and undertake economic structural adjustment has been the invisibility of resin tappers to policymakers. The ability of FEHCAFOR to negotiate higher prices showed what could be accomplished through organization. But some farmers, including FEHCAFOR manager Salvador

Meza, thought that something more than organized reaction was needed. "It would be better," he said, "if we could expand our business by processing our own resin."

Institutional Capacity

The success of a cooperative or other community group involved in natural resource management depends on its usefulness to the people who join it. There must be an economically and legally secure activity if the enterprise is to get off the drawing board. Once people have come together, dynamic leadership and the development of managerial skills are needed to maintain the consensus and transform the enthusiasm of shared ideals into the nuts and bolts of essential services. The experiences of the Cooperativas Villa Santa and San Juan de Ojojona offer clues about why some community institutions gel to form a workable consensus while others cannot.

One might think that the crucial failure limiting the San Juan cooperative was its lapse in leadership when a former president embezzled funds. Surprisingly, both the Villa Santa cooperative and the federation FEHCAFOR itself suffered similar lapses, with the latter actually dissolving before being revived in 1984 by the Confederación Hondureña de Cooperativas (CHC). Before turning to the national level, it is instructive to see what can be learned from the resiliency of Villa Santa at the local level.

Four lessons can be learned. First, members shared a powerful experience of common participation in a community movement. Genaro Osorio, one of the twelve *primitivos* present at the outset, says, "It was the strike to block the sawmill from tearing up this place that got us motivated to start this co-op." The mystique of acting together to protect the forest adhered to the organization that followed, binding its members together.

Second, the Villa Santa area is plentifully endowed with natural forest tracts and a climate favorable for resin production. Most members have access to parcels in excess of one thousand trees, allowing them to earn enough to conserve the resource rather than cash it in. Mild temperatures in the area are conducive to the sulfuric-acid tapping method, which effectively doubles traditional yields. Good roads have facilitated the transport of resin, and the payoff from group marketing has encouraged diversification into other forest-based production activities. Multiple use strengthens the conservation ethos, and allows the cooperative to weather erratic price swings in one commodity.

Third, members were able to obtain credit to buy modern tapping equipment and learned how to use it from the beginning of the cooperative. "People from Maya [the resin-processing company that supplied the equipment] taught don Luis Alonso how to attach the cup and canal," recalls

Felipe Alemendares, one of the first members. "He experimented with this and showed me; it was quite easy and we all caught on quickly."

Almost by default, since COHDEFOR did not provide communities in the Social Forestry System with much in the way of credit or technical assistance, the cooperative stumbled on the "farmer first" adaptation of appropriate technologies that has been at the heart of numerous other successful rural development programs (Chambers et al. 1989). These methodologies, which have been pioneered by nongovernmental organizations (NGOs) throughout much of the developing world, show that farmers teaching farmers what they have learned from tinkering with new technologies in their own fields are often far more likely to succeed than extension agents trying to recreate experiments created by scientists at centralized research stations. Ironically, because the "farmer first" approach led to local adoption of the state-recommended cup-and-canal method, the cooperative earned the respect of COHDEFOR, gaining the ear of influential people who could help stop encroachment by sawmills into the forests around Villa Santa.

Finally, the strong participation within the cooperative led to the diffusion of leadership skills so that when the first president drained the organization dry, a new group of leaders rose up to reclaim those resources and reenergize the community enterprise. Remembering those days in 1985, Rosalio Espinal, one of the new leaders, says, "It was sad the way previous managers had robbed us of what we had worked so hard to make, but we younger men decided to fight back and recover the car and the money that was taken." The capital that was saved allowed the cooperative to buy its truck, start the consumer store, and make new investments.

The deficiencies of the Cooperativa San Juan de Ojojona are a mirror image of Villa Santa's strengths. The diffuse membership scattered among several communities, the already depleted ecological base of the area, the inability to sustain production or diversify its sources to make forestry attractive, and the weak leadership have undermined the ability to form a strong consensus around tenure rights and manage those claims effectively to curtail outside encroachment.

The common property literature revolves constantly around this theme: A breakdown in group decision making is the prime cause of common property regimes passing into open access and overexploitation. Community forest organizations must be sufficiently strong to exclude outsiders. The apparent failure in San Juan should not obscure a silver lining that might one day be mined if it is not overlooked by outside agencies. Five new cooperatives joined FEHCAFOR in 1990, raising the total membership from 2,700 to 3,145 individuals. What this suggests, despite the still unresolved conflict endangering what remains of the commons, is that resin tappers understand they must join together at some level to cut transport costs, market their product competitively, and broker outside support.

If that vision is to become a reality and a force for protecting the commons, it is vital to strengthen institutional coherence and decision-making capability. An Inter-American Foundation (IAF) grant of $249,000 to FEHCAFOR in 1986 has provided resources to strengthen both the federation and its member cooperatives. A rotating loan fund has been established so that member cooperatives can finance efforts to diversify production and boost yields. The establishment of such funds is crucial since few rural communities in Honduras have sources of informal credit, much less banks. Firefighting equipment has also been purchased that helped extinguish two blazes in Ojojona and another in Protección in 1989 alone. Leadership training programs and technical assistance to improve management, bookkeeping, and production skills were offered by FEHCAFOR, the Instituto de Formación Cooperativa, and the CHC.

Today, Rosalio Espinal, who helped revitalize Villa Santa, is the president of FEHCAFOR, which has undergone a rebirth of its own. Wrecked by leadership abuses in the late 1970s, it was reborn when the national confederation of cooperatives decided that an umbrella organization was needed to facilitate market transport and to negotiate higher prices for resin tappers. Since 1984, it has tripled in size to forty-eight affiliates, representing over half the country's six thousand resin tappers and accounting for nearly 70 percent of production.

Espinal must be satisified that since FEHCAFOR's reemergence, resin prices paid to tappers have more than tripled. Yet he must also be aware from his experience in Villa Santa that market diversification is key. Efforts by COHDEFOR to manage its own resin-processing plant to compete with the big three failed in the mid-1980s, so that might be too ambitious a step for the federation right now. Plans are under way, however, to construct a large warehouse and plant for filtering resin, which could then be exported to processors in the United States and Europe.

Pending an in-depth study of the economic, social, and political feasibility of such an undertaking, there are other signs emerging from local cooperatives that point to new opportunities and a looming danger. When the revolving loan fund was established to diversify production activities, many groups chose to bypass forest diversification to intensify grain production, plant coffee bushes, or start small-scale animal husbandry projects. In one sense this reflects the uncertain market conditions for resin, and the promising markets for other crops being opened up by NGOs such as World Neighbors in Guinope, where farmers have been able to increase their corn and bean yields fourfold in the past five years through intercropping, soil conservation, and organic manures. Since resin tappers are also farmers, channeling investments for maximum return is only natural.

However, it may also signal a growing unease at what is happening to the forest itself. Trees are often seen as "a gift of God," which will regrow naturally to provide resin, firewood, fence posts, animal fodder, shade, and building materials. It is still rare to think of trees as a source of water or, as a national radio program says, "the lungs of the nation." Yet farmers in Villa Santa and Ojojona have begun to complain that rainfall has decreased markedly during the past twenty years and that the soils are "tired." Even though the resin-tapping cycle lasts from twenty to forty years, farmers cannot help but notice that among the 500 to 1,000 trees currently being worked, only 100 to 200 new saplings are growing up naturally to replace them.

To avoid long-term decline, forest community members must have access to training in reforestation and in how to integrate farm and forest management for sustainability. Farmer-to-farmer efforts, such as those that led co-op members to replace plastic cups with recycled metal cans, or the experiments in San Juan de Ojojona that showed the cup-and-canal method could be just as productive without using sulfuric acid, suggest that innovation is available at the local level. The question is how to harness it. There is no effective federation-wide program to share what is being learned in individual co-ops, and COHDEFOR technicians are rare visitors to the field and have yet to even devise an education campaign to make the cup-and-canal technology widely available.

The experience of the Cooperativa Villa Santa shows the promise of what can be done; the remaining question is what will be done. Many developing countries such as Honduras still have valuable forest cover remaining, and community groups in place to undertake successful natural resource management. The question is whether governments and international donors have the will to support full and secure tenure rights for these groups and the wisdom to structure market incentives that will make their businesses economically viable. If the answer is yes, then the rural poor will have the opportunity to improve their livelihoods while securing their future and our own.

Sources

Bromley, Daniel. 1989. "Property Relations and Economic Development: The Other Land Reform." *World Development* 17:867–77.

Braugh, H. 1991. "A New Lay of the Land." *Worldwatch*, January–February 1991.

Chambers, Robert et al. 1989. *Farmer First: Farmer Innovation and Agricultural Research*. London: Intermediate Technology Development Group.

Ciriacy-Wantrup, S. V. and Richard Bishop. 1975. "Common Property as a Concept in Natural Resources Policy." *Natural Resources Journal* 15:713–27.

Demsetz, Harold. 1967. "Toward a Theory of Property Rights." *American Economic Review* 57:347–59.

Fortmann and Ridell in Raintree et al. 1987. *Land, Trees, and Tenure: Proceedings of an International Workshop on Tenure Issues in Agroforestry*. Nairobi, Kenya, and Madison, Wisconsin: ICRAF and the Land Tenure Center.

Hardin, Garrett. 1968. "The Tragedy of the Commons." *Science* 162:1242–48.

Hecht, S. and S. Schwartzmann. 1989. "The Good, the Bad, and the Ugly: Amazonian Extraction, Colonist Expansion, and Livestock in Comparative Perspective." Working paper for UCLA Graduate School of Architecture and Urban Planning.

Love, Thomas. 1989. "The Political Ecology of Green Movements in Western Amazonia: Applying the Extractive Reserve Concept in SE Peru." Paper prepared for the XXIV Latin American Studies Association Congress. Miami, Florida.

Murray, Gerald, in D. Brinkerhoff and J. Zamor. 1986. *Politics, Projects and People in Haiti*. New York: Praeger.

Nations, J. and D. Komer. 1983. "Central America's Tropical Rainforests: Positive Steps for Survival." *Ambio* 12:5.

Netting, R. 1976. "What Alpine Peasants Have in Common: Observations on Communal Tenure in a Swiss Village." *Human Ecology* 4:135–46.

Panayotou, Theodore. 1989. *The Economics of Environmental Degradation: Problems, Causes and Responses*. Cambridge, Massachusetts: Harvard Institute for International Development.

Rodríguez, J. 1988. *Estudio sobre la Comercialización de Trementina y sus Derivados*. FEHCAFOR/IFICOOP consultant's report.

SECPLAN/DESFIL/USAID. 1989. *Honduras Environmental Profile*. Tegucigalpa, Honduras.

Swallow, B. 1990. "Strategies and Tenure in African Livestock Development." Land Tenure Center Paper No. 140. Madison, Wisconsin.

---

23 A. B. Cunningham ◆
Indigenous Knowledge and Biodiversity

As the concept of preserving the rainforest for its genetic diversity and pharmacological potential becomes more widely accepted, so does the need to acknowledge and reward the people who can tell us how to access that potential. A. B. Cunningham suggests that ethnobiologists and nongovernmental organizations (NGO) ought to serve as intermediaries

From *Cultural Survival Quarterly* 15, no. 3 (Summer 1991): 4–8. Reprinted by permission of Cultural Survival, Inc., 53-A Church Street, Cambridge, MA 02138.

between tribal peoples and commercial interests, facilitating equitable agreements regarding the distribution of profits from commodities with natural ingredients whose properties were discovered by indigenous peoples.

This selection is an overview of the ethical and practical issues involved in the capture and distribution of benefits from the centuries of accumulated knowledge held by traditional healers (shamans) and other keepers of tribal wisdom. It originally appeared in 1991 as part of a special issue of Cultural Survival Quarterly *on the topic of intellectual property rights (or "The Politics of Ownership," as the issue was subtitled). Cultural Survival is an NGO that supports projects designed to help indigenous peoples physically and culturally survive the rapid changes brought about by development. It has been in the forefront of thought and action regarding the issues of both intellectual property and ancestral (land) property rights of tribal peoples.*

The developing world is home to the bulk of the world's genetic diversity and customary knowledge of plant uses. The developed world, with its growing sophistication in biochemistry, genetic engineering, and biotechnology, holds the means to develop such resources. With cultural and environmental change, however, both biodiversity and customary knowledge are being lost at an increasingly rapid rate. The race for this wealth of information has begun.

Ethnobiologists, economic botanists, and anthropologists work on the cusp of traditional and urban-industrial culture, recording indigenous knowledge accumulated over many generations, knowledge that is often the key to particular active ingredients within plants. In many cases, it can only be obtained from specialists (herbalists, diviners, beekeepers, master-fishermen) after the researcher has established credibility with the society and a position of trust with the specialist. But how far does this trust extend?

In general people with the richest customary knowledge have the least formal education. They also have the least bargaining power in urban-industrial society—particularly hunter-gatherers, whose traditional knowledge is disappearing most rapidly. Ethnobiologists and anthropologists play an essential role in preventing this tragedy, not only for its own sake but for its utilitarian value to a much wider sector of society as a key to new drugs, insecticides, and other industrial products. Researchers working with traditional specialists are not only in a relationship built on trust, they are also at the "sharp end" of urban-industrial society, gathering data and publishing it. Should a community's knowledge be made public freely or at a price? Many traditional healers in southern Africa feel that this knowledge should certainly not be available to the public; even within their own societies, much of this knowledge is kept private through ritual and taboo. Many traditional healers recognize the value of their knowledge and want part of the benefits arising from its use—and why not?

Industrial Parallels

If a private company in our urban-industrial society accumulates unique and useful knowledge through trial and error, it patents that knowledge and receives a percentage of the profits from its use. For more than a century ethnobotanists have been recording customary knowledge, much of which relates to medicinal plants. Traditional knowledge, like industrial knowledge, has also been accumulated by trial and error; but it has been made public with no patent rights attached. As workers trying to bridge cultures, ethnobiologists and anthropologists are in a position to act as brokers to facilitate a partnership agreement for the benefit of both rural communities and urban-industrial society.

What are the ethics behind recording customary knowledge and making it publicly available without adequate compensation? Surely this perpetuates the historical errors and attitudes that have characterized industrial society's exploitation of other more tangible resources from developing countries. With the growth of genetic engineering and biotechnology, ethnobiologists need to clarify their code of ethics. Encouragingly, this is already happening. The International Society for Ethnobiology (ISE), the Botanical Society of America (BSA), and the Society for Economic Botany (SEB) all have established ethics committees to develop professional codes (Boom 1990)—an important first step. But what strategies need to be adopted to put them into practice, and what pitfalls need to be avoided?

Conservation, Chemical Compounds, and Plant Genetic Resources

The question of rights to tropical-zone chemical or genetic resources is a controversial one, and the debate has grown more heated as biotechnology and genetic engineering become more prevalent (Mooney 1983). The conservation and social implications of this dilemma make a timely resolution on both issues essential. It has become widely recognized in international funding circles that innovative funding mechanisms will be required to support conservation, and that this support should come from those who benefit from biological resource use. A policy of treating both traditional knowledge and biological material as "free goods" discounts their value; this has important implications for any attempt to justify conservation as a form of land use through economic benefits in addition to aesthetic, religious, and other values.

The more complex a vegetation type in terms of species (or life-form) diversity (and this usually means those with the highest conservation value), the more complex, expensive, and labor-intensive it becomes to manage sustainable use of forest resources such as timber or "minor forest products." In most cases, conservation bodies in developing countries do not have the financial or human resources to carry this out. In instances where demand is high, then, "mining" rather than "managing" occurs, and the fine line between sustainable use and overexploitation is crossed. This negates the rationale behind "sustainable use" being a means for justifying conservation as a form of land use. The primary reason for maintaining core conservation areas is for long-term habitat and species diversity. We see results in Africa, Asia, and South America, particularly for commercially valuable products (whether timber, rattan, medicinal plants, or craftwork resources). The tropical zone countries, however, are rich in resources that have great value globally and can be harvested with low impact: genes, chemical compounds, and knowledge. The problem is that these resources are largely viewed by urban-industrial society as a "global commons" rather than as a regional resource.

This attitude, often unknowingly fostered by people from temperate-zone countries, thus "devalues" the resource that could best justify maintenance of species-rich vegetation if financial value were placed on those resources. As Scholtz (1989) puts it with regard to the rosy periwinkle plant, the source of a drug used to treat childhood leukemia: "But why should Madagascar preserve the rosy periwinkle? The world community reaps benefits from this plant, but what are the benefits to the local people or to the Madagascan government? The answer is: none at all. No money flows back to Madagascar for the drugs produced, and it is unlikely that the drug itself is available to the poor peasants of Madagascar, should they need it. There is on the face of it no reason whatsoever for Madagascar to preserve the rosy periwinkle."

What Are "Benefits"?

In the past, the sovereignty of renewable (timber, rattan, latex, etc.) and nonrenewable (bauxite and other minerals) tropical-zone resources has been recognized (although prices paid for renewable resources may have borne no resemblance to replacement costs). Why not protect genes, chemical components of plants, and the knowledge that enables them to be collected and identified? The same applies to plants with horticultural potential, such as the US$30 million per year from the sale of African violets (*Saintpaulia*), which come from the Tanzanian forest (Lovett 1988); none of this money is linked to Tanzanian forest conservation.

If nothing is done, then an already politicized conservation issue will worsen, and we will all lose out. Internationally based researchers will be excluded from collecting either traditional knowledge or plant genetic material. Prolonged war, coupled with economic and ecological devastation in many African countries, will severely limit national capacity to record traditional knowledge or effectively conserve habitat or species diversity in a number of key areas. If neither in situ (in core conservation areas) nor ex situ (in gene banks and botanical gardens) conservation can take place due to a ban on data or seed collection, then the result is a double tragedy where no one wins. We need a mechanism linking the recognition of the origin and value of these resources *and* a mechanism for "capturing" a portion of the profits arising from the use of these resources for local communities and habitat conservation in the tropical zone.

Benefits: Passive Trickle or Active Capture?

At present, what benefits do trickle down to traditional societies or regions when local traditional knowledge is used or when local plant resources are developed? If patent rights are secured, what form should benefits take and how should they be distributed? The answers to these key questions vary by country and therefore need to be resolved at a regional level using a broader ethical framework. Certain generalizations can be made, however.

First, in many of the tropical or subtropical countries concerned, the ratio of MDs to total population is low, even in urban areas (that is, one MD per 16,400 versus one traditional doctor per 110 in Benin City, Nigeria (Oyenye and Orubuloye 1983). The traditional knowledge that leads to new pharmaceuticals often comes from people with the least formal education and from very remote areas, so there is certainly less access to modern pharmaceuticals, particularly in a barter economy. Certain modern pharmaceuticals can deal with ailments that traditional medicines can not; as Schultes (1988) points out, they are dispensed by mission doctors in certain areas. The constancy of these handouts undoubtedly varies. If a sustained primary health care scheme collaborated with traditional practitioners, the community would have the best of both worlds.

Second, surely it is worthwhile to consider the *active* direction of benefits from new drugs resulting from customary knowledge rather than to rely on the passive trickle-down of modern pharmaceuticals (some of the cake rather than the crumbs)? If 74 percent of the 110 known useful plant-derived drugs have a related use in traditional medicine (Farnsworth 1988) and the dollar value of prescription drugs sold in the United States containing active ingredients from higher plants totals $8 billion per year (Farnsworth and Soejarto 1985), then we are looking at a substantial financial resource—even at royalties of a fraction of 1 percent.

Finally, what attraction is there in this for pharmaceutical companies? For those relying on a chemical synthesis of drugs, none. For others, who see the potential for drug development from higher plants with the advances in phytochemistry, genetic engineering, and patent law, they see the opportunity to get ahead of competitors through supporting an equitable partnership between traditional herbalists and urban-industrial society. They would have quicker access to material for new drug development.

Capturing and Distributing Benefits

Labeling Sources

Active "capture" of benefits can take a wide variety of forms depending on local needs and the products involved. Simply recognizing the research input of traditional specialists through a note on a package can be an important—albeit nonmonetary—benefit. Wider recognition of the value of traditional knowledge would be particularly important in countries with racist attitudes and an emphasis on the "superiority" of urban-industrial society. The same would apply to industrial products developed from tropical-zone resources, as this could help highlight the need for conserving biological diversity.

Researchers as Advisers

By more formally recognizing traditional specialists as partners, researchers from a wide variety of fields can facilitate reciprocal arrangements in information flow. This already takes place when scientists provide copies of their reports to the communities with whom they have worked. Researchers can also serve as advisers in land-use conflicts, land-rights issues, or resource management problems. Chemists and pharmacologists could provide additional detailed information on toxic medicinal plants and their antidotes, and food chemists could give input on the nutritional values of wild food resources. In all cases, referral and information transfer channels need to be set up, and the extent and limits of the assistance need to be defined from the start.

Patents and Legal Contracts

The experience that patent lawyers have built in urban-industrial society certainly provides some useful examples. What need to be avoided, however, are legal wrangles from which only lawyers will benefit. The past five years have seen a great increase in patent rights applications relating to new drugs, plants, or organisms for industrial use (Crawford 1988). Discovering plant species that have useful active ingredients (such as those from traditional medicines, dyes, fish toxins, fungicides, and insecticides) is certainly an inventive, intellectual process. Even more so is the selection by trial and error of a few plant species for their synergistic effect from vegetation that may contain hundreds of plant species. The same can apply to specific genes identified from key plant species, which may be used through genetic engineering techniques to produce a particular chemical.

While the ethical arguments behind the patent rights debate may be clear cut, the same does not apply to strategies for capturing benefits; it is essential that false expectations not be raised. On the surface, for example, patenting seems to hold great promise. Again the vinca alkaloids from the Madagascar rosy periwinkle are a well-publicized recent example. The plant was discovered to have antitumor activity in 1958 (independent of any guidance from traditional medicine) and was patented and marketed by 1963. The sale of pharmaceuticals from this source totaled an approximate $100 million by 1985, 88 percent of which was profit for the company (Farnsworth 1988). This is a rare case, however. The average value and life of patents is considerably lower. For example, the average value of patent rights between 1951 and 1981 in Great Britain was only $7,000; in France, just over $6,000; and in Germany, $18,000. More than half the patents were canceled after eight years, and only 25 percent survived beyond thirteen years.

Usually patents are applied only to material that has not yet been made publicly available. Published data culled from decades of ethnobiological research, however, have already been made public. The same would apply to genetic material of widespread plants, either as weeds, ornamentals, or crops. (The rosy periwinkle has spread throughout much of the tropical and subtropical world as a weed of disturbed areas.) Any claims to rights of published information or already widespread plant resources are a case of shutting the stable door after the horse has bolted, and are all the more reason why guidelines are developed to facilitate capturing benefits from newly recorded, unpublished information and natural resources not found under cultivation or dispersed as weeds.

Legal contract agreements, such as one developed by the National Cancer Institute, provide a very useful alternative mode; but again, any false expectations must be avoided. All groups involved in the research need to know that only a fraction of potentially valuable industrial products will reach the commercial market, since many are unsuitable (due to side effects of new drugs, for example).

Researchers as Brokers

An additional possibility for capturing benefits is by linking the legal approach to a "brokerage role" played by ethnobiologists—who bridge the gap between urban-industrial culture and traditional cultures—and university-based organic chemists and pharmacologists, forming a buffer between ethnobiologists and pharmaceutical companies. Ethnobiologists would provide plant samples for screening, but would maintain confidentiality through identifying the sample by code number only, combined with maceration of botanically identifiable material such as leaves, flowers, and fruits. Once a potentially important new ingredient is identified, these "brokers" can negotiate an agreement with a large company, enabling traditional healers (or other specialists) and ethnobotanists to determine the terms of the contract, not the pharmaceutical company.

"Green Consumerism"

A different approach, taken by Cultural Survival and other groups, is the concept of green consumerism. This could be applied to horticultural products such as the African violet as well as to industrial products, foods, and cosmetics. Companies marketing natural resources would hook up with the people harvesting them to facilitate better prices and therefore benefits to local communities and possibly to conservation.

Distributing the Monetary Benefits

Even if the problems surrounding the capture of benefits are circumvented, the problem of how to distribute and administer them remains. Anders (1989), for example, has documented the social problems among Alaskan peoples as money flowed into communities from oil and land revenues; it would be ironic and tragic if attempts to channel benefits to regions or communities ended up destroying those same communities. Misappropriation of funds has been a feature of many administrations, governmental and nongovernmental alike, and that would have to be guarded against, too.

Incomes from the capture of benefits are unlikely to accrue to a specific community, however (as plant uses are often known through much of the range of a plant species), unless a highly localized, endemic species is involved. Why not base regional funds on biogeographic or phytogeographic boundaries rather than on political ones? A regional fund, perhaps administered by an appropriate NGO through community leaders, would be one way; but the issue requires serious debate. Benefits could take the form of legal resources, primary health care, medicinal plant nurseries for overexploited or popular species, or educational bursaries.

In all cases, however, the position of developing countries in capturing some of these benefits would be greatly improved through access to the training, infrastructure, and technology for screening and developing new products. With few exceptions, Africa does not yet have this expertise; parts of Asia (India, for example) and South America (Brazil) are in a stronger position. The same applies to forming partnerships or legal expertise in developing countries because there is a similar imbalance of power. The majority of patents in developing countries, for example, are owned by foreign corporations—Germany, France, the United States, and Britain. In the short term, partnerships with organizations such as Lawyers for Human Rights need to be explored to improve local access to legal expertise relating to patents and contract agreements.

Clearly there is no single answer to this complex issue that encompasses all research areas or fields. Because patent rights to knowledge involve people, resources, and access to technology, the issue is inevitably politicized. It is essential that ethical guidelines and a strategy for developing equitable partnerships be developed as soon as possible. Encouraging examples such as the Kuna in Panama (the Kuna require researchers working on their land to pay fees, use a Kuna field representative, and provide copies of final reports to the community) already exist. The sooner pragmatic partnerships are developed, the better.

Literature Cited

Anders, J. C. 1989. "Social and Economic Consequences of Federal Indian Policy: A Case Study of the Alaskan Natives." *Economic Development and Cultural Change* 285–303.

Boom, B. M. 1990. "Giving Native People a Share of the Profits." *Garden* 14(6):28–31.

Crawford, M. 1988. "Patent Claim Buildup Haunts Biotechnology." *Science* 239–273.

Farnsworth, N. R. 1988. "Screening Plants for New Medicines." In E. O. Wilson, ed. *Biodiversity*. Washington, DC: National Academy Press.

Farnsworth, N. R. and D. D. Soejarto. 1985. "Potential Consequences of Plant Extinction in the United States on the Current and Future Availability of Prescription Drugs." *Economic Botany* 39(3):231–240.

Lovett, J. C. 1988. "Practical Aspects of Moist Forest Conservation in Tanzania." Monogr. Syst. Bot. Missouri Bot. Gard. 25:491–496.

Mooney, P. R. 1983. "The Law of the Seed." *Development Dialogue* 1–2:1–172.

Oyenye, O. Y. and I. O. Orubuloye. 1983. "Traditional Health Manpower Resources in Nigeria: The Case of Bendel State." *Aman: Journal of Society, Culture and Environment* (cited in Kemwin and Kemwin. "The Apothecary Shop in Benin City." *African Arts* 22(1):72–83).

Posey, D. A. 1990. "Intellectual Property Rights and Just Compensation for Indigenous Knowledge." *Anthropology Today* 6(4):13–16.

Scholtz, A. 1989. "Conserving Biological Diversity: Who Is Responsible?" *Ambio* 18(8):454–457.

Schultes, R. E. 1988. Letter to the Editor. *Tradition, Conservation and Development: Occasional Newsletter of the Commission on Ecology's Working Group on Traditional Ecological Knowledge* (October):10.

24 Rhona Mahony ◆ Debt-for-Nature Swaps: Who Really Benefits?

One of the most promising and highly touted innovations in the conservation world during the 1980s was the idea of the debt-for-nature swap. In these swaps an environmental organization such as World Wildlife Fund purchases deeply discounted loans from creditor banks and then offers to retire the debt if the debtor country implements an agreed-upon conservation project, such as the creation or expansion of a national park. Writing in 1992, Rhona Mahony criticizes the debt-for-nature swap concept as fundamentally flawed, pointing out two major miscalculations. First, the buying and canceling of relatively small amounts of foreign debt will not appreciably help the debtor nations of the Third World. Second, the approach fails to recognize the forces at work against real protection of park land, which leads to the phenomenon of "paper parks"—parks without infrastructure or protection. She argues that because the concept is a top-down approach, it neglects to involve local populations in the land-use decisions that directly affect their livelihoods.

Environmentalists thought they had found a new ally in the 1980s—Wall Street. In 1984, a vice-president of the US World Wildlife Fund, Thomas Lovejoy, suggested that northern environmentalists enter the financial markets, buy up some of the loans which developing countries owed to US or European banks and which the banks were offering for sale at discounted prices, and then cancel those foreign debt obligations in return for good behavior by these countries.[1] Good behavior would include making payments in local currency, equal to the dollar face value of the debt or a little less, to a local environmental nongovernmental organization (NGO).

Scores of environmentalists took up the suggestion. The deals they struck were called debt-for-nature swaps and seemed an excellent idea. By mid-1991, nineteen debt-for-nature swaps had been completed in ten countries. For paying out a small sum in U.S. dollars, environmentalists received a large amount of local currency in return. But, despite superficial appearances, they did not get something for nothing.

The conservation funds generated by the swaps in Costa Rica, the Philippines, Ecuador, and Madagascar account for 95 percent of the total funds generated. They will be used mainly to administer national parks, to buy land to expand the parks, to train park personnel, to research habitats

From *The Ecologist* (May-June 1992): 97–103. Reprinted by permission of the author and *The Ecologist*, Agriculture House, Bath Road, Sturminster Newton, Dorset DT10 1DU, England.

and species, and to carry out environmental education. The environmentalists have worked hard and creatively to arrange these swaps.

From the beginning, however, the effort put into debt-for-nature swaps by environmentalists has been flawed by two miscalculations. The first was their belief that buying and canceling small amounts of debt would help the indebted countries; the second was that simply drawing park boundaries on a map could protect sensitive ecosystems from invaders propelled into them by powerful economic forces, defended by private armies and bribery, and hidden by thousands of hectares of wilderness. Parks supposedly gaining from swaps in all four major beneficiary countries are being invaded by loggers, miners, or the landless.

Third World Debt

Those Third World governments which borrowed heavily during the 1970s from foreign commercial banks, foreign governments, and multilateral institutions, such as the World Bank and the International Monetary Fund, now owe sums of money so staggering that they will never be able to repay them.

In 1990, the developing countries' long-term debt totaled $1.05 trillion of which $293 billion was owed to commercial banks. Developing countries can try to earn dollars to repay these foreign loans by exporting more goods and services than they import. In 1990, however, the developing countries ran a trade deficit of over $28 billion which was projected to rise to $38 billion in 1991.[2]

This disturbing state of affairs is reflected in the low prices the commercial banks have been willing to accept when they sell Third World debt obligations on the secondary, or resale, market. The secondary market began in 1982 after Mexico announced in the same year that it could not make its scheduled loan repayments. Other highly indebted countries, including Argentina, Brazil, Nigeria, the Philippines, Costa Rica, and Peru soon made the same announcement.

Faced with nonpayment of their loans and therefore keen to reduce their risk by diversifying their portfolios, some U.S. and European banks began selling individual loans at a discount. They calculated the discount by estimating a country's ability to repay in the future, considering aspects such as a country's foreign exchange reserves and its expected net income from foreign trade. Other banks and some private investors, who had made slightly differing assessments of the likelihood that debtor countries would repay, bought up these loans.

By 1989, the total annual volume of debt traded was over $20 billion.[3] The discount on these Third World loans has varied from country to country and over time. Sample secondary market prices, in cents per dollar of face value, in early 1991 were: Colombia 67 cents, Philippines 47 cents, Morocco 46.75 cents, Brazil 26.625 cents, Ecuador 26 cents, Zaire 16.5 cents, Panama 14.25 cents, Ivory Coast 6 cents, Peru 5.5 cents.[4] Most countries participating in debt-for-nature swaps are heavily indebted.

Who Benefits?

Who actually benefits from the purchase of a country's debt? Suppose your best friend has $100,000 in assets, but owes $2 million. You consider going to the lenders and buying back some of the debt so as to cancel it, in effect paying off some of your friend's debt—or so you think. They would sell it to you for five cents on the dollar, a rate calculated on how much your friend, or rather your friend's assets, are worth. If your friend cannot pay the debt, the most the lenders can hope to get back is the assets, their only security. Thus $100,000 assets divided by $2 million debt equals a discount price of five cents. For only $50,000, you could relieve your best friend of half— $1 million—the burdensome debt ($1 million multiplied by five cents equals $50,000). Should you do it?

The answer is no. If you repurchased half the debt, your friend would still have assets of $100,000, but now owe $1 million. The price of the debt, however, on the resale market, would probably go up to ten cents on the dollar ($100,000 assets divided by $1 million equals ten cents). The lenders would still expect your friend to repay the same amount as before ($1 million debt now multiplied by ten cents is the same as $2 million debt before multiplied by five cents). Your friend would be no better off than before the repurchase. But you would have given $50,000 to some of the lenders, and also increased the value of the debt held by those lenders who did not sell; their IOUs would have doubled in value.

Although this is a simplified example, these price changes do happen in real life. Bolivia repurchased some of its own debt in March 1988. Donors said they would give Bolivia the money to buy back about 46 percent of its debt and cancel it; they did not ask for anything in return, so this deal was not a debt-for-nature swap.

Before the buy-back, Bolivia's commercial bank debt had a face value of $670 million. Its secondary market price was six cents on the dollar which meant that banks expected Bolivia to repay $40.2 million ($670 million multiplied by six cents).

After the buy-back, Bolivia had only $362 million of commercial bank debt outstanding. The secondary market price, however, had gone up to eleven cents which meant that after the swap, banks expected Bolivia to repay $39.8 million ($362 million multiplied by 11 cents).

The benefit to Bolivia from the buy-back can be considered as a reduction in the amount the banks *expected* it to repay—$0.4 million. The keenest, most self-interested observers of the situation still expected Bolivia to pay back roughly the same amount as before the debt purchase.

Bolivia, therefore, got very little for its troubles, or for its donors' troubles. In fact, it did not cost the donors some $18.5 million as it would have done when the deal was first mooted (46 percent of the total debt of $670 million multiplied by its discount price of six cents). Instead it cost them $33.9 million, because news of the impending buy-back had driven the price of the debt on the secondary market up to eleven cents *even before* the purchase.[5]

It was the commercial banks which really received the benefit. Those that sold the debt earned eleven cents on the dollar for something that, until the buy-back, had been worth only six cents, giving them $33.9 million. Those that did not sell suddenly found that the debt they owned had almost doubled in value.[6]

The system works the same way when environmentalists buy back debt. Swap advocates have spent $16.7 million so far to buy debt.[7] That money went directly to such needy institutions as Bank of America, Citibank, National Westminster Bank plc, Dresdner Bank, Banque de l'Union Européene, Crédit Commercial de France, Salomon Brothers, Lazard Frères, and Shearson Lehman. Moreover, for the banks that did not sell, the value of the debt they held went up in value.[8]

Misplaced Enthusiasm

Even if advocates of debt-for-nature swaps realized that the swaps are not a panacea for a country's debt crisis, many of them are still enthusiastic about the conversions because they believe that the discount at which the Third World debt is sold helps multiply the donations. They are confident that they enable the donor to leverage quantities of funds for rainforest conservation at a higher exchange rate than would normally be available, as long as inflation does not whittle away the advantage gained.

Costa Rica carried out a typical swap in February 1988. A Costa Rican NGO, Fundación de Parques Nacionales (FPN), used $215,692, donated by the U.S. World Wildlife Fund (WWF), to buy official Costa Rican debt with a face value of $1.3 million. FPN then cancelled the debt in return for the Costa Rican Central Bank making donations in *colones*—the local currency—equivalent to $978,000 to the Guanacaste and Corcovado National Parks and the Monteverde Conservation League.

WWF paid $215,692 to buy debt for which the Costa Rican government paid the equivalent of $978,000 in local currency to have cancelled. Thus

WWF's contribution resulted in a donation from the government to local environmental groups which was 4.5 times larger, a result that swap advocates enthusiastically call the multiplier effect. But there is nothing magic about it.

The Central Bank's donation to the park authorities and the Monteverde Conservation League was in the form of five-year bonds, denominated in *colones*.[9] These groups will have to wait five years before they can get the funds—assuming the government redeems them. There is no guarantee that Costa Rica will honor these bonds in five years' time any more than it will pay back the rest of its debt. Remember, there is a reason for that secondary market discount in the first place—the Costa Rican government cannot pay its debts. But even if the government did honor this new debt, it could cut its other environmental spending to make up the cost.

What happened in this Costa Rican example, and in most of the other eighteen debt-for-nature swaps worldwide, is that a First World environmental group has given money to First World commercial banks while a Third World country has promised to give money to its environmental groups. No transfer has taken place from north to south.

Unprotected Parks

How do environmentalists spend the money they pry out of Third World governments? They mostly create, enlarge, or administer national parks. Unfortunately, calling an expanse of natural, and possibly threatened, habitat a park by drawing a line around it on a map and issuing uniforms to a few rangers gives it no more protection than it had before. Natural areas will not be safe until governments stop subsidizing the destructive activities of humans, stop theft and violence by the well-off, and fulfill the basic needs of the poor.

Ecuador

The government in Ecuador contributed the equivalent in the local currency, *sucres*, of $10 million, in the form of bonds to an NGO, Fundación Natura. This organization will spend all the money to maintain national parks, mark boundaries, draw up management plans, and carry out environmental education. The parks include the Galápagos Islands; over one million hectares on the western and eastern slopes of the Andes (Cayambe-Coca Ecological Reserve, Cotacachi-Cayapas Ecological Reserve, Sangay National Park, and Podocarpus National Park); and one million hectares in the Amazon (Cuyabeno Wildlife Reserve and Yasuní National Park). They also include Machalilla National Park, a forty thousand-hectare site on the northwestern coast.[10]

The rangers will face a formidable job in all these places. Poachers and illegal loggers have invaded the Andean Podocarpus park. Foreign oil companies and landless farmers from western Ecuador, many of whom are part-time oil-company employees, are active in both the Amazonian parks. On the Andean slopes, large-scale plantation operators have invaded Cotacachi-Cayapas, while landless farmers threaten Cayambe-Coca and Sangay. Local people's tree-cutting for fuel and overgrazing of goats and cattle may soon desertify parts of northwestern Machalilla.[11]

Many of the people of Ecuador have no other option but to survive in this way. With a per capita GNP of $1,020, Ecuador has a population of 10 million which grows at a rate of 2.8 percent a year; 38 percent of children under five are malnourished.[12] The government depends heavily on its revenues from petroleum, all of which comes from—and is expected to come from—reserves in the Amazon. The roads built by the petroleum industry, which has not been subject to environmental regulation, are the main way the poor colonists enter the rainforest.[13]

Land-tenure laws cause environmental destruction as well. Most of the Amazonian region has been declared "unoccupied," even though indigenous people live there. To receive a title to land, a person must clear the forest, replacing it with crops or pasture. The government gives preferential credit to cattle ranching, even though it is not sustainable on the poor soils of the Amazon.[14] Indigenous people cannot obtain land titles by carrying out shifting agriculture, which is sustainable. When their land rights are granted to them, however, they get no help in enforcing their boundaries against outsiders.[15]

To overcome environmental destruction, the government should help farmers in the coastal areas and mountains produce more for their own consumption and for local sale, or to find city jobs, which at present are too few and pay barely enough for a family to live on, so that they will not be forced to migrate to the Amazon. More spending on education, especially for women, would help as well. . . .[16]

Costa Rica

The Costa Rican wildlife parks cover over 11 percent of the country's land area and have become international tourist attractions.[17] The swap program in Costa Rica has been the largest of any country so far in terms of number of swaps, face value of the debts, the amount paid for them, and the conservation funds generated. As part of swap agreements, the government has contributed the equivalent in *colones* of roughly $42.9 million to environmental projects. But in spite of its reputation as a pioneer in trying to protect national parks, Costa Rica has problems too.

Much of the government's donation will be spent on buying land from private owners and administering parks. Guanacaste National Park, which used to be a tropical dry forest, has been badly degraded by cattle ranching and is still threatened by tree-cutting. Gold miners started working in the Corcovado National Park, part of the Osa Peninsula on the Pacific coast, about ten years ago, many of whom now refuse to leave. Monteverde Cloud Forest in the northwest is beset by illegal loggers. Landless farmers are encroaching on many other parks and reserves.[18]

Reforms

Many environmentalists who have arranged these debt-for-nature swaps know that creating a park is not enough. Some have tried to incorporate social development assistance and reform into their projects. In Madagascar, WWF will help train three hundred villagers to teach contour farming, strip composting, and other techniques to improve farmers' productivity, protecting the local environment in the process. They are considering demonstrating simple, more fuel-efficient cooking stoves, so women would not need to search for, carry, or use so much wood.[19] In Costa Rica, WWF and the Nature Conservancy support environmental lawyers working to issue titles to land on the Osa Peninsula where only 10 percent of the land is held under secure title.[20]

In another project on the Osa Peninsula, WWF and the Nature Conservancy have come up with an idea called Community and Family Rainforests. Landless farming families living in the forest will be issued land titles and receive a lump-sum payment and annual salary thereafter to become caretakers and guardians of the forest under an agreement to fulfill certain duties. Violators will lose title and possession of the land. The success of such schemes remains to be seen.[21]

To protect sensitive ecosystems in the Third World and the indigenous people who rely on them, the underlying forces causing their destruction, which include extreme poverty, government subsidies for forest clearing, and insecure land tenure, need to be addressed. Development, environment, and economics need to be perceived as indivisible.

Within a wide-reaching framework which attempted to tackle economic, demographic, political, and environmental issues with equal force, debt-for-nature swaps could perhaps play a minor role. But in their current form, despite some good intentions, they are not the mechanism to address or affect any of these problems which have invariably led to the resource degradation in the first place. The only beneficiaries of debt-for-nature swaps at present are the northern banks.

Notes

1. *New York Times*, 4 October 1984, opposite editorial.
2. World Bank, *World Debt Tables, 1991–92, Vol. 1, Analysis and Summary Tables*, Washington, DC, 1991.
3. US Agency for International Development (USAID), *Innovative Development Approaches* No. 4, Washington, DC, January 1991, p. 8.
4. Bid prices, that is, the prices buyers were willing to pay, on 29 April 1991. Information taken from Salomon Brothers, *Indicative Prices for Developing Country Credits*, New York. The loans to Colombia, Morocco, and the Philippines are benchmark performing loans, that is, those countries are up-to-date in making their interest payments; other countries are not.
5. The secondary market, like most markets, reacts to supply and demand. The price of the debt is likely to go up if the seller feels there must be an underlying cause for confidence in the country's finances, illustrated by a buyer's eagerness to purchase the debt.
6. Bulow, J. and Rogoff, K. "Buyback Boondoggle," *Brookings Papers on Economic Activity*, No. 2, 1988, pp. 678–682.
7. The donors who contributed the money for the debt-for-nature swaps include foundations, corporations, individuals, the US Agency for International Development (USAID), and the Swedish and Dutch governments. USAID contributed $1.4 million for debt-for-nature debt purchases between 1987 and 1990 and plans to grant another $29.6 million for swaps currently being negotiated, mostly to buy Philippines' sovereign debt. See USAID, *Innovative Development*, p. 2.
8. Conversation with Kurt Low, US World Wildlife Fund (WWF), Conservation Finance, on 14 May 1991. Information about National Westminster Bank plc, Dresdner Bank, Banque de l'Union Européene, and Crédit Commercial de France from WWF news release, *WWF and Madagascar Announce First Debt-for-Nature Swap for Africa*, 3 August 1989.
9. WWF, *Compliance Review of 1988 Costa Rican DFN Swap*, undated memo concerning review carried out during the week of 5 March 1990.
10. WWF, *Amended and Restated Debt-for-Nature Agreement between WWF (US) and Fundación Natura*, 4 April 1989.
11. Ibid.
12. World Bank, *Social Indicators of Development 1990*, Washington, DC, 1990.
13. World Bank, *Ecuador's Amazon Region: Development Issues and Options*, Discussion Paper No. 75, Washington, DC, 1990, p. 12.
14. As S. Nugent points out: "Exportable beef is simply not the profit inspiration for forest-felling. Amazonian beef production is highly unprofitable, in fact, each hectare of cleared forest producing only twenty-two kilograms of meat. The value of such land from the cattle-ranchers' point of view is that it holds its value well in inflationary times." (Nugent, S. *Big Mouth: The Amazon Speaks*, Fourth Estate Limited, London, 1990, p. 226). For further discussion, *see also*: Hecht, S. B., "The Sacred Cow in the Green Hell: Livestock and Forest Conversion in the Brazilian Amazon," *The Ecologist*, Vol. 19, No. 6 Nov/Dec. 1989, pp. 229–234.
15. World Bank, Ecuador's Amazon Region, Annex 2, pp. 35–38.
16. World Bank, Ecuador's Amazon Region, p. 23.
17. WWF, *World Wildlife Fund and the Nature Conservancy: A Quarter Century in Costa Rica*, undated, obtained in May 1991.

18. WWF, *Attachment to Debt-for-Nature Agreement*, undated, obtained in May 1991; and conversation on 15 May 1991 with Randy Curtis, the Nature Conservancy.

19. Conversation on 14 May 1991 with Ira Amstadter, WWF.

20. CEDARENA and Fundación Neotrópica, *Towards Community and Family Rainforests*, March 1991.

21. Ibid.; and Curtis, R., conversation.

25 James D. Nations ◆ Protected Areas in Tropical Rainforests: Five Lessons

Among the issues that anthropologist James Nations covers in this summary of the factors involved in conservation of the wildlands in Latin America is how the consumerism of the developed countries helps cause the destruction of tropical rainforest. In addition, in this 1990 essay, he emphasizes the importance of balancing human and conservation needs when establishing national parks, and the urgency of doing so before the rapid rate of deforestation makes it a moot question.

Nations, however, does not cover all of the questions raised by the wholesale adoption of the national park concept by underdeveloped countries, which have economic and social conditions very different from the United States, where national parks were first created. Some critics have claimed that conservation strategies based on the establishment of national parks exemplify a colonialist attitude toward Latin America on the part of the United States and other developed countries. They fault conservation groups such as the Nature Conservancy for aligning themselves with and enriching Latin America's landed elites by purchasing their land for reserves. The rural poor therefore tend to view environmentalists as their enemies, which could eventually defeat the efforts of some activists to forge alliances with peasants and Indians. These critics consider national parks to be playgrounds for the world's elites. Other observers, however, consider parks to be the last line of defense against the destruction of the natural patrimony of the countries in which they are established, so that in the long run they fare better than those countries that squandered their natural resources in the name of development.

In the tropical rainforest of Yasuní National Park, the sound of the future is the drone of a Super-Puma helicopter lifting off from the Daimi Uno oilwell site. Inside the helicopter are twelve exhausted oilfield workers, headed home after twenty-two days of exploratory drilling in Ecuador's

From *Lessons of the Rainforest*, ed. Suzanne Head and Robert Heinzman (San Francisco, 1990), 206–16, by permission of Sierra Club Books.

Amazon jungle. Finally, the men are en route to Quito for a week of drinking, carousing, and rest. As the backwash of the helicopter fans across the rainforest canopy, the men look down on an ocean of green that stretches as far as they can see in all directions.

Eight miles into their flight toward the oil company's jungle headquarters at Waimo Base, the chopper pilots pass unknowingly over three small huts with palm thatch roofs. On the ground below, a pair of Waorani Indians, dressed in G-strings and balsa earplugs, aim three-meter blowguns at the helicopter's metal underbelly. Part of Ecuador's last uncontacted indigenous group, the Waorani pretend to knock the intruders from the sky with poisoned darts they normally reserve for monkeys. But the aircraft is gone in a blur, and the sound of the jungle once again becomes the whine of insect voices that passes for quiet in the Amazon.

Yasuní National Park, Ecuador's largest protected area and one of the largest rainforest parks in the world, covers one million hectares (ten thousand square kilometers) of lowland tropical rainforest near the conjunction of Ecuador, Peru, and Colombia. The park is designed to protect part of the forest area that botanists call the most biologically diverse spot on the Earth's land surface.

It would have been enough for Nature to stop there. But Yasuní holds more than a wealth of plant and animal species. Beneath its thin red soils lie Ecuador's largest petroleum reserves. And in a nation dependent on oil exports for 70 percent of its income, oil is big business. The whir of the future has met the whine of the jungle, and the big money is betting on oil.

As I write this, smartly dressed engineers sit at their desks in Houston and Quito, sketching lines across maps of places they've never been. These lines are the roads their company will bulldoze across the face of the Amazon jungle during the fall of 1989. The mass of upturned soil and twisted trees the bulldozers push aside will become jungle roads used to construct an oil pipeline. The pipeline will transport its liquid cargo across the width of Ecuador, pumping it over the Andes to the coastal city of Esmeraldas. There, the oil will gush into the holds of giant tankers. A week later, the tankers will unload the oil at a refinery on the Texas coast. Transformed into gasoline and a hundred other products in a belch of stench and smoke, Yasuní's oil will filter its way through the veins of America's economy. You and I will pump it into our cars to drive to the Safeway to buy meat and vegetables packed in plastic that may also be made from the oil of Yasuní.

As we are pushing our shopping carts across the parking lot, a jaguar will be stalking a frightened capybara someplace in the Ecuadorean rainforest, and a dark-skinned Waorani child will be whimpering in her sleep, turning restlessly in her hammock.

Lesson one in the conservation of tropical rainforests: We are all involved in their destruction and their protection.

In our interconnected world of global markets, we are involved in rainforest destruction whether we like it or not. With our wooden picture frames, with the teakwood bowls we place on mahogany coffee tables, we destroy the tropical forest. With our gasoline, our food packaging, our boats and paneled offices, we eradicate the jungle. Living the lives of modern consumers, we eat the tropical forest.

While we work to change those habits and the institutions responsible for those destructive products, we must work hard to conserve the rainforests that remain. Unless we work deliberately and forcefully to preserve tropical rainforests, we will lose the little that remains. A large part of our work is to support national and international organizations that create and manage rainforest parks, to protest rip-and-burn business schemes that make a few families rich at the expense of biodiversity, and to watch what we eat and buy and burn.

Lesson two: In the struggle to protect tropical rainforests, the job must be done now or never. This day in Guatemala, as I write, the National Congress is in session to vote on the proposed creation of thirty-five new national parks and protected areas. If the yes votes carry, the parks the legislators declare will be the last large wilderness areas ever designated in Guatemala. More than half of the new park territory, sixteen thousand square kilometers, will focus on tropical forests.

Similar events have taken place in scores of nations around the tropical belt during the past two decades. National parks and wildlife reserves now protect more than two hundred thousand square kilometers of tropical rainforest throughout the world.[1] Some of these areas conserve undisturbed forest wilderness filled with tapirs, pacas, reptiles, monkeys, and a range of unknown plant species. Others are small pockets of rainforest remnants surrounded by human populations. Some are also home to indigenous tribes that have lived in the forest for centuries.

The sobering side of this news is that the decade of the 1980s, perhaps the first few years of the 1990s, will see the protection of the last rainforest areas on Earth. Rainforest regions not protected by the end of those years—not just by law, but in actuality—will never survive in their original state. In the name of progress, profits, and simple human needs, they will be transformed into less biologically diverse, less interesting, and probably less useful ecological systems. The majority of rainforest regions outside of parks and protected areas will be cleared and burned for a few more years of crops or cattle during your lifetime.

We are groping our way through humankind's final opportunity to protect, in their original condition, the forests that have been called "the richest, most exuberant expression of life on land."

So far, only 3 percent of the rainforest of Africa has come under protection, only 2 percent in Southeast Asia, and only 1 percent in South and Central America. Yet conservationists estimate that we must protect 10 to 20 percent of the world's remaining rainforests if we hope to conserve samples of all the world's rainforest habitats.[2]

The recent push for the declaration of new tropical forest parks has been advanced by two realizations. The first is the realization that tropical rainforests are vital to the future of the human species. They are vital as sources of direct, immediate benefit through watershed protection and as sources of timber, animals, and medicinal plants. They are also valuable as sources of future benefits such as new agricultural crops, natural insecticides, and medical discoveries.

The second realization is that these crucial ecosystems are being eradicated at alarming rates around the world. The benefits, both present and potential, that rainforests hold for humankind are evaporating in the smoke of agricultural fires and beneath the reservoirs of hydroelectric projects.

Taken together, these two realizations are prompting conservationists to redouble their efforts to create national parks and protected rainforest areas. They have learned that, in most rainforest regions, only those areas protected by law and by human beings on the ground are likely to survive intact past the turn of the century.

Lesson number three is a caveat: Not all of the protected rainforests will survive. As population growth, agricultural frontiers, and national development push up hillsides and into wilderness areas throughout the tropics, people are coming into conflict with national parks and protected areas that are critical to rainforest survival. Economic and political realities force rural families to exploit tropical forests and wildlife within and on the edges of parks and protected areas. Few pristine rainforest areas—parks or not—are likely to survive in places where people must struggle simply to provide their basic daily needs.[3]

But rainforest parks are destroyed by greed as well as need. As oil companies push roads through the Amazon, loggers file down the roads to wrench timber trees from the forest to sell on foreign markets. Following close behind the loggers come businessmen with visions of cattle ranches and oil-palm plantations. Few of them are driven by need.

Even some of the colonists are in the forest for the money, knowing that access to land is their only hope for putting together a nest egg for the future. A section of one of Ecuador's protected rainforest areas is already being colonized by rural families seeking land to clear and sell. Most migrated into the area before park guards were hired or a park manager was on the spot. They followed oil roads into the Cuyabeno Wildlife Reserve and cleared and planted farm plots before the parks department was even aware they had arrived.

By national law, Ecuadorean colonists are allowed to settle on national forest lands and seek legal title to a fifty-hectare plot (finca) from the Institute of Agrarian Reform and Colonization. Colonists' de facto occupation of the Cuyabeno reserve forced the Ecuadorean parks department to cede the cleared land to the families and move the reserve boundaries several kilometers to the east.

Although families were allowed to settle and seek title to only one finca at a time, censuses have revealed families in which husband, wife, and each child all hold fifty-hectare plots. Even newborn babies are landowners.

In addition, half the families in some regions of the Ecuadorean rainforest begin clearing a second finca deeper in the forest while waiting for legal title to their first. When they receive title to the first finca, they sell it to speculators or other colonists and move on to their second plot to begin anew. Viewing the same process in the Brazilian Amazon, Marianne Schmink, a University of Florida anthropologist, called this pattern "the land rights industry."[4] An official with the Federation of Indigenous Communities of the Province of Napo, Ecuador (FCUNAE) called colonists who follow the practice "*negociantes de tierra*," or mini-land developers.

The threats to protected tropical forests do not come only from landless families, eager businessmen, and overzealous colonists. Corrupt and incompetent officials are also a threat. In Yasuní National Park, already threatened by oil development, the local head of the Institute of Agrarian Reform and Colonization has been deeding land and promoting colonization within the park along its eastern border with Peru. Called to task by Yasuní's only park guards (two of them for one million hectares), the official justified his action in the name of *fronteras vivas*, "living frontiers," to protect Ecuador from Peruvian invasions. Park officials in Quito roll their eyes when they hear the story and speak in soft asides of bribes and local corruption.

Lesson number four: In the face of population growth and expanding demands for land and tropical resources, working with tropical forest peoples—both indigenous communities and immigrant colonists—is the most important focus for rainforest conservation from this day forward.

Conservationists, biologists, and development planners have come to realize that the crucial need to conserve tropical rainforests must be balanced with the social and economic requirements of human beings. If families are forced to invade national parks or exploit forest reserves in order to stay alive, we can be certain that they will do so. Because of this realization, park planners will tell you that national parks and reserves must go beyond the goals of protecting species and preserving habitat; the objectives of conservation must take into account the needs of local people.[5] The goals of rainforest conservation must also be balanced with the broader interests of tropical nations at large. In the words of Jeffrey McNeely, of the International Union for the Conservation of Nature and Natural Resources, "Protected areas must serve human society if they are to survive in a period of increasing demands on nature."[6]

Far from being a compromised position for conservation, this interdependence of protected areas and human needs can present the opportunity for new patterns of cooperation that benefit both resources and human families. But to ignore the needs of neighboring communities is to create a volatile future that can impoverish both parks and people. Mexican ecologist Arturo Gómez-Pompa states the concept simply: "We can no longer earmark an area as a 'Nature Reserve: Keep Out' and have it policed, while multitudes of starving peasants in the vicinity are looking for a suitable spot to plant next season's crop. This colonialist approach to conservation is doomed to failure."[7]

Or more bluntly, as one tropical park manager has stated it, "The people, the forest, and the wildlife, either thrive together in a balanced environment, or stagnate together in a wretched one."[8]

Thus, the crucial questions for rainforest parks have become: How can conservationists balance the need for wildlands with the needs of human communities? How can protected forest areas contribute more to human societies? What are the economic and social incentives to ensure the forest's survival? Where do we go from here?

One of the initial answers to these questions comes in the form of biosphere reserves, a type of conservation unit first promoted by the United Nations Educational, Scientific, and Cultural Organization (UNESCO). In line with conservation's new way of viewing wildlands and human needs, biosphere reserves combine forest preservation with the needs of surrounding settlements.

Biosphere reserves usually have a series of zones, each with its own particular rules. At least one zone is always an unviolated core of natural vegetation that is permanently protected. This core area is surrounded by concentric rings of land used in increasingly intensive fashion. Moving outward from the protected center, first are buffer zones where local families gather medicinal plants and harvest wild resources. Scientists and tourists enter to collect specimens or take photographs. In the next ring out, local families may farm and collect wood. And in the outermost rings appear houses, hotels, and highways.

In UNESCO's biosphere reserves, indigenous peoples are encouraged to use the outer rings of the reserve as they have used the forest for centuries. Immigrant farm families living on the edges of the reserve are included in planning so they have an interest in the reserve's survival. The families serve as guardians for the buffer zones and for the protected inner core.

Almost 250 biosphere reserves exist in 65 countries, though only one fourth of these protect tropical rainforest.[9] More biosphere reserves are proposed every year. The most crucial aspect of their success is that local people are included in their planning and development.

Creating and properly managing wildland areas is one of the key strategies for protecting tropical rainforests. When well staffed and well funded, protected areas give us the assurance that while we work with the citizens of tropical nations on the underlying problems that cause rainforest destruction, there will still be something left to defend when we finally have the chance to look up.

Meanwhile, on a local level, the basic strategy has to be to ensure that rural families are allowed to prosper by conserving natural resources instead of by destroying them. We need protected areas, but we also need intensive agriculture, fuelwood lots, and soil conservation that will allow us to set aside protected areas in the first place.

Lesson number five is a challenge. The most important step in rainforest conservation is not what happens inside the forest so much as outside, in the fields and in the lives of rural families and in the courtrooms and offices of decision makers in Indonesia, Brazil, Washington, and Tokyo. One new jungle road or one new tropical dam can have more impact than a generation of forest farmers.

In addition, we need more field research. We need to understand how problems in land ownership can prompt people to clear forest instead of conserving it. We need to identify the laws that work against sustainable use instead of for it. We must know more about the economics of land speculation and its role in forest destruction. We must study traditional agricultural systems and learn how to transform them into new, sustainable systems of crop production on infertile tropical soils. We must find out more about the plants and animals that live in the tropical rainforest in the first place. And we must know how to make these species more valuable alive than dead.

There are countless lessons in the conservation of tropical rainforests, most of them still unlearned. Because the threats to tropical forests are dynamic, it follows that the lessons and strategies to counter these threats must also be dynamic. Every case is different; flexibility and adaptability should be our watchwords. Guidelines and experience are crucial, but there are few fixed rules in rainforest conservation.

Still, we can learn the most important lessons of rainforest conservation, and apply them, if we are willing to work with the citizens of tropical nations, and if our vision is of a world where destroying one of our fellow species is a violation of our own rights as living creatures. Our vision should be one of a world where human beings and the creatures we share the planet with can live together, dependent on one another and benefiting one another, as long as the Earth continues to turn. At its basis, that is the major lesson of the rainforest and of life itself.

Notes

1. Thomas E. Lovejoy, "The Science of Amazon Conservation," *The Environmentalist* 3:5 (1983), pp. 57–61; Norman Myers, *The Sinking Ark: A New Look at the Problem of Disappearing Species* (New York: Pergamon Press, 1979), p. 222.
2. Myers, *The Sinking Ark*.
3. Edward C. Wolf, "Challenges and Priorities in Conserving Biological Diversity," *Interciencia* 10:5 (1985), pp. 236–42.
4. Marianne Schmink, "The Rationality of Tropical Forest Destruction," in Julio C. Figueroa et al., eds., *Management of the Forests of Tropical America: Prospects and Technologies* (Río Piedras, Puerto Rico: Institute of Tropical Forestry, U.S. Department of Agriculture Forest Service, 1987).
5. Jeffrey A. McNeely and Kenton R. Miller, eds., *National Parks, Conservation and Development: The Role of Protected Areas in Sustaining Society* (Washington, DC: Smithsonian Institution Press, 1984).
6. Ibid., p. 4.
7. Thomas Holzinger, "Preserving the Ecology in Tropical Areas," *R & D Mexico* 2:11 (Mexico: CONACYT, 1982), p. 29.
8. McNeely, *National Parks*, p. 183.
9. William P. Gregg, Jr. and Betsy Ann McGean, "Biosphere Reserves: Their History and Their Promise," *Orion Nature Quarterly* 4:3 (1985), pp. 41–51.

---

26 John O. Browder ◆ Alternative Rainforest Uses

Complex, interlocking economic and social forces, rather than single issues such as population growth, contribute to the destruction of forests. Consideration of the full social dimensions of tropical deforestation must be a part of successful conservation planning. In this 1991 essay, John O. Browder examines three basic strategies for linking economic development and conservation objectives: plantation forestry, agroforestry, and natural forest management. He quickly eliminates plantations as a major player in sustainable development and focuses on agroforestry and natural forest

From *Economic Development and Environmental Protection in Latin America*, 45–54, ed. Joseph S. Tulchin with Andrew I. Rudman. © 1991 by the Woodrow Wilson International Center for Scholars. Reprinted by permission of Lynne Rienner Publishers.

*management. In particular, he indicates the value of sustained-yield forest
exploitation modeled after the systems developed by indigenous societies or
long-term forest dwellers, such as the rubber tappers and Brazil nut collectors
of the Amazon. Above all, Browder stresses that no single strategy will work
everywhere. Different strategies must be devised for the various conditions
found in different geographic locations. In other words, public policy must
be sensitive to the diversity of ecological and socioeconomic systems of
Latin America.*

Forests cover more than a quarter of the Earth's surface; 27 percent of
these forests are found in Latin America. Although many traditional
forms of cutting enable tropical forests to recover cleared areas, the large-
scale conversion of tropical forests has become one of the most controversial
and widely publicized issues of our time. Estimates of the annual rate of
tropical forest conversion range from 113,000 square kilometers—an area
roughly the size of the state of Oklahoma—to 205,000 square kilometers.[1]
Many legitimate concerns are being raised about the long-term environmental
impact of extensive tropical forest conversion on biodiversity and species
extinction, indigenous human populations, climate, hydrology, and soil
conservation. Although the social costs associated with significant human
disturbance of tropical forests are by no means precisely understood, there
is a rapidly emerging consensus among scientists, economists, and
conservationists that present patterns of tropical forest degradation are
portentous. Calls throughout the 1980s for concerted international action to
manage an unfolding ecological crisis included the UN Food and Agriculture Organization's Tropical Forestry Action Plan.

Underlying the ecological crisis of tropical forest destruction is a dense
amalgam of troubling social, economic, and political issues: rural poverty in
developing countries, rapid population growth, food and energy deficiency,
territorial sovereignty, foreign debt, and misguided modernization policies.
The structure of the "deforestation problem" is multidimensional and organic;
no single component of the problem exists in total isolation from the others.
Tropical deforestation is not just an event that sets in motion a chain of
devastating ecological consequences. It is also a social process, reflecting a
continuum of human responses to diverse and changing economic and
political conditions—responses that range from desperate hunger to out-
right greed.

Responsibility for the deforestation problem and its consequences is
not confined to the tropical countries of the Third World alone. Effective
control of tropical deforestation requires confrontation of numerous
seemingly intractable social ills and injustices that are both country-specific
and global in nature. Conservationists and enlightened growth economists

face the task of finding long-term human uses of tropical forests that are compatible with the economic development objectives of vastly different countries, and land development strategies capable of reconciling the inherent ecological heterogeneity of the forest with the relatively homogeneous, but often conflicting, economic demands placed upon them by differing social groups.

Development Alternatives for Tropical Forests

There are three basic strategies for tropical forest land use that might link economic development and conservation objectives: plantation forestry, tropical agriculture and agroforestry, and natural forest management.

The Limits of Plantation Forestry

Industrial wood plantations are widely considered to be an essential part of any long-term strategy of sustainable forest resource management in the developing world. Annual timber production rates range from ten to twenty cubic meters per hectare. There are currently about thirteen million hectares of plantation forests in the developing world (excluding China), seven million of which are found in Latin America. However, by the year 2000 the developing countries will require approximately fifty million hectares of fuelwood plantations, mainly in the arid tropics.[2] The rate of natural forest conversion currently outstrips the rate of forest plantation establishment by ten to one, making the production and long-term supply of wood to meet energy and raw material needs an issue of strategic concern to both conservationists and development economists. In short, many believe that industrial wood plantations, especially in degraded or secondary forest areas, can be used to reduce pressure on natural forests while providing essential energy for industry and households.

Plantation forestry alone, however, like other tropical forest develop-ment alternatives, is not a panacea for Third World energy inadequacy. Nor is it always an appropriate vehicle for achieving economic development objectives. Forest plantations tend to obtain maximum efficiency at high levels of output over relatively long production cycles (seven to thirty-five years), thereby precluding extensive participation by smallholders.[3] They are relatively expensive to establish, although they yield a moderate to high rate of return (10 to 20 percent).[4] Employment on forest plantations is usually cyclical, being more intensive in the early stages of seedling growth. Thus the economics of fuelwood production tends to favor large enterprises over small producers, often requires government subsidization, and offers little promise of significantly serving household energy needs.

Plantation forestry has also been considered or undertaken to produce sawlogs, pulpwood, and fuelwood for electrification of small urban areas in various parts of Latin America. These experiences have not yet been systematically studied, but in most cases the hazards facing monocultural tree production include increased probability of fire damage, reduction in biodiversity, depredations of insects and fungi, short-term decline in soil fertility, soil compaction, and weed competition. These environmental dangers combine with high start-up costs, little permanent job creation, and long-term dependency on excessively hybridized or imported plant stock. Thus monocultural tree farming has, at best, a relatively minor role in sustainable forest use strategy.

Tropical Agriculture and Agroforestry

Because most of Latin America's food supply is produced in small traditional farming systems, conservation development initiatives should seek to stabilize rather than replace small farms. Additionally, the majority of the region's economically active population is engaged in smallholder farming. There are between fifty and one hundred million Latin Americans who make their living from farming, a small fraction of whom live and work on tropical rainforest lands. In many cases, these small farms supply most of the food for domestic consumption.

Although Amazonian smallholder farming systems vary, they share several general characteristics. First, they tend to be low-impact systems; that is, they have low capital/output ratios and low-to-moderate use of labor and industrial inputs. Second, production is commercially oriented toward national markets and tends to be limited to a few commercial food crops. Very few forest products are harvested for sale or consumption. Third, colonist farmers often use agronomic knowledge gained in farming different ecological zones—knowledge that is ecologically inappropriate for the rainforest. Retention and utilization of a natural forest component in farming is, to them, an alien concept. Fourth, these characteristics often reinforce another trait—the sensitivity of smallholders to even minimal exposure to risk. Because risk aversion takes precedence over profit maximization it is difficult to diffuse new agroforestry technology. Finally, unclear land tenure generally discourages smallholder investment in long-term perennial tree-cropping systems. Whereas tree *planting* frequently establishes specific land-use rights in many parts of Africa, tree *removal* usually serves the same function in Amazonia.

There are three main objectives for agricultural development and environmental conservation in most tropical forest areas: increased productivity of agriculture through intensification or increased frequency of cropping; diversification from monoculture to polyculture; and incorporation of productive tree or forest components.

Relatively little attention has been paid to soil management techniques employed by indigenous residents of the Amazon. Recent research suggests that some of these traditional systems are more productive than conventional smallholder agriculture. A comparison of crop yields obtained by the indigenous Kayapó and by smallholder colonists and ranchers in the Brazilian Amazon found that the indigenous farming system produced three times greater yields than the colonist farming system. The difference reflects the fact that the Kayapó recognize many more plant products as crops than do most colonists.

The objective of diversifying crop production is not limited by farm size. In Mexico, for example, small farms ranging from 0.3 to 0.7 hectares are known to produce between thirty-three and fifty-five useful species.[5] Thus farm size alone does not determine farm viability. Smaller farms require intensive management of a more diverse resource base. Short-term yields per unit area in a monoculture will likely exceed the yield of any single crop in a polycultural system but the total useful yield over the long term may be significantly greater in the polycultural system. Research shows that diversified cropping helps to overcome three important limiting factors to tropical agriculture: soil nutrient depletion, weed competition, and plant disease.

The type of farming system most appropriate to a given area depends on topography, soil and hydrologic factors, access to basic physical infrastructure and consumer markets, and policies that affect market prices for different agricultural products. The key is that a wide range of small-scale agroecosystems exist and tend to share certain characteristics: they produce a wide range of products in a relatively small area, they retain and utilize a significant area of forest, their reliance on natural and locally available sources of fertilizer makes them resource regenerating rather than resource depleting systems, and the sequencing of cropping provides continuity in the supply of food and income. The key issue, therefore, is how to transfer these characteristics successfully to the "modern" smallholders who use resource-depleting monocropping systems on tropical soils.

Natural Forest Management

A wide range of activities, aside from sustained commercial timber harvesting relying on natural regeneration, are now included within natural forest management. Recent research of cultural ecologists suggests that many traditional forms of natural forest management can provide greater financial return on investment of labor than many strictly silvicultural and agricultural activities, provided that they are integrated into larger agrosilvicultural land-use systems or complemented by other small-scale agricultural activities.

One of the best examples of such financial return is seen in northeastern Mexico. A relatively small tropical forest (350,000 hectares) is managed by Huastec Maya and other small farmers. They produce a traditional mix of commercial and subsistence crops (sugar, coffee, maize) through the use of a unique component—the *te'lom*, or natural forest grove. Ninety percent of the more than three hundred plant species found in the *te'lom* are used by the Huastec.[6] Although a *te'lom* alone cannot support a family, its functions within the larger Huastec economy are indispensable. The *te'lom* produces a wide variety of important subsistence goods that would otherwise be expensive or unavailable to farmers, provides nutritionally important additions to the diet (thus preventing the deterioration of diet quality that generally accompanies a shift to commercial agriculture), provides a variety of marketable goods to supplement farm income, supports the production of livestock (often an important source of cash for women), and serves important ecological functions that farmers value by protecting the region's genetic diversity for future generations. The Huastec agroecosystem is capable of sustaining an averge family on four hectares of tropical forest land. The potential financial benefits of replicating the Huastec production model are especially impressive. If market prices are applied to nonmonetized production factors, the analysis reveals that the average Huastec household earns a net benefit equivalent to $2,459 per year (in 1987 dollars) from farm production, excluding ecological benefits.[7]

Traditional forest management practices are low-input, highly productive uses that can be practiced on either large or small areas of tropical forest lands; they often are more land efficient (that is, they use less land per capita) than many conventional land uses, even though they are associated with low population densities; they have minimal adverse impacts on ecological stability; and they are characterized by a high rate of resource utilization (up to 80 percent of forest tree species) and a diversity of income sources.

Traditional practices are often integrated with various complementary productive activities that ensure continuity of income flows over time. Where such management is a cooperative venture within a large area, the active participation of the local (often indigenous) population is essential. Such areas are generally found in situations where effective private (or tribal) property rights have long been established and recognized, or where public land-use controls have been effectively enforced.

Although these production systems involve the extraction or cultivation of a variety of products, they frequently are dominated by at least one important cash crop, such as sugar for the Huastec. The financial viability of these production systems is constrained primarily by market distance and secondarily by market acceptance, emphasizing the importance of geographic location and marketing infrastructure (not necessarily roads).

The productive potential of low-impact forest management has been demonstrated, but several questions about the possibility of widespread application of these strategies remain unanswered and should be included in any research agenda for natural forest management-based conservation and development: How can such technologies be successfully transferred, in whole or in part, from one cultural group to another? If such systems are replicable, can they be deployed at scales of production that significantly increase employment opportunities without depending upon costly subsidies, swamping local consumer markets with minor forest products, or endangering local habitats from overzealous adoption? What are the likely gender implications (household division of labor) associated with transferred technologies? What is the prospective market demand for the commercial goods produced under managed natural forest systems? What support services (credits, marketing, technical extension) and exogenous inputs (fuel, fertilizers, pesticides) would be necessary to ensure stable production of tranferred or expanded natural forest management systems? And finally, under what circumstances of land use and tenure are such systems socially acceptable, especially when they entail the restricted use of large areas of forest land?

The application of traditional natural forest management strategies relies largely on restrictive land-use zoning (reserves), often in areas where surrounding land uses are incompatible with intended forest management activities. Under these circumstances, reserves must be treated as one component of a larger land-use strategy that accommodates the competing land uses surrounding them. Low-use-intensity reserves favorable to one group of people undergoing rapid land-use transition may unfairly discriminate against others, resulting in social conflict. "Extractive reserves," in which lands are set aside especially for the harvesting of tree products (for example, nuts or rubber) but not for tree cutting, can work, but only if cattle ranchers, landless peasants, and other forest land users pressing at the edges are simultaneously incorporated into complementary solutions to their respective needs for land and forest resources.

Conclusions and Recommendations

Tropical forest destruction in Latin America is largely the result of public policies that promote the expansion of commercial agriculture and ranching, as opposed to in Africa and South Asia where the destruction is caused by timber harvesting and rural poverty. No single land-use strategy will successfully harmonize conservation and economic development objectives for the entire Amazon. Different strategies must be adapted to diverse local conditions. These strategies should share three common characteristics: they should be decentralized and their benefits widely distributed; they should be diversified to promote heterogeneity, not homogeneity, of production; and they should focus either on activities that can be adapted to small-scale production or on low-impact activities that can be adapted on a socially acceptable large scale.

Brazilian conservation efforts in particular should consider three important realities. First, between five and seven hundred thousand rural households depend on precarious small-scale short-cycle monocropping for their livelihood; thus, successful development strategies must provide small farmers with the proper technology and financing to incorporate the lessons about continuous cultivation that can be derived from traditional Amazonian agroecological systems. Second, most of the region's population growth is urban based, so joint poverty and environmental development strategies must consider the implication of growing urban demand for food, energy, and building materials on the region's natural resource base. Third, areas of secondary forest growth are becoming increasingly prominent features of the Amazonian landscape. These degraded pastures and abandoned fallows represent an important untapped resource that appropriate strategies should incorporate.

The following conclusions and recommendations for tropical rainforest regions, especially in the Americas, address small-scale farming, plantation forestry, natural forest management, and diversification of production.

Small-Scale Farming

Appropriate land-use strategies for small-scale farming should promote (1) expanded low-impact extractive utilization of natural forest remnants on existing productive farm lots; (2) the planting of trees by farmers in conjunction with ground cropping—not only for commercial gain but also planting of those trees that preserve vital ecological functions such as nitrogen fixing; (3) diversification of farm production, especially through the planting of "useful" tree species; and (4) intensification of farm cultivation—continuous cropping with greater reliance on natural fertilizers. Major impediments to all four of these objectives include insecure land tenure, a lack of agroecological knowledge, poorly staffed and underfunded extension institutions with parochial work programs, inadequate technical

and ethnological knowledge, and the continued subsidization of monocultural cash cropping and cattle ranching through tax incentives and other
governmental policies that promote large-scale forest destruction often to
make way for desultory land uses.

More attention must be given to indigenous agroecological knowledge.
Obviously, such knowledge must be blended with modern approaches to
tropical agriculture and fit existing sociocultural situations. Much indigenous
knowledge is culturally esoteric and alien to contemporary commercial
farming. Nevertheless, many indigenous practices do show the way toward
techniques that may be able to overcome ecological and financial constraints
facing agriculture in moist tropical forest areas. Future funding should
emphasize the practical management aspects of applying existing indigenous
and traditional knowledge at the farm level.

Plantation Forestry

Four potential applications of plantation forestry will continue to receive
attention: electrification of small urban areas, urban household firewood
production, industrial fuelwood production, and industrial sawn-wood production. Decentralized small-scale tree farming by rural inhabitants in areas
surrounding small towns is an income-spreading and ecologically preferable alternative to centralized or monocultural plantations. An important
first step toward the adoption of tree-planting strategies in combination with
annual cropping would be a localized response to urban-driven demand for
fuelwood and sawlogs.

Natural Forest Management

A number of promising strategies for traditional forest management and
agroforestry have been largely neglected by donors in land-use planning for
Amazonia. Opportunities to utilize more fully the diverse resources of
natural forests in conjunction with agriculture need to be further refined, not
only as potential development models for extensive protected forest areas
but also for application at the small farm level. Additional research is
needed on the following issues: (1) the market potential, both local and
national, of promising minor forest products and lesser-known timber species;
(2) technical production aspects of local industrial processing of marketable
forest products, especially minor forest products; (3) marketing requirements
for diverse natural forest products (for example, grouping by general use
characteristics); (4) potential uses of different natural forest products as
inputs to farm production; (5) financial performance and employment impact

of different management procedures that increase yields and minimize damage to natural forest vegetation; and (6) financial analysis of forest management at the farm level and the use of secondary forest growth areas on farm lots for commercial tree planting and agroforestry demonstrations.

Diversification of Production

Diversification of production must become the central and guiding tenet of sustainable tropical forest land use. In one sense, diversity of production runs counter to conventional economic development wisdom advocating specialization around a comparative resource advantage. The reductive conversion of biotically diverse forest communities, supporting tens of thousands of living species for thousands of years, to genetic cesspools capable of supporting one or two commercial species for five or ten years must be rejected as an economic development model. The comparative advantage of tropical forests is their biodiversity.

In those countries where subsidies play a major role in forest land use, the shift from subsidies for commodities to subsidies for biotically diversified land uses should be considered. Instead of rural credit to convert forest land to upland rice fields, policies could entice farmers to productively utilize the biodiversity of the natural forest for financial benefits.

Notes

1. Norman Myers, *The Primary Source* (New York: W. W. Norton and Co., 1984), p. 2; and "FAO's Tropical Forestry Action Plan," extracted from *Unasylva*, Vol. 38, No. 152 (1988): 40.

2. John Campbell, "The World's Third Forest," *Commonwealth Forestry Review*, Vol. 59, No. 4 (1980): 533.

3. Michael Nelson, *The Development of Tropical Lands* (Baltimore: Johns Hopkins University Press, 1973), p. 155.

4. See John Spears, "Replenishing the World's Forests: Tropical Reforestation—An Achievable Goal?" *Commonwealth Forestry Review*, Vol. 64, No. 4 (1985): 318.

5. Stephen R. Gleissman, "Local Resource Use Systems in the Tropics: Taking Pressure off the Forests," unpublished manuscript, n.d.

6. Janis Alcorn, "An Economic Analysis of Huastec Mayan Forest Management," in John Browder, ed., *Fragile Lands of Latin America: Strategies for Sustainable Management* (Boulder, Colo.: Westview Press, 1989).

7. Ibid.

27 Kathryn Phillips ◆ Peru's Rainforest: The Kindest Cut

This reading, first published in 1992, describes a model of production forestry for the tropics that is more ecologically and socially desirable than the existing methods of large-scale forest clear-cutting. The new model, developed by scientists from the Tropical Science Center in Costa Rica, is based on the tropical rainforest's natural ability to recover from small disturbances such as tree falls. The forestry model uses small cuts, called strip-shelterbelts, that allow quick recovery by natural reseeding from surrounding forests. Production is organized in a cooperative that benefits the forest-dwellers rather than wood-products companies based in distant cities. The pilot study with Yánesha Indians in the Peruvian Amazon proved to be a success, and the model is now being adopted by other Indians in the western Amazon.

Patches of bare pastureland scar Peru's lush Palcazú Valley. A half-century ago, Swiss and German colonists introduced cattle to this isolated, rain-soaked region, stripping trees from virtually every riverbank to accommodate their herds. More recently, Peru's government planned to import thirty thousand colonists into the area from around the country. The aim: to turn this valley east of the Andes into a vast logging and cattle-grazing region.

Like most residents, thirty-seven-year-old Emilio Sanchoma saw ranching as the only hope for his family's future. A dark-eyed Yánesha Indian whose ancestors arrived in the area four thousand years ago, Sanchoma figured he, too, must destroy his forest home to survive.

Now it seems he figured wrong. Today, forest loss in Palcazú has not spread much farther than the riverbanks. The government has dropped its sweeping plans. And fellow tribesmen have elected Sanchoma *jefe de campo*, or chief of forestry, for an innovative new program in sustainable forestry management.

Using what's called a strip-shelterbelt system, which relies on the forest's natural ability to reseed itself, Sanchoma and fellow tribe members are reaping profits from local woodlands without wiping them out. The program is only part of a long-term conservation strategy, researchers caution. Yet results are so encouraging that it has become a model for other indigenous people locked in a cycle of poverty and destruction that claims 2.5 acres of the world's rainforest every second.

From *International Wildlife* 22 (May-June 1992): 17. Reprinted by permission of the author.

The idea came from a group of scientists who had come to Palcazú in 1981 to look into the potential impact of the government's massive development plan. These dozen or so anthropologists and foresters funded by the U.S. Agency for International Development saw the need for a program that would make the forest so valuable that ranching would lose its appeal.

At first, the Yánesha were less than receptive; history had made them leery of outsiders and their promises. But after two years, five of the valley's eleven Yánesha communities formed a committee to look into the proposal. The result was the Yánesha Forestry Cooperative, which, under the leadership of elected tribe members, began a logging and sawmill operation in 1985 using the strip-shelterbelt system.

The concept is based on research by tropical ecologist Gary Hartshorn, now vice president for science at the World Wildlife Fund. He discovered that many tropical trees grow only in natural gaps in the forest. People can mimic these gaps, he suggested, by cutting trees in narrow strips and leaving wide sections of forest intact. With the help of seed-carrying animals, the gaps regenerate in thirty years—a fraction of the time it takes a razed forest to replenish itself.

Today, more than two hundred Indians earn their living as members of the Yánesha cooperative. Workers with chain saws cut strips thirty yards wide and three hundred yards long through the forest. Oxen haul the logs to a processing plant, where other tribe members convert them into boards, fence posts, and charcoal. From an airplane, the harvested strips are barely visible. "You would be hard-pressed to find them," say Robert Simeone, a forestry consultant who serves as an adviser to the Yánesha.

The Indians have found a developing market around the world for their ecologically benign wood products. Project workers also act as traveling consultants, sharing their expertise with tribes such as the Quichua of Ecuador's Napo Valley, who recently launched a similar program. Now, with luck, perhaps Emilio Sanchoma and others struggling to save their homes can finally see the forest for the trees.

---

28 William Booth ◆ U.S. Drug Firm Signs Up to Farm Tropical Forests

As described here by William Booth in The Washington Post, *in September 1991 a landmark agreement regarding the rights to commercial exploitation of tropical rainforest organisms was reached between a pharmaceutical*

From *The Washington Post* (September 21, 1991): A3. © 1992, *The Washington Post*. Reprinted with permission.

company (Merck) and a Costa Rican parastatal institution, the National Institute of Biodiversity (INBio). Costa Rica has already earned an international reputation for its national park system, and this agreement enhances its reputation as a leader in conservation among Third World nations. In fact, this agreement is regarded as a model for conservation-based economic development strategies. The Costa Rican government officially launched INBio in 1989, its task to inventory and catalog the country's enormous biological wealth. INBio's mission was furthered by its agreement with Merck to "prospect" for possible pharmaceuticals in Costa Rica's forests, thereby encouraging forest preservation.

In what is said to be the first deal of its kind, the world's largest pharmaceutical company announced yesterday it will pay a Costa Rican conservation organization $1 million for the right to screen plants, microbes, and insects gathered in the forests for their possible use as drugs.

The agreement between Merck & Co. and the National Institute of Biodiversity of Costa Rica promises to help the Central American country protect its natural resources by finding new ways to exploit the forests without destroying them.

Cornell University biologist Thomas Eisner, who helped broker the deal, calls the arrangement "chemical prospecting" in which biologists and others would comb the tropical forests for plants and animals that might be made into useful products, such as drugs.

As an example, Eisner suggested that a leaf on the forest floor covered with mold might be the source of a new antibiotic or a plant untouched by insects might contain a good repellant.

In the deal, local people who live around Costa Rica's twelve thousand square kilometers of protected lands are being trained and paid to gather plants and other materials, which are collected and cataloged by the biodiversity institute, a nonprofit scientific organization.

Merck would then be sent any promising organisms for screening. If a product became a marketable drug—something Merck scientists say is a long shot—the Costa Ricans would be given a share of the royalties, which would be earmarked for conservation.

This is not the first time Merck has pursued natural substances as a source of drugs. Indeed, the pharmaceutical industry was originally based on the use of natural compounds, mostly derived from medicinal herbs. Many drugs still in use were discovered first as natural substances.

Merck already markets four drugs made from soil organisms. A substance called Mevacor, for instance, is made from a microbe dug up in Spain and is used to control high cholesterol. Merck sold $735 million worth of Mevacor in 1990.

While Merck scientists say they are skeptical the forests will ever be the "virtual cornucopia of drugs" that some environmentalists have suggested, they say it is worth a look.

"You read papers today, all those medicines they say are supposed to be in the rainforests," said Georg Albers-Schönberg, head of the natural products chemistry branch at Merck. "I feel some skepticism. But I say, 'Why not give it a try? Let's try.' "

Albers-Schönberg said that while plants and insects are difficult to work with as potential drugs, the pharmaceutical industry is now more willing to explore natural substances. Merck also has a deal with the New York Botantical Gardens, whose botanists send promising plants to Merck, which has agreed to share royalties with the country of origin if a marketable drug is developed.

When Merck researchers get an interesting plant from Costa Rica or elsewhere, they grind it up and produce an extract that is then tested for activity against certain enzymes or specific receptors on cells associated with human or animal disease.

If the extract shows activity, the scientists can synthesize batches of the compound. In almost all cases, the forests would not be harvested for more of the plant.

"It's a very productive way to preserve the great biological diversity of land we have, our great greenhouses," said Anna Sittenfeld, a microbiologist and head of science programs at the Costa Rican institute.

"These types of agreements will help us preserve our natural areas by increasing opportunities for people who are living around them. We can hire more people. Create jobs. Maybe one day a drug company can move and develop their drugs here," said Sittenfeld. "It also helps people here in Costa Rica understand that the forests are important, not just for land, grazing, and trees, but for drugs and medicines."

---

29 Ty Harrington ◆ Tourism Damages Amazon Region

The simultaneous increase in environmental consciousness and specialty tourism during the 1980s has given rise to a new economic boom in Latin America—ecotourism. As entrepreneurs tapped into the growing interest in environmental issues, especially tropical rainforests, ecotourism—promoted as a good way to blend nature conservation and economic development—

From *The Christian Science Monitor* (June 6, 1989): 6. Reprinted by permission of the author.

began to grow exponentially. Although nature tourism is in theory a nonconsumptive use of forests and other natural environments, in reality it creates a number of environmental impacts, as the U.S. National Park Service has discovered. The explosive rate at which ecotourism has grown in Latin America has exacerbated pollution, erosion of trails, wildlife disruption, and degradation of the culture of native peoples. Many governments have moved belatedly to control the negative impacts of tourism before they destroy the very attractions that tourists come to see and experience. In this reading, originally published in 1989 in The Christian Science Monitor, *Harrington shows that ecotourism must be carefully controlled if it is to live up to its promise as a path to sustainable development. In particular, care must be taken to ensure that a significant proportion of the economic benefits remain in the local area and that local environments are not degraded by overuse.*

Tourism's negative impact on Brazil's Amazon is now being recognized by José Sarney's government as a serious new threat.

The tourism industry has already contributed to extensive damage, including widespread pollution, destruction of wildlife, and cultural erosion among the aboriginals.

But President Sarney is moving to prevent further destruction by expanding preservation programs. Key to the Brazilian government's efforts to regulate a rising flood of visitors, and to stop the decimation of a region already smoldering under siege of development, are programs for ecologically conscious tourism.

In April, Sarney announced the first step of a broad preservation package: a $100-million, five-year plan to divide the entire 1.9 million square-mile Amazon basin into separate zones for economic and environmental use—making easier the control of land use. Forty-nine newly signed environmental regulations include the creation of new parks and recreational preserves. And the most significant program, which will give the government more control over tour operators, requires that their staff be tested, licensed, and intensively trained in environmental concerns.

Ironically, the worldwide media focus on the Amazon's impending destruction and the need to prevent it, is also responsible for attracting the increasing numbers of visitors. Brazilian "nature tourism" operators confirm the surge, reporting 1989 bookings up more than 300 percent over 1988—predominantly from Europe, North America, Japan, and urban Brazil.

In fact, wilderness tourism is growing so quickly that experts question whether these new preservation measures are not largely cosmetic—a public relations' effort by the government to stave off intensified international outcry against destruction of the rainforests. Environmentalists contend that the limited funds allocated will not be sufficient for the programs to take effect in time. Instead, the environmentalists are seeking a rapid increase in public awareness that will foster self-restraint in the marketplace.

Says Carlos Quintela of the Nature Conservancy, a private conservationist agency, "The words eco- and nature-tourism are so easy to sell that the marketing has begun before an infrastructure has been set up." And growth is outstripping the government's ability to put controls in place.

But Amazon tourism is a profit-driven industry, unencumbered by ecological considerations, and offers the Brazilian interior its biggest potential since the discovery of rubber.

"It's not the fact that tourism is business," says Dr. Quintela, "but that it is big business."

However, the greatest obstacle to regulating the interior tourism industry is its chaotic state. José Carlos Fonseca, spokesman for the Brazilian embassy in Washington, says the Ecological Tourism Program can only begin to tackle the situation, and will be limited until it gains local financial support from the state governments.

Even now, experts say it may be too late to regulate an industry composed of hundreds of small businesses peppering a territory two thirds the size of the United States. The vast majority are mom-and-pop operations which spring up wherever visitors will pay to sightsee.

Officials compare controlling tourism in the Amazon with trying to stop a gold rush. They note that a savvy tour operator can earn an average year's wages in a single day. And, usually, they add, at the expense of the environment.

A wide swath of litter forms a paper chase along the jungle highways, and pollution, from plastic containers to sanitary napkins, defaces the serene surface of nearly every lake in the central state of Mato Grosso. Snack bars and lodgings, scattered along roads, hundreds of miles from the nearest building or health codes, are run without consideration or concern for the environment.

There are no provisions for garbage collection or sewers. High water carries waste down the millions of miles of tributaries into the Amazon River, through which flows one fifth of the world's fresh water.

Unregulated fishing is so extensive that many districts are reported nearly depleted of some species, the Forestry Department says. And local operators confirm that explosives have been fired into rookeries to frighten birds into the air and provide tourists with video footage.

The impact upon wildlife has been devastating. One of the largest rookeries in the Pantanal province has been abandoned, and the young left to hawks. Wildlife has become more sparse over the past three years in the southern sections of the Amazon region, as visitors routinely throw stones to make the wild animals react.

Dr. Lee Harper, a biology professor at St. Lawrence University in New York, comments that "those developing tourism in Brazil haven't realized that people would rather see a live caiman than a dead one."

Hunting, which is illegal in Brazil and carries severe penalties, can nonetheless be booked easily, either locally or from the United States. Quintela of the Nature Conservancy says the proportions of poaching are enormous. "Between the sportsmen and the poachers, hunting is so big for some species that it is not just killing or harvesting, it is comparable to strip mining," he said, "and little game is left for the Indians' subsistence."

To make matters worse, free-lance jungle guides openly solicit travelers at ports and airports, luring them with inexpensive trips into the Amazon's Stone Age villages, and bush pilots offer flights to restricted Indian reservations.

Jesus Delgado, professor of preservation management at the University of Sao Paulo, says that the cultural effects are even worse than the environmental impact. President Sarney has banned all visits to primitive Indians, except for authorized scientific purposes, but here also enforcement is sparse and ineffective.

A Brazilian TV news reporter was recently shown interviewing a federal guard in Araguaia National Park when a large boat roared past loaded with illegal tourists. The guard shrugged and said he stood powerless, being one man in a territory the size of Belgium. Professor Delgado, who says the entire forestry agency has only five hundred employees, calls the reserves "paper parks."

The Brazilian Interior Ministry responds that the government is buying up private land as fast as possible. The ministry says the Ecological Tourism Program will inspire local governments to assist in tourism management as they realize that their communities will benefit from tourism income.

The hope, Fonseca says, is that the tourism industry has the potential to be the least damaging form of development. He sees in the president's programs "a hope of a growing governmental awareness of ecology." "Brazil is changing its tune," Fonseca says, "and is listening to what the developed world has learned instead" of repeating its mistakes.

Delgado feels it is the tourists themselves who will have the final say about whether the controls work. He views them as both the problem and the solution. "No matter how complete the controls and tourism management," he warns, "preservation measures will not be effective until travelers themselves learn not to throw rocks, and stop encroaching upon restricted Indian reservations, no matter how alluring."

He adds, "Tourism can no longer be separated from other man-made disruptions of the ecology, such as mining and deforestation."

30 Michael Lipske ◆ How a Monkey Saved the Jungle

Athough recent experience in Amazonia has made it painfully clear that ecotourism can grow out of control and become a destructive force (Selection 29), small-scale ecotourism can be successful when based on nature sanctuaries that involve local participation. Here, in a 1992 article for International Wildlife, *Michael Lipske takes this approach to combining environment and development.*

A biologist studying howler monkeys in the forests of Belize sought to promote a rural development strategy that would strike a compromise between the needs of the local farmers and the forest-dwelling monkeys. This strategy involved managing the forest fallows in the local slash-and-burn farming system so that there were always forest corridors ("monkey freeways") to connect patches of forest. The villagers suggested that tourists might pay to visit the monkey sanctuary—and ecotourism was added to the development strategy. The local people's involvement in the project and its small scale have contributed to its success, at least in the short run. The Community Baboon Sanctuary of Belize may prove to be a model for the development of successful grass-roots ecotourism projects elsewhere in Latin America.

Two men with a large net stand under a tree in the Belize jungle, waiting for a drugged monkey to fall to earth. Injected with an anesthetic fired from a CO_2 rifle, the unhappy animal does not go gently into dreamland. High above the ground, the coal-colored creature has wedged its body in the crotch of a branch and wrapped its tail around a smaller limb. The men shake the tree until their quarry finally pops loose and tumbles safely into the net.

The reluctant acrobat is a black howler—or "baboon," as the black Creoles of this Central American nation call the monkey. In recent years, the species has become the centerpiece of a unique experiment in human-wildlife relations. Now, instead of stripping all their land, subsistence farmers along a stretch of the Belize River leave parts of the forest standing. That's obviously good for the monkeys. And because it preserves soil nutrients, the practice also benefits the local farmers.

For scientist Robert Horwich, who has orchestrated the capture, spreading the word about this new style of conservation has become a crusade in partnership with residents in the flat bush country of northcentral Belize. He

Reprinted with permission from *International Wildlife* 22 (January-February 1992): 38–42. © 1992 by the National Wildlife Federation.

is acting on his belief that the world's rural farmers hold a vital key to preserving tropical forests and the wildlife they contain.

Local farmers, in turn, have bought into the notion that what's good for monkeys is also good for them. For one thing, preserving the forest lets them harvest dollars from tourists who come to Belize to gaze at wild monkeys in the treetops. Result: The project—called the Community Baboon Sanctuary—has emerged as an example of grass-roots conservation at its best, a tool for tackling the problems of rural people and wildlife, and a model for developing countries around the world.

Horwich, a stout, affable man with a gray bird's nest of a beard, is studying black howlers to learn more about how the animals make a living in the rainforest along the Belize River. Not long ago, a half-dozen biologists joined him in the village of Bermudian Landing for a whirlwind monkey hunt that left dozens of howlers documented and tagged, readied as research subjects for years to come.

A soft-spoken, fifty-year-old ethologist who lives most of the year in Gays Mills, Wisconsin, "Dr. Rob" (as some villagers call Horwich) has studied the behavior of mockingbirds, gray squirrels, Nilgiri langurs, and sandhill cranes. A decade ago, he turned his attention to black howlers. A survey he conducted revealed that the monkeys (one of six howler species in Latin America) were declining in Guatemala and Mexico as their jungle habitat was cleared. He found, however, that howlers were doing better in heavily forested Belize, particularly along the Belize River.

Living in small troops headed by a dominant male, the primates travel from treetop to treetop, feeding on fruits, flowers, and leaves. Seldom coming to the ground, the slow-moving monkeys usually walk on branches (rather than swinging on them), using their prehensile tail as a fifth hand.

The animals sleep at night and rest more than 70 percent of the day. Still, they make their presence known. In Bermudian Landing, the voice of the howler comes crashing out of the jungle every morning and afternoon. The roar rolls out past houses built on stilts, mixing with the din of barking dogs, clucking chickens, screaming kids, and scolding parents.

The monkey's bellicose cry begins as a raspy roar and ends in an agonized wheezing moan. Audible up to a mile away, the howl is generated by special throat structures that funnel sound into a hollow, resonating bone. The volume is astonishing, all the more so for coming from a bunch of nine- to twenty-pound vegetarians. Like the roar of traffic in Mexico City or lawn mowers in suburbia, monkey song helps define life along the Belize River.

It was in Bermudian Landing, a village of about three hundred that straddles the dirt highway slicing through the forest, that Robert Horwich broached the idea of establishing a sanctuary to benefit people and monkeys.

Having spent time studying howler roaring rhythms and breeding behavior on the outskirts of the village, he says, "I felt like I wanted to do some conservation. You're really just taking if you only do research."

Horwich outlined the concept at a village meeting in 1985. From the start, his goal was to stake out a compromise position between the requirements of forest-dwelling monkeys and the needs of people.

Farmers in the region practice slash-and-burn agriculture, cutting down forest and burning it to create a milpa, or small cleared area, for planting. They grow rice, beans, or yuca [manioc] on this patch for one to two years, then switch to banana or coconut trees. After five years, they abandon that milpa and clear another. As the old field lies idle, soil nutrients build up, and in fifteen years or so the young forest that has sprouted on the abandoned land can be cut and farmed again.

But trees in that regenerating jungle can serve as a howler food source as soon as six years after the land goes fallow. "The monkeys will use regenerating forest if they can get to it," says Horwich. Hence, he proposed, if farmers could retain skeletal strips of forest along field edges, these strips could act as elevated "freeways." Howlers could then travel through the sanctuary's patchwork of active milpas and young and mature jungle. Leaving strips of forest, especially along the river, he argued, would also reduce soil erosion, cutting siltation and yielding richer fish stocks.

Natural Creole tolerance helped Horwich sell the idea. "I think people in the different communities had strong respect for the monkeys even before Dr. Horwich came around," explains Fallet Young, manager of the sanctuary. Elsewhere in Belize howlers are hunted for food, but farmers along the Belize River leave them alone. And other than raiding cashew trees for the fruits that villagers prize for making wine and jelly, the monkeys "don't actually eat anything the farmers plant," says Young.

In the beginning, Horwich and Jonathan Lyon, a plant ecologist doing graduate work at Pennsylvania State University, took a count of howler monkeys around Bermudian Landing. They mapped out a three-square-mile area to determine vegetation types and property-ownership lines. For each participating landowner they prepared a tailored land-management plan. Farmers signed pledges saying they would follow practices beneficial to monkeys. Once people understood that participation would be voluntary, Horwich says, they were enthusiastic about helping.

Now, more than one hundred landowners voluntarily leave monkey food trees standing and maintain corridors of trees to serve as howler highways around fields and pastures. "We work on the premise," says Horwich, "that, if it doesn't take too much from their land, people will follow practices that are decent for wildlife."

As a result, the eighteen-square-mile Community Baboon Sanctuary is home to an estimated 1,100 howler monkeys. The success of the operation, which has spread from one village in 1985 to eight today, owes everything to the willingness of farmers to manage their land for the sake of the environment. "If anyone in Belize has really done a major sacrifice for conservation where it hurts—in the pocketbook—it is these people," says Victor Gonzalez, former president of the Belize Audubon Society.

In fact, it was the villagers who suggested that tourism figure into the equation. At first, Horwich admits, the notion struck him as "kind of a joke." Plenty of tourists came to Belize's tropical coast to snorkel or scuba dive on the world's second-longest coral reef. But few outsiders had cause to visit the isolated villages in the bush. Now, thanks to the sanctuary and its celebrity monkeys, tourism is fast becoming a vital industry.

If Robert Horwich brought the seed for a sanctuary to Bermudian Landing, it is Fallet Young who has nurtured it. The thirty-seven-year-old father of five traces his roots in the village back to the 1890s. Bamboo thin, he is the flexible diplomat who fosters a happy meshing of interests among farmers, scientists, and tourists. One of Young's jobs is to coordinate the comings and goings of the growing number of sanctuary visitors. Last year, six thousand people came from as far away as Denmark to visit the sanctuary and catch glimpses of its loudmouthed monkeys.

"The things they desire, they are all here," Young says of the tourists, and he works to keep it so. He persuaded one tour organizer to stop having visitors bring box lunches packed by a Belize City hotel. Instead, Young has the tourists dining on meals cooked by the women of Bermudian Landing, thus ensuring that visitors "give a little benefit" to the local economy.

Lucky tourists get their first look at monkeys within minutes of arriving in Bermudian Landing. Walking tours led by villagers start at the edge of town, where a giant fig tree often holds feeding howlers. "Here's a little narrow way," Young says over his shoulder one day, leading a covey of eco-tourists into the dark forest. The nine visitors follow along the muddy path. A few have come to observe some of the sanctuary's nearly two hundred species of birds, others to see an ocelot or one of the big, endangered Morelet's crocodiles patrolling the river.

Young leads his charges through a green dreamscape of hanging vines and clinging orchids. Cigar-shaped hummingbirds flit through steamy shafts of sunlight, while white-collared manakins, all but invisible in the tangled undergrowth, make finger-snapping sounds with their wing feathers.

Dreamers are regularly pinched awake as jungle mud sucks at shoes, spiny bamboo grabs at clothing, and mosquitoes double-park on foreheads and backs of hands. But no one complains when Young steers the group beneath a treetop full of howlers deep in the sanctuary.

"Oh, beautiful! Oh, have a look!" cries an ecstatic visitor, handing over her binoculars. Tripods are positioned in the path, spotting scopes and cameras aimed upward, while four monkeys—indifferent as film stars—placidly munch white flowers in the canopy.

"Tourism is beginning slowly," says Young, sitting on the gnarled trunk of a cashew tree after a van has carried the tourists back to Belize City. "We have a saying in Creole: 'You have to creep before you can walk.'" Already, a half-dozen villagers lodge tourists overnight in their spare rooms, charging from $2.50 to $5 a head. Bring in jobs, he says, and "a lot of stress would be taken off the forest."

Tourist facilities in Bermudian Landing should improve dramatically, thanks to a recent ten thousand-dollar grant from the Inter-American Foundation, based in Washington, DC. Administered by the Belize Audubon Society, the money is being paid out as revolving loans to villagers building guest rooms or starting businesses.

The sanctuary got another big boost one recent spring, when a team of biologists descended on Bermudian Landing for the great baboon hunt of 1990—where all the bullets were tranquilizer darts and every victim was tucked safely into its treetop by nightfall.

Scientists and villagers beat the bush around Bermudian Landing for more than a week, downing forty-seven monkeys in all. While darted animals plummeted into nets or outstretched arms, other "hunters" set off to catch and record data on whole troops of howlers at a time.

Spread out on plastic drop cloths in jungle clearings or village back-yards, the snoring monkeys were prodded, probed, and pricked with needles. "I feel if we're going to knock 'em down we should learn as much as we can from them," said Horwich as kneeling researchers collected blood and tissue samples, pulled back lips to examine teeth, took temperatures, measured limbs, recorded weights, and dusted paws with inky black powder to make howler footprints.

With the released monkeys now sporting color-keyed ankle tags, Horwich and other scientists hope to follow the animals, learning if the local population is stable, how far individuals move within the sanctuary, and how troops form and break up. They also want to find out more about how monkeys make use of the sanctuary's changing forest as farmers cut down patches, then allow them to regrow.

"What we're discovering is that it doesn't take much forest to support the primates," says Kenneth Glander, a Duke University primatologist who participated in the hunt. In twenty years of studying plant-primate interactions in Costa Rica, Glander has learned that vegetarian monkeys must be careful to avoid overdosing on toxic compounds naturally present in many plants. Fortunately, he says, young forests such as the generating patches around Bermudian Landing tend to contain fewer toxic compounds.

Like many scientists, Glander has seen less successful conservation projects err by focusing only on trees and wildlife while ignoring the needs and rights of forest-using people. As he points out, "If people are already there, you can't go in and say, 'You're out of here.' "

Perhaps one reason for the apparent success of the Community Baboon Sanctuary is its founder's low-key, grass-roots approach. "Too many scientists come to a community and pontificate. They might as well come in and speak Chinese or Russian," says Mick Craig, a former director of the Belize Audubon Society. Robert Horwich, by contrast, would "drink rum with them, go to church with them. He didn't try to indoctrinate."

These days, Horwich is working on ensuring the sanctuary's financial security. He has established a foundation—Howlers Forever—to build a permanent endowment that will pay operating expenses for sanctuary staff and programs. He believes that too many well-meaning conservationists, while sincere in their wish to slow destruction of the tropical forest, overlook the socioeconomic cause of deforestation. "It is the rural farmer," he has written, "that will decide the fate of the forests as he or she weighs the needs of a hungry family against the external pressures to leave forests standing."

Only time will tell whether this peculiar blend of wildlife management, ecotourism, and sustainable agriculture will hold together. "It's a concept that's kind of ethereal," says Horwich. "I want ten years to look back and see if it's working. Will the village change so much I'll be disgusted? Will tourism get so big it destroys the monkeys?"

Still, he has no doubts about the validity of "the model" or the need for new approaches that respond directly to the plight of the people who use the forest. Now Horwich, looking the part of the prophet in his long beard, intends to spend more time preaching the gospel of this new kind of conservation to fellow scientists around the world. "Spreading the community sanctuary idea—that's my main goal," he says.

One hopes that any converts he makes will hold fast to his first principle of practical conservation: involving local people. "I want to help," says the scientist. "But I'm a guest here, and I have to *ask* if I can help." It all boils down to those two little words: "You ask."

Suggested Readings

A large and growing literature exists in both the natural and social sciences regarding the tropical forests of Latin America. The following list is nowhere near exhaustive but does represent some of the best sources for further exploration of the causes and consequences of tropical deforestation and alternatives to destruction of the forest in the name of progress.

Anderson, Anthony B., ed. *Alternatives to Deforestation: Steps toward Sustainable Use of the Amazon Rain Forest*. New York, 1990. The essays in this book, written by experts in a wide range of fields, analyze the ecological dynamics of tropical rainforests and the impacts of deforestation. The collection emphasizes appropriate management of tropical forests and contains a number of essays on innovative technologies and approaches that will permit simultaneous use and conservation of the Amazon rainforest. *Alternatives to Deforestation* is written by scholars for readers with some background in ecology.

Browder, John O., ed. *Fragile Lands of Latin America*. Boulder, 1989. This collection of essays grew out of an academic symposium on fragile lands in Latin America, whose goal was to explore strategies for sustainable development. Many of the authors are geographers or anthropologists who analyze nature-society relations from the perspective of cultural ecology. The essays expand on many of the concepts introduced in *Tropical Rainforests: Latin American Nature and Society in Transition*.

Caufield, Catherine. *In the Rainforest*. Chicago, 1991. This book is a good place to start learning about the tropical rainforest. It is a beautifully written, easily accessible account of the social and environmental factors involved in tropical rainforest destruction. Although the scope is global, much of the book is about Latin America—especially the Amazon.

Cowell, Adrian. *The Decade of Destruction*. New York, 1990. This well-researched book documents the destruction of the Amazon rainforest and its traditional inhabitants with a passion born of the author's ten years of work in the region. It is the companion book to the documentary film of the same name that aired in the United States on the *Frontline* television series.

Davis, Shelton H. *Victims of the Miracle*. Cambridge (UK), 1977. The subtitle of this book, "Development and the Indians of Brazil," indicates its focus. The first in-depth analysis of the social and environmental impacts of Brazil's approach to developing the Amazon, it also provides an excellent overview of Brazil's Indian policy since 1940. This book is aimed toward a more academic audience than are the books by Caufield, Cowell, and Head and Heinzman.

Goodman, David, and Hall, Anthony, eds. *The Future of Amazonia*. New York, 1990. This collection of essays, primarily by social scientists, analyzes the ecological and social impacts of Brazil's approach to developing the Amazon. The authors emphasize the social tensions and struggles caused by the destructiveness of current policies in Amazonia. Included are essays that suggest strategies for sustainable development of the Amazon rainforest.

Head, Suzanne, and Heinzman, Robert, eds. *Lessons of the Rainforest*. San Francisco, 1990. Head and Heinzman have put together a comprehensive collection of essays by many of the leaders of rainforest conservation, both academics and activists. The essays are written for the general public by experts in their fields, making *Lessons of the Rainforest* both readable and informative.

Hecht, Susanna and Cockburn, Alexander. *The Fate of the Forest*. New York, 1990. *The Fate of the Forest* is an exquisitely written, sophisticated analysis of the forces that are destroying the tropical rainforest and indigenous cultures of Amazonia. An excellent example of the perspective of political ecology, which considers how political economy affects the relationship between society and nature, it is written for a general, educated audience.

Hemming, John, ed. *Change in the Amazon Basin, Volume 1: Man's Impact on Forest and Rivers*. Manchester (UK), 1985. This volume of wide-ranging essays reflects the diversity of its contributors, who come from both the natural and social sciences. All are experts in their disciplines, with a wealth of field experience in Amazonia. The result is a collection of informative reports on environmental change in the region. Various alternatives for sustainable development are explored.

Leonard, H. Jeffrey, ed. *Divesting Nature's Capital*. New York, 1985. This volume is a collection of interesting essays on the political economy of environmental abuse in the Third World. It includes an excellent essay by George Ledec on "The Political Economy of Tropical Deforestation," which is an exhaustive analysis of the complex factors involved in the destruction of the tropical rainforest, with significant coverage of Latin America.

Meggers, Betty. *Amazonia: Man and Culture in a Counterfeit Paradise*. Chicago, 1971. In this classic of cultural ecology, Meggers analyzes the relationship between the environment and the cultural adaptations of several indigenous groups in the Amazon. Meggers was one of the principal exponents of the theory that the tropical rainforest is fragile and lacking in the subsistence resources that humans need, thereby limiting population growth and cultural development.

Mendes, Chico (with Tony Gross). *Fight for the Forest: Chico Mendes in His Own Words*. London, 1989 and 1992. This fascinating book came out of the last major interview given by Chico Mendes before his assassination. Composed of segments by Mendes interspersed with explanatory material provided by the interviewer, Tony Gross, *Fight for the Forest* provides a good summary of the social history of rubber in the Amazon, with a description and justification of the political resistance by forest-dwellers against environmentally destructive development of the rainforest. The 1992 updated version includes information about the trial of Mendes's alleged assassins and about Brazil's environmental policy under President Fernando Collor de Mello.

Moran, Emilio. *Developing the Amazon*. Bloomington, Indiana, 1981. Moran, an anthropologist, analyzes the government-directed colonization program along the Transamazon Highway and reaches somewhat different conclusions than does geographer Nigel Smith. (Geographers and ecologists have tended to focus more on negative impacts than Moran does.) Moran suggests that some aspects of the homesteading program were succeeding and criticizes the Brazilian government for abandoning the entire program rather than fine-tuning it to respond to variations in the environment and in the colonists themselves.

Moran, Emilio, ed. *The Dilemma of Amazonian Development*. Boulder, 1983. This collection includes essays by specialists from a wide range of disciplines, including ecology, soil science, geography, anthropology, and economics. The emphasis of the volume is on various strategies for making a living in Amazonia—from traditional indigenous methods to urban middle-class approaches. The authors analyze the social and ecological impacts of various development strategies in a variety of Amazonian environments.

Schmink, Marianne, and Wood, Charles, eds. *Frontier Expansion in Amazonia*. Gainesville, Florida, 1984. Based on papers given at a Latin American conference in 1982, this volume focuses on the effects of social change and public policy on development in the Amazon. The authors, primarily social scientists, consider the impact of development on both the environment and on the populations of the region.

Smith, Nigel J. H. *Rainforest Corridors: The Transamazon Colonization Scheme*. Berkeley, 1982. This book exemplifies the approach that cultural geographers use in studying land use and environmental change. Smith analyzes a broad spectrum of impacts on both people and environment created by the construction of the Transamazonica during the 1970s. He emphasizes the negative impacts of settlement along the highway more so than Moran does in *Developing the Amazon*.

Tomlinson, H. M. *The Sea and the Jungle*. New York, 1964. Tomlinson's witty and eloquent account of his travels up the Amazon to Rondônia on a steamer early in the twentieth century offers modern readers a different perspective than is currently fashionable. Tomlinson was a British journalist who shared his contemporaries' belief in their own cultural superiority and their ambivalence about tropical nature.

Wallace, David Rains. *The Quetzal and the Macaw*. San Francisco, 1992. Naturalist-writer Wallace has produced a highly readable account of the history of Costa Rica's acclaimed national park system. In the process he identifies key social and political factors involved in nature conservation. He points out that Costa Rica's efforts to preserve its forests have made it a model for all Latin American countries on how to balance political enlightenment, environmental concerns, and economic development.

Wilson, E.O., ed. *Biodiversity*. Washington, DC, 1988. This comprehensive volume contains essays by experts from many fields. It explores the importance of biodiversity, the threats to it, and strategies for preserving it. Although the collection is global in scope, many of its essays focus on Latin America. The volume is aimed at academic readers and presupposes basic knowledge of both biology and economics.

The following journals publish articles on tropical rainforests relatively frequently, and those marked with an asterisk (*) are especially good sources of information on tropical rainforest topics: *BioScience, *Cultural Survival Quarterly, Environment, *Interciencia, International Wildlife, Natural History, *The Ecologist*.

Suggested Films

The tropical rainforest and its rapid decimation have been portrayed in many recent videos. The following list offers a sample of some that are both interesting and informative. Unless otherwise indicated, most are about one hour long.

"Amazonia: A Celebration of Life." 1984. Director: Andrew Young. Twenty-three minutes long, this is a short but comprehensive introduction to the ecology of the Amazonian rainforest and its value to humans.

"Costa Rica: Paradise Reclaimed." 1987. Director: David Heeley. From the *Nature* series, this video provides a fascinating look at veteran tropical ecologist Daniel Janzen's attempt to recreate an ecosystem that is even more endangered than the tropical rainforest—the tropical dry forest. Filmed in Costa Rica's Guanacaste province, it highlights Janzen's efforts to involve local people in environmental conservation.

"Gertrude Blom: Guardian of the Rain Forest." 1989. Director: Robert S. Cozens. Focusing on photographer Gertrude Blom's long-term relationship with the Lacandon Maya in the Mexican state of Chiapas, this video shows efforts to save the last remaining rainforest in southern Mexico and reveals how the fate of the Lacandon Indians is tied to that of the forest.

"The Hidden Power of Plants." 1987. Director: Kathleen Bernhardt. Part of the *Nova* series, this documentary explores the complex chemical activities of plants and their pharmacological importance. The video focuses on the tropics, although other regions are shown as well. Part of the video emphasizes the importance of the botanical knowledge of rainforest shamans (traditional healers or "medicine men") in helping Western scientists unlock the biochemical wealth of the Amazon rainforest.

"Hope for the Tropics." 1991. Director: Pamela Hogan. Describing various efforts to save the remaining tropical forests in Costa Rica, this *National Audubon* special is somewhat unusual in its focus on the positive aspects of human-forest interactions.

"In the Name of Progress." 1990. Director: Katherine Carpenter. An outstanding example of social ecology, this segment from the television series *The Race to Save the Planet* contrasts the environmental and social impacts of top-down megaprojects, such as Greater Carajás in Brazil, with grassroots, small-scale development projects, such as extractive reserves in Amazonia. Although the video includes segments on India, these illustrate phenomena that are also part of Amazonian "development" based on the destruction of the rainforest and the culture adapted to it.

"Murder in the Amazon." 1989. Director: Adrian Cowell. From the *Frontline* television series, this documentary explores the forces responsible for the destruction of the Amazon rainforest, concentrating on the conflict between rubber tappers and ranchers. The central figure of the video is Chico Mendes, whose assassination gave the film its title. Cowell also made a five-part series, *Decade of Destruction*, which explores the process of deforestation in the Amazon in more detail. *Frontline* aired the series in 1990.

"Nomads of the Rainforest." 1984. Director: Adrian Warren. This segment from the *Nova* series offers an engaging look at life among unacculturated Huaorani Indians of Ecuador's Amazon region. Their homeland and way of life are now threatened by oil exploration and production and the expansion of African oil-palm plantations. This film may someday represent a historical record of a vanished way of life.

"Rainforest." 1983. Directors/photographers: Carol and David Hughes. Filmed in Costa Rica, this *National Geographic* special provides a good introduction to the ecology of the tropical rainforest. "Rainforest" has the outstanding photography for which *National Geographic* has become famous.

About the Editor

Susan E. Place is associate professor of geography at California State University, Chico. For the past fifteen years she has researched various aspects of the relationship between nature and society in Latin America, particularly in Costa Rica. Her research has explored the ecological and social impacts of deforestation, the relationship between newly created national parks and local communities, and women's participation in agricultural restructuring.

Jaguar Books on Latin America

William H. Beezley and
Colin MacLachlan
Editors

Volumes Published

John E. Kicza, ed., *The Indian in Latin American History: Resistance, Resilience, and Acculturation* (1993). Cloth ISBN 0-8420-2421-2 Paper ISBN 0-8420-2425-5

Susan E. Place, ed., *Tropical Rainforests: Latin American Nature and Society in Transition* (1993). Cloth ISBN 0-8420-2423-9 Paper ISBN 0-8420-2427-1